TRYST
with
PERFIDY

Praise for the book

In this sharp dissection of the powerful network of institutions that constitute the Pakistani Deep State, Lieutenant General Davar chronicles the birth and subsequent entrenching of extra-constitutional interests in various branches of Pakistan's government, putting forward a fresh perspective on the country's fractious relations with India, in prose that is brisk, punchy and stimulating.

—Dr Shashi Tharoor,
Member of Parliament

In this book which makes for compelling reading, General Davar objectively analyses the Pakistan Army's undue influence in shaping the destiny of its country, right from its stormy birth till date. A must read for not only strategic experts interested in the geopolitics of South Asia, but importantly, for institutions and students engaged in the study of the complexities of Pakistan's continuing quest for an identity and its eternal, albeit myopic, anti-India policies.

—General (Retd) N.C. Vij, Director,
Vivekananda International Foundation and
former Chief of Army Staff

The illusions, misperceptions and ambitions of Pakistan's army have led the country and its people to a life of continuing violence, instability and misery. As Lieutenant General Davar lucidly brings out, rather than concentrating on creating an atmosphere of peace and security within the country and its neighbourhood, the army has focused predominantly on using radical Islamic elements to spread mayhem and violence in all its immediate neighbours—India, Afghanistan and Iran. The blowback of these policies is being felt within Pakistan and indeed worldwide. This is essential reading for all those interested in understanding the challenges that the army dominating the country's national life poses, within and beyond its borders.

—G. Parthasarathy,
former High Commissioner of India to Pakistan

TRYST
with
PERFIDY

The Deep State of
PAKISTAN

KAMAL DAVAR

Published by
Rupa Publications India Pvt. Ltd 2017
7/16, Ansari Road, Daryaganj
New Delhi 110002

Sales Centres:
Allahabad Bengaluru Chennai
Hyderabad Jaipur Kathmandu
Kolkata Mumbai

Copyright © Lt. Gen. Kamal Davar 2017

The views and opinions expressed in this book are the author's own and the facts are as reported by him which have been verified to the extent possible, and the publishers are not in any way liable for the same.

All rights reserved.

No part of this publication may be reproduced, transmitted, or stored in a retrieval system, in any form or by any means, electronic, mechanical, photocopying, recording or otherwise, without the prior permission of the publisher.

ISBN: 978-81-291-4897-1

First impression 2017

10 9 8 7 6 5 4 3 2 1

The moral right of the author has been asserted.

Printed by Parksons Graphics Pvt. Ltd. Mumbai

This book is sold subject to the condition that it shall not, by way of trade or otherwise, be lent, resold, hired out, or otherwise circulated, without the publisher's prior consent, in any form of binding or cover other than that in which it is published.

Contents

Foreword vii

Preface xi

1. A Troubled Legacy and the Paradox — 1
2. J&K: Accession to India and the First Kashmir War — 12
3. Inside Pakistan's Armed Forces — 28
4. ISI: Symbol of the Deep State — 46
5. Genocide in East Pakistan — 69
6. Strategic Deterrence through Nuclear Sabre-rattling — 80
7. Armed Forces and Their Corporate Interests — 97
8. Stirring the Pot in J&K — 103
9. Fomenting Communal Troubles and Secessionism in India's Punjab — 111
10. Northeast: India's Backdoor Beckons the ISI — 120
11. Eternal Quest for Strategic Depth in Afghanistan — 126
12. The Deep State and the US: A Turbulent Relationship — 144
13. Enduring Sino–Pak Relationship — 160

Epilogue: India–Pakistan: The Way Forward 168

Appendix 1: Resolution adopted by the United Nations Commission for India and Pakistan on 13 August 1948 — 194

Appendix 2: Simla Agreement, 2 July 1972 — 198

Appendix 3: The Lahore Declaration — 202

Appendix 4: Major Terrorist Organizations Based in and Operating from Pakistan — 204

Bibliography — 213

Index — 215

Foreword

For our ancient land, which had seen centuries of invasions, domination and exploitation by foreigners, the dawn of freedom in August 1947, and emergence as a nation state was indeed a 'tryst with destiny'. The bliss of the moment was, however, sadly diminished, because the nation was vivisected at the moment of its birth. If Jinnah was dismayed at what he saw as 'a maimed, mutilated and moth-eaten Pakistan', Nehru had cause for even greater angst at his beloved India being amputated at both shoulders, with the creation of East and West Pakistan.

Given India's historic tradition of tolerance, forbearance and open-mindedness, there is no doubt that we would have found a modus vivendi to live in peace and harmony with our sibling neighbour and share the fruits of joint economic prosperity. However, as the history of our tormented subcontinent shows, this was not to be. If post-independence Indo–Pak relations represent a huge missed opportunity for India, it has been far worse for a smaller and poorer Pakistan; with national resources and energies being frittered away in hostility, bitterness and an arms race, interspersed with violent conflict.

No Indian can (or should) ever forget the chilling message conveyed by Pakistan's Foreign Minister Zulfikar Ali Bhutto in 1965, 'Pakistan will fight for a thousand years. If India builds the bomb, Pakistan will eat grass, even go hungry…but we will get one of our own.' If Pakistan is bent upon protracted hostility, Indians need to acquire a comprehensive insight into the Pakistani mind and decipher the basis of its perception of an everlasting 'existential threat' from India and its visceral hostility towards Indians.

However, this is easier said than done, because Pakistan cannot be judged or assessed by standards that apply to most other countries. There are a number of reasons for this. Firstly, the country was created to be an 'Islamist state' and an exclusive homeland for subcontinental Muslims. Secondly, a corrupt and weak polity surrendered power to a praetorian military soon after the creation of Pakistan. Thirdly, the military, instead of adopting a national agenda of socio-economic development, decided to focus national resources and energies on a self-created Indian bogey and on grabbing Kashmir. Finally, to consolidate its grip on the country, the military decided to adopt religious fundamentalism and sharia as the glue to hold this Islamic republic together.

Pakistan is, uniquely, a schizophrenic nation; an archetypal military dictatorship masquerading as democracy. As sociologist Samuel P. Huntington has pointed out that in countries where elected representatives are incapable or unwilling to exercise 'civilian control of the military', the function of strategic decision-making is seized by the military.

The absence of civilian control, thus, results in the military managing national politics as well as foreign policy; leading to the creation of a 'state within a state' or what is termed as a 'Deep State'. In Pakistan's case, the Deep State has been formed through an unholy nexus of the army's General Headquarters and its Inter-Service Intelligence (ISI) Directorate. This is the entity which has been guiding the destiny of a benighted Pakistan, and tormenting India for seven decades.

It is against this backdrop that Lieutenant General Kamal Davar endeavours to enlighten the reader in his maiden opus, *Tryst with Perfidy: The Deep State of Pakistan*, about our consistently hostile and often treacherous and volatile neighbour.

Commissioned into one of India's oldest cavalry regiments, the 7th Light Cavalry, General Davar has had a distinguished career, with extensive combat experience and wide exposure in command appointments, crowned by his last assignment—establishing India's Defence Intelligence Agency and serving as its first Director General. After hanging up his uniform, the General has taken to academic pursuits; writing and speaking on security-related, counter-terrorism and intelligence issues.

While examining contemporary Indo-Pak relations, India's security elite often fails to view them through a historical prism as a continuum. Perhaps that is the reason why we have found ourselves being repeatedly surprised by Pakistani actions; militarily by the 1947, 1965, and 1999 incursions and politically by the Punjab and Kashmir insurrections. It is this intellectual myopia that the book attempts to remedy.

Combining a soldier's grasp of military history and strategy with a spymaster's insight into the internal dynamics of India's neighbourhood, the author attempts to analyse, what he terms, '...the motivations and machinations of Pakistan's Deep State to unravel what propels them to adopt policies and stratagems which, by conventional wisdom, are hard to fathom.'

Painting on a broad canvas, General Davar starts his account by tracing the historical roots of Muslim separatism in undivided India, and then takes the reader, step by step, through the evolution of the Pakistani state, its armed forces, foreign relations and conflicts from 1947 till today. Along the way, he provides thoughtful commentary and insights into the birth and transformation of the ISI from a minor political tool in 1948, to a dreaded component of the Pakistani Deep State; a hydra of domestic and foreign state policy in South Asia and beyond, wielded by the army's general headquarters.

With the real power in Pakistan residing in its Deep State, and the elected civilians being circumscribed by the limits acceptable to it, Indians need to be clear that any forward movement in Indo-Pak relations has to be within the parameters laid down by the latter. A breakthrough in relations will occur only if and when the Deep State wants it. In this context, this timely book, written in uncomplicated prose, provides much food for thought and could be a primer for security professionals, academic researchers and laypersons alike.

At the end of the book, the author despairingly asks, 'Will the strategic manipulations of China...the unbridled powers of the omnipotent Pakistani Deep State, the powerless civil government in Pakistan...ever let India-Pakistan relations assume normalcy?'

One can only offer fervent support to his own fond hope, expressed earlier, that, 'Objectively dissecting the Deep State may, perhaps, lead us to comprehend regional dynamics better as we look for the betterment of lives in our troubled neighbourhood.'

Dabolim, Goa

Admiral (Retd) Arun Prakash,
Former Chief of Naval Staff

Preface

After serving the Indian Army for forty-one years with great pride and a childlike joy, I ventured into a long-suppressed love—writing and lecturing on matters concerning security, counter-terrorism and geopolitics. With over a hundred articles and commentaries published in national and international media and many military journals, not only my friends but, more importantly, my family has also encouraged me, since some years, to explore the fascinating world of writing books. It is a pity that I have listened to their well-meaning advice rather late; but as they say—better late than never!

I now embark upon a book concerning an institution which is driven by a medieval ideology, and has acquired unbridled powers which, in my considered view, has accentuated unnecessary and uncalled for troubles and travails for South Asia. What the world predicted fifteen to twenty years back—that the twenty-first century would be an 'Asian century', exemplified by the transition, and thus the rise, of billions of suffering people into a better future—has just not happened. If there is one nation in South Asia which is at the core of creating regional instability and unleashing and fostering fundamentalist violence, not only for other nations in this expanse, but also for itself, it is unquestionably, Pakistan.

Although Pakistan was born from the womb of Mother India—so similar in a million ways to its elder offspring—since India's independence on 15 August 1947 and the violent partition which ensued, it has been running away from its roots—directionless. Since then, it has consistently traversed a myopic, self-destructive path. Pakistan has been overly obsessed with its larger and powerful neighbour, and thus, India looms large singularly, albeit illogically, in all its politico-strategic formulations. Constantly whipping up tensions with India has been an existential self-defeating mission for Pakistan. Where it will lead a revisionist Pakistan to is anyone's guess.

As universally acknowledged, Pakistan has a Deep State, which is the focus of my book. Its Deep State, like that of many other nations, historically speaking, has been and, likely, may be responsible for its downfall in the future, as feared by many eminent and sane Pakistanis both in their writings and otherwise. I am thus endeavouring, in my debut book, to analyse the motivations and machinations of Pakistan's Deep State and unravel what propels them to adopt policies and stratagems which, by conventional wisdom, are hard to fathom. That Pakistan over the years has earned the dubious distinction of being the epicentre of global terror, is an outcome directly attributable to its Deep State. It may wish to remember that its attempt to obfuscate its global perception as a nation is difficult and not easily forgotten by the international community. Among the countless names Pakistan has been referred to, the most common ones are 'ideological state', 'garrison state', 'client state' and 'terror state'.

As a proud soldier, I love my country and its values and would unhesitatingly die fighting for them, which is the unstated mission and motivation for all soldiers. However, hyper nationalism based upon mere religious fanaticism or the unbridled ambitions of a general gone astray or any other base motivations are out of place in today's increasingly dangerous world. The Deep State has constructed itself over a self-defeating narrative based upon a lethal cocktail of religion, an anti-India cacophony and ever-increasing radicalism. But is it suffering only from this serious malaise or else determinedly furthering and trying to perpetuate its own selfish interests rather than of its nation? I have embarked on this research and hopefully, by the end of this book, we all will reach some sound and logical conclusions. Objectively dissecting the Deep State may, perhaps, lead us to comprehend regional dynamics better as we look for improvement of our lives in our troubled neighbourhood. It goes without saying that the road of peace and sanity is far more difficult to traverse than the path of violence, terror and perdition. But whether a Deep State, whenever it has existed or wherever it is, recognizes this historical truism is a moot question.

I dedicate this book to my parents, Lilavati Davar and Dr M.C. Davar. My father was a renowned freedom fighter under Mahatma Gandhi's leadership who fought to prevent India's partition. As a matter of fact, my father left the Indian National Congress and, along with Muslim League's Fazl-ul-Haq (later Governor of East Pakistan) and some other like-minded people from both parties, briefly formed the United Party of India to fight the British mischief of vivisecting India. In his later years, as president of the Council of Indo–Pak Affairs, he was a keen votary of Indo–Pak amity and, as a prominent Congress leader, he had advocated the creation of a confederation between India, Pakistan and later with Bangladesh to promote regional peace and progress. Though a renowned pacifist, but a realist, he sent two of his four sons to serve the Indian Army.

I also thank my wife, Madhu, without whose gentle prodding, this book may not have seen the light of day.

I would like to express my gratitude to my old friend and a valued former naval chief, Admiral Arun Prakash, for writing the Foreword to this book. Also, my thanks to former Army Chief General Nirmal Vij, former Union Minister Dr Shashi Tharoor and former High Commissioner to Pakistan, Gopal Parthasarathy, for their valuable endorsements.

For his guidance while writing this book, I would like to express my gratitude to an uncommonly distinguished gentleman–soldier, Brigadier Sukhjit Singh, MVC, the former Maharaja of Kapurthala. He taught me, in my formative years in the army, not only about the various nuances and importance of staff work, but also, importantly, the value of probity. For his assistance during my research, I would like to also thank Brigadier Kuldip Singh, my erstwhile Staff Officer at the Defence Intelligence Agency, which I had the privilege to raise after the Kargil conflict.

I would like to acknowledge the contribution of some of my valued colleagues and friends including Vikram Sood, former chief of the Research and Analysis Wing (R&AW) and senior R&AW

official, Rana Banerji, who shared his extremely well-researched monograph on the Pakistan Army with me. I would also like to acknowledge the support of Lieutenant Generals Kuldip Khajuria and Harwant Singh, Chayanika Saxena, research associate at the Society of Policy Studies, New Delhi, Yamini Chowdhury, Senior Commissioning Editor, and Prerna Mathur at Rupa Publications. I would also like to thank Colonels Rajesh Negi and Sanjeev Khurana for their administrative assistance.

Every ordinary Indian, as is his civilizational mooring, believes in the equality of different religions and fraternal and friendly relations among all. Thus, I cannot but empathize with the long-suffering ordinary people of neighbouring Pakistan, who have been trampled many times over by the jackboots of the powerful military elite. As this book unfolds, an underlying concern for the Pakistani civil society gets underscored with the hope that one day they will be able to live in a country that is secular, civilized and at peace with themselves and their neighbours as envisioned by their Quaid-e-Azam (The Great Leader), Mohammad Ali Jinnah. The chief instigator of India's partition would be more than uncomfortable if he saw the plight of today's Pakistan where Muslims, other than those who follow the Sunni faith or the northern Punjabis, have been ostracized legally and socially. If religion was the overwhelming glue, Pakistan hardly exemplifies the same. The hapless people of Balochistan, Sindh, Khyber Pakhtunkhwa (KPK) and those in Pakistan Occupied Kashmir (POK) and Gilgit–Baltistan regions continue to be at the mercy of the Pakistani establishment, whose worse-than-medieval brutality towards its own people is inexplicable and unpardonable by basic human value systems.

Before I venture further, it will be in the fitness of things to amplify the nuances of what constitutes a Deep State. Basically, it is a 'state within a state'—some institutions of a nation, like its armed forces, bureaucracy, intelligence agencies, police and the like which are in 'de facto' control over the nation, and not 'de jure'. These institutions do not pay much heed to the duly elected political dispensation of the nation. These are primarily powerful, self-interest perpetuating groups who essentially control the levers of power behind the seat of the government.

Though the term Deep State is of recent origin—it is derived from the expression 'derin devlet' in Turkish after the 1996 Susurluk incident—the concept is as old as governments. It has its birth originally in Greek, but its concept got virtually formalized in the Latin term 'imperium in imperio' (state within a state). Former US President Dwight D. Eisenhower, in the mid 1950s, dubbed the American military-industrial-congressional complex as those wielding awesome power within the US government. Another former US President, Harry S. Truman had, some years earlier, also lamented that the 'Central Intelligence Agency was turning into an operational and policymaking arm of government far beyond its laid-down charter.' Former US President Theodore Roosevelt, too, had succinctly expressed that 'behind the ostensible government sits enthroned an invisible government, owing no allegiance and acknowledging no responsibility to the people.' Over the centuries, many nations of differing ideological hues have had various forms of the Deep State overly influencing their respective governments albeit without any form of legitimate sanction.

The Deep State in Pakistan has been in existence virtually since its early years as a nation-state. Through its uneasy years from 1947 to date, it has been a rather unholy amalgam of its army, intelligence agencies, primarily Inter-Services Intelligence (ISI) and, since some years, the countless terror 'tanzeems' (outfits) which thrive in Pakistan with state patronage. Some like-minded diplomats and radicalized intellectuals do lend their knowledge and accord a veneer of sophistication and credibility to this state within a state. The Pakistani Deep State has, as universally accepted, conceived the contours of and formalized the employment of terror as an extension of state policy.

The Deep State has been giving its own perverse interpretation of their founder Jinnah's vision with regard to the ideological path Pakistan should follow and its relations with India. Thus, the country's 'tryst with destiny' appears uncertain, though most in India wish them well. But this is a belief that the Pakistan terrorist conglomerate and its mentors, the army and the ISI, assiduously endeavour to erase from the minds of the common man. But I have met some from the Pakistani establishment and their sane, though rapidly shrinking, civil society, whose principles are definitely different than those of their Deep State. In the larger interests of the neighbourhood and mutual well-being, we wish those who broke away from us, seventy years back, well.

1
A Troubled Legacy and the Paradox

The partition of India in mid-August 1947 by the departing imperial power, Britain, was one of the most seminal events of the twentieth century. India's independence heralded the end of colonialism in the world with dozens of nations getting their independence in the coming decade or so. This turning point, and globally a momentous event has, unfairly, not been given enough significance in the pages of history. However, and very sadly, India's freedom from the colonial yoke was marked by the largest migration of people in human history, besides unprecedented and unanticipated violence. Hindus and Sikhs left their centuries-old ancestral homes and hearths to migrate to a new India, and most Muslims to the newly carved state of Pakistan. In actual fact, the erstwhile state of Punjab was bifurcated into two, with the western part going to Pakistan and the eastern portion to India. Similarly, East Bengal was rechristened East Pakistan, while the western portion remained with India. The two wings carved out for Pakistan, purely on religious lines, were separated by a thousand miles of intervening Indian territory—a factor which significantly came into play twenty-five years later. The Partition also incorporated a separation of personnel, arms and equipment of the British Indian Army, the other two armed services, as also a division of the monetary assets with India's Reserve Bank for the two emerging nations.

The Partition displaced over fourteen million people, according to the figures from the United Nations High Commissioner for Refugees (UNHCR). Horrific violence between Hindus and Sikhs on one side with Muslims on the opposing side resulted in a communal genocide that left nearly a million people dead. Thus, the seeds of discord and hostility were sown right from the birth of Pakistan, and its visceral hatred for everything Indian has been the cornerstone of its shortsighted policies since 1947.

Envisioned by a small group of Urdu-speaking Muslim elite to have a homeland for Muslims of the Indian subcontinent, the tragic events leading to the partition of India—the 'jewel in the crown' of the British Empire—need to be recounted, at least in brief, to comprehend the primeval animosity that many Pakistanis have consistently displayed towards India. It is equally important to understand the factors that have gone on to shape the Pakistani Deep State, its psyche and motivations, which essentially, if not wholly, are a by-product of the development of Muslim consciousness in the subcontinent in the late nineteenth and twentieth centuries in particular.

HISTORICAL PERSPECTIVE

It has been seventy years since the Partition, but it will be unanimously accepted by most in the Indian subcontinent that the raison d'être for the division of India has hardly been met as it was visualized. The overall objective for the Partition was that once achieved as a homeland for Muslims of the subcontinent, both nations would live in peace and harmony with each other. Both the first heads of the governments of the two nations, Pandit Jawaharlal Nehru and Mohammad Ali Jinnah, had voiced the same aspirations. That virtually the same number of Muslims preferred to stay back in India, as ultimately was Pakistan's Muslim population, was a pointer to the hollowness of the concept of the 'two-nation theory' which was the basis of Jinnah's struggle for a separate Muslim homeland. That the Partition created more problems than it resolved was apparent soon after 1947. In the last seven decades, Indo–Pak relations have been consistently bedevilled by hostility, conflict and mutual suspicion. The thoughts of two eminent authors reproduced here are relevant.

Since the beginning Pakistan has been confronted with the monumental task of formulating a national identity distinct from India. Born out of a schism of the old civilization of India, Pakistan has debated over the construction of a culture of its own, a culture which will not only be different from that of India but one that the rest of the world can understand.

—Mubarak Ali, *Dawn*, 7 May 2000

The tensions between the countries were seeded early. Jinnah's conciliatory approach was not shared by many in the Muslim League nor by Pakistan's civil and military bureaucracy who saw advantage in maintaining the frenzy of Partition while they consolidated control over the new country. The unwillingness of India's government leaders, notably Prime Minister Jawaharlal Nehru and Home Minister Sardar Vallabhbhai Patel, to be generous to the new state, especially in the division of assets, also made reconciliation difficult.

—Husain Haqqani, *India vs Pakistan, Why Can't We Just Be Friends?*

Before we delve into the aspect of how the idea of Pakistan germinated—its many contradictions notwithstanding—thus gained acceptability and finally fruition is indeed a more-than-interesting exercise for historians. Some, if not all, answers lie in the study of the complex socio-ethnic origins of Indian Muslim separatism which started emerging at the end of the nineteenth century.

ORIGINS OF INDIAN MUSLIM SEPARATISM

Since the tenth century, several Muslims invaders have attacked India and a few of them stayed on in the country. The Lodi and Mughal dynasties became a part and parcel of the land they conquered and assimilated themselves thoroughly in local traditions and lifestyles, primarily in north and central India. Nevertheless, down the centuries, most Muslim invaders and rulers including the Mughals converted millions of local Hindus, especially of the lower castes, into the Islamic faith, by employing the tactics of medieval cruelty, rape and loot.

The Mughals ruled India for over 300 years. However, relative harmony among the majority Hindu population and Muslims truly came about in the mid-nineteenth century with the combined efforts by both communities to rid India of the oppressive British rule, prevalent in the country since the early eighteenth century. The 1857 Sepoy Mutiny, also referred to as the First War of Indian Independence, was the turning point in the Hindu–Muslim amity since centuries.

The end of the nineteenth century witnessed the stirrings, after many decades, of the phenomenon of Muslim political separatism in India. This was primarily fostered by some Urdu-speaking Muslim intelligentsia in North India. The leading light nurturing the idea of separatism was Sir Syed Ahmed Khan, founder of the Anglo-Mohammedan Oriental College in Aligarh in 1877. Popularly dubbed as the Aligarh Movement, the aforesaid college became the fountainhead of Muslim separatism. Subsequently, this led to the birth of the Muslim League as a political party representing the aspirations of the Muslims in the Indian subcontinent, a fact which the other major political party, the Congress, contested even till the Partition. As early as 1906, the Muslim League won its first political victory when it forced the more-than-eager British government to grant a separate electorate status for Indian Muslims, much against the wishes of the nationalist Congress party. Thus, the wily British government, as early as in the first decade of the twentieth century, eminently succeeded in dividing the major political parties.

That the Muslim League over the next three decades became the principal voice of Indian Muslims portended ominous tidings for India's political integrity. Even hardliners of the party had never dreamt or asked for a separate state during that era but then history is witness to how a small spark can grow into a conflagration.

In the latter part of the nineteenth century, the two leading Islamic seminaries at Deoband and Barelvi, though intrinsically opposed to each other, also contributed in widening the chasm between Muslims and Hindus. Even the British administration in

India exploited the differences between these two Muslim schools of thought to counterbalance the Deobandis and seduce the Barelvis to their camp. All throughout the coming decades, the British continued to reinforce the dictum commonly called, 'Divide and Rule'.

It is an interesting fact of subcontinental history that the quest for Pakistan predates the Partition by just thirty years. A young student at Cambridge University, Chaudhary Rahmat Ali, wrote a monograph in 1933 titled, 'Now or Never'. In his writings, Rahmat Ali advocated a separate homeland for the future well-being of the Muslims of South Asia, particularly in British India, where the Hindus were in majority. This homeland for Muslims was to be called 'Pakistan' and would comprise Afghanistan, North-West Frontier Province (NWFP), Punjab, Jammu and Kashmir (J&K), Sindh and Balochistan. Surprisingly, the pre-Partition Muslim League of India 'rejected Ali's idea describing it as chimerical and unpracticable'. However, in the late 1930s, the renowned poet and philosopher Allama Iqbal (ironically, the lyricist of the moving and patriotic poem, 'Sare Jahan Se Achha Hindustan Hamara'), revived the idea of a separate homeland based on Rahmat Ali's suggestion. Subsequently, Jinnah proposed the idea, and at the Lahore Session of the Muslim League in 1940, the 'Pakistan Resolution' was passed and Assam and Bengal were also included in the Muslim League's proposed homeland. However, by 1945–46, as Jinnah was bargaining with the British on the shape and size of future Pakistan, most Muslim leaders maintained that India's Muslims demanded Pakistan without really knowing the outcome of that demand. By May 1947, Jinnah was reportedly confiding to a foreign visitor that 'even if driven into the Sind desert he would insist on a sovereign state'.

It is also a fact that the ascendancy of the Muslim League in India's political environment is virtually synonymous with the political journey of the Scotch-sipping, pork-eating, westernized Bombay-based lawyer, Mohammad Ali Jinnah. How did a liberal constitutionalist, an Indian nationalist, also labelled as an 'ambassador of Hindu–Muslim unity' become the chief architect of the division of the very land and its values he intensely loved? Perhaps, somewhere the pursuit of personal power propelled by latent ambitions clouds the judgement of even sane and highly educated people.

In his seminal book on Jinnah, India's former external affairs minister and defence minister, Jaswant Singh, has delved into the historical perspective of the journey of Islam onto its long journey in the Indian subcontinent leading ultimately to the partition of India. In his well-researched book, *Jinnah: India-Partition-Independence*, he succinctly elucidates that, 'India's involvement with these diverse strands of Islam covered the entire range of human experience, encapsulating within the geographical spread of the subcontinent a journey that travelled from arriving as a conquering faith, adopting the country as home and then finally dividing this very homeland with the faithful abandoning it.'

Singh further self-inquires that, 'How do you divide a geographic (also geo-political) unity? Simply by drawing lines on maps? Through a "surgical operation," Mountabatten had said, and tragically Nehru and Patel and the Congress party had assented. Jinnah, in any event having demanded adopting to just such a recourse.' The Muslim League in that sense triumphed under Jinnah's leadership. The League was his political instrument and his acumen enabled him to exploit the accumulated weaknesses of the Congress party's mistakes, principally from the 1930s which he heaped on the British Empire's critical enfeeblement post World War II. This enabled him to carve out for himself a Pakistan, even if it was 'moth-eaten' from birth. How and why did Mohammad Ali Jinnah become, in Viceroy Lord Wavell's phrase, a 'Frankenstein's monster', working to dismember that very world which had so generously created him?

TWO-NATION THEORY

Led by Mahatma Gandhi, a large number of Indians of many political hues, including in the Congress, and of different religions and regions within India were against the Partition, notwithstanding Jinnah's constant and determined refrain that 'Muslims were a separate nation'. Accordingly, an equal number of Muslims repudiated Jinnah's assertion and stayed on in India. The understanding of many Muslim stalwarts in India was different to the adherents of the two-nation narrative. The Congress party's Maulana Azad, a renowned Muslim scholar, elucidated that being a staunch Muslim did not push him to deny the composite Indian heritage. In a stirring speech at the All India Congress Committee Session in 1940, as part of his presidential address, Maulana Azad spoke for Muslims who renounced Jinnah's communal diatribes. He eloquently reiterated that, 'I am a Muslim and proud of that fact. Islam's splendid traditions of thirteen hundred years are my inheritance. In addition, I am proud of being an Indian. I am part of the indivisible unity that is Indian nationality. It was India's historic destiny that many human races and cultures and religious faiths should flow to her, and that many a caravan should rest here... One of the last of these caravans was that of the followers of Islam. Full eleven centuries have passed by since Islam has now as great a claim on the soil of India as Hinduism. If Hinduism has been the religion of the people here for several thousand years, Islam has also been their religion for a thousand years. Eleven hundred years of common history have enriched India with our common achievement. Our languages, our poetry, our literature, our culture, our art, our dress, our manners and customs...everything bears the stamp of our joint endeavour. There is indeed no aspect of our life, which has escaped this stamp.'

Ashutosh Varshney, a professor of Political Science at Brown University, USA, in his writings on the two nation theory says that, 'the followers of the two-nation theory sometimes use the horrific violence during India's partition as evidence that Hindus and Muslims could not live with each other and the two-nation theory had mass legitimacy, not simply the approval of educated and propertied Muslims...this argument is a non sequitur. It derives causes from consequences. The violence only proved that once Partition was accepted, unspeakable havoc was unleashed on the masses, even though they had little to do with its creation. Post-Partition violence cannot demonstrate that Partition was a voluntary choice of the Muslim masses on an ideational or ideological basis.'

As India and Pakistan commenced their independent journeys, the two-nation theory received further blows. The unwillingness of the highly popular Muslim leaders of a Muslim-majority Kashmir, stalwarts such as Sheikh Abdullah, to join Pakistan was the first bruising disappointment for Jinnah and his ilk. Subsequently, the reasonable success of India as a democracy under Nehru in the 1950s, despite the odds raised by the violent horrors of Partition, increasingly suggested the viability of a multireligious India.

Pakistan's identity fostered exclusively on Islam and consequently the two-nation theory was once again thrown to the winds twenty-five years later with a rebellion in its eastern wing leading to the emergence of a sovereign nation. In 1971, the birth of a Muslim-majority Bangladesh as a nation, breaking away from Pakistan, wrote the epitaph of this theory.

Pakistan, however, largely blames India rather than its policy and acts of genocide against its own Bengali people in erstwhile East Pakistan. Thus, its eastern wing's separation has also played adversely on Pakistan's psyche in its continuing contentious relations with India. Soon after the birth of Bangladesh as an independent nation, the Pakistani Deep State lost no time to unleash its hidden, and not-so-hidden, agendas against India. Its well-coordinated plans to foment communal trouble in Bangladesh met some success in the early years after the country's independence. It assassinated the nation's founder, Sheikh Mujibur Rahman, through agents in the nascent Bangladesh Army, and supported fundamentalist forces in the new nation. However, right to this day, the Pakistan Army and Inter-Services Intelligence (ISI) are smarting over the defeat suffered by them at the hands of the Indian Armed Forces in December 1971 and publicly, time and again, continue voicing their resolve to avenge their East Pakistan debacle.

Another significant geopolitical factor of the subcontinent which has psyched the Pakistani establishment since 1947 has been its continual fears, inordinately inflated though, of an Indian–Afghan encirclement of Pakistan. The latter has also always harboured unrealistic ambitions for the land of Hindu Kush, which persists even till date. In the years preceding India's division, Pashtun nationalism was resurrecting itself in the subcontinent. The principal leader of this nationalism under the British Raj in NWFP was Khan Abdul

Ghaffar Khan, popularly known as Frontier Gandhi, an ardent supporter of the Congress and a secular Pathan. He also commanded the loyalty of millions of Pashtuns on both sides of the Durand Line (the border between Afghanistan and India, later Pakistan, which the former does not recognize to date). The Frontier Gandhi ensured that in 1946 the Congress secured more Muslim votes than the Muslim League in the NWFP. After Independence, Ghaffar Khan complained that Pakistan's rulers, most of whom were not sons of the soil, sought to keep the Pakistani people under control by making them live in a nightmare of riots, assaults and 'holy war'. Even the prominent Sindh leader, Ghulam Murtaza Syed, had criticized the heavy influx of alien people and 'planned colonization' in Sindh, a reference to Punjabis and Urdu-speaking Mohajirs moving into Sindh after the Partition.

In June 1947, the then Afghan prime minister, Mohammad Hashim Khan, had declared, '...If an independent Pukhtoonistan cannot be established, then the Frontier Province should join Afghanistan.' In September of the same year at the United Nations (UN), Afghanistan was the only nation which opposed Pakistan's entry as a member of the UN. The Afghan delegate to the UN had expressed that his country will not 'recognize the North West Frontier as part of Pakistan so long as the people of the North West Frontier have not been given the opportunity free from any kind of influence to determine for themselves whether they wish to be independent or to become part of Pakistan.' The close relations between India and Afghanistan have been referred to as a 'pincer movement' designed to encircle Pakistan, by former Pakistan dictator, General Ayub Khan. Nevertheless, the Pakistani Deep State, since decades, has left no stone unturned to establish a pro-Islamabad regime in Kabul and assiduously endeavoured to keep Indian influence out of Afghanistan.

The major bone of contention between India and Pakistan since the Partition is unquestionably the J&K imbroglio, which remains a permanent scar on the contentious relations between the two nations with no signs of any resolution. That J&K has been the prime driver and casus belli for Pakistan's four wars against India (1947–48, 1965,

1971 and the 1999 Kargil conflict) cannot be denied. Pakistan's virtual humiliation at the hands of India in each of these conflicts only appears to have strengthened its resolve to avenge the embarrassment.

CREATION OF AN IDEOLOGY

Before Partition, Jinnah's thoughts and ambitions for Pakistan to be just an ideological state nurtured exclusively on one religion were virtually non-existent. Though having won Pakistan on the plank of communalism, Jinnah was indeed a realist and appreciated that a nation could not develop amidst religious strife and thus opposed theocracy as his nation's plank. He addressed Pakistan's Constituent Assembly on 11 August 1947, in what is oft-quoted as articulating his inner voice, far more mellow than when he had whipped up sentiments of Muslims being a separate nation as the reason to seek the division of India. Pakistan's Quaid-e-Azam eloquently expressed that,

> You are free to go to your temples, you are free to go to your mosques or to any other places of worship in this state of Pakistan. You may belong to any religion or caste or creed—that has nothing to do with the business of the State...and in the course of time, Hindus would cease to be Hindus and Muslims would cease to be Muslims, not in the religious sense, because that is the personal faith of each individual, but in the political sense as citizens of the State... We should begin to work in that spirit, and in course of time all these angularities of the majority and minority communities, the Hindu community and the Muslim community—because even as regards [to] Muslims, you have Pathans, Punjabis, Shias, Sunnis and so on, and among the Hindus you have Brahmins, Vaishnavas, Khatris, also Bengalis, Madrasis and so on—will vanish.

Nevertheless, it will be easily accepted by both Pakistanis and non-Pakistanis that Jinnah's secular and sane advice to his people was unceremoniously expelled from the Pakistani psyche even before their founder had breathed his last, a year later. How many Pakistanis would know that their founder had publicly expressed a desire to retire to his favourite city, Bombay, after his tenure? Pakistan has been running away from its roots and the vision of its creator and, unnecessarily, attempting to divide the common heritage, thus germinating unnecessary problems.

Pakistan's Commander-in-Chief and first military dictator, General (later Field Marshal) Ayub Khan, despite having a Western orientation in his personal habits, has explained the paradox in Pakistan's creation and thence existence. In an article* in 1960 in *Foreign Affairs*, he elucidated Pakistan's contradictions stating that until the 'advent of Pakistan, none of us was in fact a Pakistani, for the simple reason that there was no territorial entity bearing that name… Prior to 1947, our nationalism was based more on an idea than on any territorial definition. Till then, ideologically we were Muslims; territorially we happened to be Indians; and parochially we were a conglomeration of at least eleven, smaller provincial loyalties. But when suddenly Pakistan emerged as a reality, we who had got together from every nook and corner of the vast sub-continent of India were faced with the task of transforming all our traditional, territorial and parochial loyalties into one great loyalty for the new state of Pakistan.' Renowned American expert on Indo–Pak affairs, Stephen Cohen, comments that under Ayub Khan, 'Pakistan began the process of official myth-creation in earnest. A large central bureaucracy was created to manufacture an ideology for Pakistan, one that glorified the army as the state's key institution.' That is the reason people, down the decades, have derisively exclaimed that if Jinnah gave Muslims a country, it was self-styled Field Marshal Ayub Khan who gave the Pakistan Army a state!

Successive governments in the country, from its inception to date, have zealously followed a policy based on three pillars—Islam, anti-India and alliance with the West, primarily the US and UK and now with the newly emerging assertive global power, China. Concurrently, the sinisterly motivated Deep State endeavours to carve out for itself a role, far beyond constitutional norms and those universally acceptable in democracies and the civilized world.

---

*Mohammed Ayub Khan. 'Pakistan Perspective'. *Foreign Affairs*, June 1960.

2

J&K: Accession to India and the First Kashmir War

The strategic significance of the state of J&K is as overwhelming as its infinite beauty. Since the Partition, and the stormy, but perfectly legal, accession of this princely state to the Indian Union on 26 October 1947, J&K has been in the eye of the storm. The restive state, so far, has quelled hopes of any rapprochement ever between the two neighbours, India and Pakistan, with many contentious issues of the state preventing a peaceful resolution. This volatile region is considered a nuclear flashpoint by the rest of the world with continuing internal conflict and three wars waged by Pakistan to wrest the state from India. Notwithstanding its successive defeats in military operations in the wars it initiated, Pakistan doggedly continues to pursue its anti-India endeavours in J&K. Since the last thirty years or so, it has introduced an asymmetric warfare in all its nuances employing the strategy of terrorism as an extension of its state policy. However, it will be in order to go into the origins of all these problems as its brutally frank analyses may suggest the way ahead for the good of all, especially the common Kashmiri people. They have grievously suffered for no fault of theirs owing to the misplaced territorial ambitions of some nations in the region.

BACKGROUND AND STRATEGIC PERSPECTIVE

The idyllic expanse of undivided J&K is literally the 'roof of the world'. It is situated between Afghanistan and Central Asian Republics (CARs) of the erstwhile Russian Empire/Soviet Union to its north, China to the northeast, Pakistan to its west and the rest of India to the south. The Himalayas, the Karakoram Range and the Hindu Kush meet in the trans-Himalayan region of Kashmir's Gilgit–Baltistan and form a strategic triangle. Kashmir's northern frontiers reach up to the Karakoram Range which forms the watershed between Xinjiang and India. In the west, the frontier merges with the Pamir and the Hindu Kush mountains. In the east, the boundary merges with the high plateau of Tibet. Historically, its snow-clad mountains and narrow valleys made this region a military nightmare for many invaders, who primarily came from Greece, CARs and Afghanistan.

At the time of Partition, J&K had an area of 84,471 square miles. In addition, two gigantic rivers of Punjab, Indus and Ravi, with two other great rivers, Jhelum and Chenab, flow through this region before they enter the fertile plains of Punjab. The waters of these rivers now irrigate and sustain both India and Pakistan. There exists, since 1960, the Indus Waters Treaty, legally binding the two warring nations in the distribution of the waters.

In the early periods, the region was ruled by Hindu and Buddhist kings. Islam came into this region as late as the eleventh century. A syncretic form of Islam had established itself in the Valley by the fourteenth century, and by this time the Mughals had full control of J&K. Accounts of the fondness of Mughal emperors Akbar, Jehangir and Shah Jehan for this 'Paradise on Earth' are part of folklore. However, the decline of the Mughals in Delhi led to a brief period of Afghan rule in Kashmir. The rise of Maharaja Ranjit Singh as the ruler in Punjab led to Kashmir coming under his suzerainty in 1819. One of the Dogra nobles in Ranjit Singh's court at Lahore, Gulab Singh, was appointed the administrator of Kashmir. Later, the British, after the Battle of Sobraon in Punjab, vanquished the Sikh emperor and ultimately forced Ranjit Singh to sell the entire state of J&K to Gulab Singh for ₹75 lakh through the Treaty of Amritsar signed on 16 March 1846.

Gulab Singh faced tremendous challenges while consolidating his newly acquired kingdom—something similar was to happen again in

1947. Gulab Singh had to contend with the rebellious Muslim ruler of Hunza who fought tenaciously, defeated the attacking Sikh troops of Gulab Singh and made the Indus River the western boundary of Kashmir. A few years later, the British, ever apprehensive of the territorial ambitions of the Russian Empire, attached the territory of Hunza to the state of J&K and appointed a political agent. Nevertheless, the passage of time witnessed the Dogra rulers and their Muslim majority populace maintaining a not-so-cordial relationship between the ruler and the ruled. As a matter of fact, the dictatorial and blatantly anti-Muslim stance of the Dogra rulers contributed many times towards unrest in J&K in the decades preceding the Partition.

Maharaja Hari Singh ascended the J&K throne in 1925 and his administration had both Muslims and Hindu bureaucracy from India. However, he had taken away the rights of the Kashmiri peasants to buy or sell land, thus reducing them to landless tenants. This oppression of the Kashmiri peasantry led to a young firebrand popular leader, Sheikh Mohammad Abdullah, to establish the Muslim Conference in 1931 to fight for the rights of local Kashmiris. However, this organization split into two factions in 1941 with Sheikh Abdullah forming the secular National Conference (NC) with a larger band of supporters and the more fundamentalist remnant retaining themselves in the Muslim Conference. The NC had a bigger base in the Valley while the latter in Poonch and Mirpur—the two Muslim-majority districts outside the Valley. It was supportive of the Indian National Congress (INC) with Sheikh Abdullah having very close relations with Jawaharlal Nehru, a leader of Kashmiri descent. On the other hand, the Muslim Conference supported the hard-line and separatist agendas of Jinnah's Muslim League. The months preceding India's partition were destined to be truly momentous for J&K as well.

At the time of Partition, there were 562 princely states, with just fourteen of them having Muslim-majority populations, and which were contiguous to or located within the territory ultimately given to Pakistan. The British rulers had given a choice to all the princely states to join either the Dominion of India or Pakistan, depending on the choice of the state itself, but independence to any state had been ruled out by the British Parliament. The INC, under Nehru and Sardar Patel, had proactively commenced negotiations with the Chamber of Princes while, by all accounts of that period, Jinnah's Muslim League was way behind in similar negotiations.

Of the 562 princely states, only six states in the initial stages were reluctant in their accession to India. Travancore and Bhopal—one with a Hindu ruler and the latter with a Muslim ruler but both with Hindu-majority populations—were reluctant to join India, and considered remaining independent. But after some behind-the-scenes, not-so-gentle persuasion by Nehru, Patel and V.P. Menon, these states agreed to join India. Meanwhile, the Hindu-majority Jodhpur, also with a Hindu ruler, contiguous to both India and Pakistan, was forcefully approached by Jinnah to join Pakistan. However, better sense prevailed and after some vacillation, Jodhpur finally agreed to accede to India. The Nawab of Junagadh, who was a Muslim ruler of a Hindu-majority state surrounded on all sides by India, had announced the accession of his state to Pakistan. As expected, the Nawab's population revolted against him. Junagadh merged with the Union of India and its Nawab migrated to Pakistan.

The accession tangle had another unique dimension as regards the two biggest states. Hyderabad, the richest and the largest state in erstwhile undivided India, had a Hindu majority but a Muslim ruler. The Nizam of Hyderabad belonged to one of India's oldest ruling dynasties. Similarly, J&K was a Muslim-majority state but with a Hindu ruler. Though the Nizam of Hyderabad was keen to maintain close relations with Pakistan, his state's geographical location way down in southern India and the wishes of his people ensured that he acceded to India. In the end, Jinnah's threat to Viceroy Lord Louis Mountbatten that India's interference with the Nizam's decision to opt for Pakistan would be met by all of India's Muslims rising against it to 'save the oldest surviving Muslim dynasty in India', turned out to be an empty boast.

The destiny of the other Muslim-majority state, J&K, was underscored with many contradictions and insurmountable problems waiting to explode in the future. According to the Indian Census

Report of 1941, J&K's population was approximately 77 per cent Muslim, and barring in Jammu, Udhampur and Ladakh, Muslims were in majority in all other districts of the state. The two major routes connecting Kashmir to British India were primarily in what was to become Pakistan—the Rawalpindi-Murree-Baramula-Srinagar road that followed the Jhelum River for part of the way, and the Sialkot-Jammu-Srinagar road that crossed the 9,000 feet high Banihal Pass in the Pir Panjal Range. An ancillary dirt road connected Punjab's Pathankot to Srinagar. The significance of these road links between J&K to Pakistan and India was awaiting much drama with the unfolding of events leading to the ensuing Partition.

With the division of India around the corner, the ruler of J&K, Maharaja Hari Singh, flirted with the idea of remaining independent. During this period, his crafty Prime Minister, Ram Chandra Kak, though a Hindu, tried to influence his ruler to opt for independence in order to exploit a grey area in the Indian Independence Act, or preferably, accede to Pakistan. Kak surreptitiously remained in touch with Jinnah without the knowledge of his ruler right through the days preceding the Partition. However, the popular and staunchly secular Muslim leader, Sheikh Mohammad Abdullah, owing to his proximity to Nehru and tremendous respect for Mahatma Gandhi, strongly advocated for J&K to accede to a secular-driven India.

Many Pakistani historians and scholars are of the view that Lord Mountbatten, owing to his close relations with Nehru, managed to influence the Boundary Commission under Sir Cyril Radcliffe. They opine that even the Muslim-majority Gurdaspur district was awarded to India in order to ensure a road link from India to J&K. The British government had set up two boundary commissions, one for Punjab and the other for Bengal, for demarcation of boundaries of the two dominions in the offing. The remit of these commissions was clear—to recommend/delineate areas of majority and contiguity for the Muslim and non-Muslim populations. Yet this arduous mission was not accorded sufficient time and both these commissions were, naturally, influenced by various pressures from the INC and the Muslim League. The original date for the two dominions to be formed was June 1948, but the Viceroy and the British government, sensing communal violence, hurriedly announced the Partition to be effected by mid-August 1947.

A first draft of the Boundary Commission's award was ready by 8 August and the final draft was delivered to the Viceroy on 12 August. However, the award was formally announced by Lord Mountbatten only after the Partition, leading to many charges and counter-charges of favouritism and illogicality in the division by both India and Pakistan.

Since then, Pakistan has always complained that in the original draft, most of Gurdaspur and the three tehsils of Ferozepur, Fazilka and Zira were to be included in Pakistan, but Lord Mountbatten and his Chief of Staff, Lord Ismay, had prevailed upon Radcliffe to award them to India instead. Former Pakistani diplomat, Husain Haqqani, in his book, *Pakistan: Between Mosque and Military*, opines that, 'Had the map of the Punjab been drawn differently, Kashmir could have ended up with road access only to Pakistan and a natural mountainous frontier with India. This would have precluded any effective Indian claim on the princely state.'

Meanwhile, in the fluid situation prevailing immediately before the Partition, to gain time for further negotiations, Maharaja Hari Singh offered standstill agreements with both India and Pakistan. While Pakistan signed the agreement with J&K, India refused to do so. According to some historians, even the Congress leadership at that time had differing views on Kashmir's political future, as a few were inclined to let Kashmir go whichever way it wished. However, Nehru and Sheikh Abdullah always wanted J&K to accede to India. It was at this juncture that Pakistan overplayed its hand and in its impatience resorted to annex J&K by force.

The months preceding the Partition had triggered communal tensions and Hindu–Muslim riots at many places in India, and J&K was no exception. Sensing trouble and having been informed of the Muslim Conference's intent in the Poonch-Mirpur region, Maharaja Hari Singh demobilized nearly 40,000 Muslims from his army, which caused resentment among them. Amidst rising communal tensions all over the state, the British, on 1 August, transferred the Gilgit Agency to the Maharaja. Brigadier Ghansara

Singh was appointed the governor of Gilgit with Major William Brown as the commander of the Gilgit Scouts. The latter was slated to play a perfidious role in the months ahead. In the weeks prior to August 1947, both the Viceroy and Mahatma Gandhi had visited the state to impress upon the ruler to make up his mind to accede to either dominion. But all along, Hari Singh continued to display his reluctance. Somewhere, he kept dreaming of independence for his huge and ethnically diverse state.

On 11 August, violence erupted in Sialkot with Hindus and Sikhs fleeing to Jammu in large numbers, and on 18 August, the Lohars and Kashmiris of Nizamabad murdered all the Hindu and Sikh passengers on the Wazirabad-Jammu train. By 20 August, the newly formed Pakistan Army conceived 'Operation Gulmarg' to organize a tribal invasion of Kashmir led by its officers. Colonel Akbar Khan was appointed the commander of the 'lashkar' (militia), who immediately got down to organizing, training and equipping his force. Meanwhile, in early September 1947, 400 armed Muslims infiltrated from Kahuta into J&K to terrorize Hindus and Sikhs even as an uprising by the demobilized Muslim soldiers commenced in the Poonch principality. To pressurize the Maharaja, Pakistan, in violation of its Standstill Agreement, cut off supplies of petrol, sugar, kerosene and salt whilst stopping all trade from J&K towards its areas. On 20 September, Pakistan PM Liaquat Ali Khan approved the plan prepared by Colonel Akbar Khan for an armed revolt inside Kashmir. Representatives were sent to the NWFP to mobilize Pashtun tribes for the impending tribal invasion. By 20 September, the Muslim Conference informed Jinnah about the oppression against Muslims in Poonch and the mobilization of the former soldiery into an 'Azad Army' loyal to the ideals of Pakistan. Muslim ex-servicemen from the Poonch and Mirpur areas revolted against their ruler and subsequently assisted the tribals who were launched, beginning the night of 3 October, from Domel and Rawalakot towards Poonch, Baramulla, Srinagar and southwards towards Naushera and Rajouri.

With intelligence reports of Pakistan's preparations to invade J&K, and rising communal tensions in the state, Mehar Chand Mahajan, a former judge who had very reluctantly consented to become the prime minister of J&K, made frantic visits to Delhi to meet Nehru and Patel. Mahajan wished to apprise them of the precarious security situation prevailing in his state. He conveyed the Maharaja's willingness to accede to India, but requested for any political reforms to be postponed. Nehru advised him that the most popular NC leader, Sheikh Abdullah, should be immediately released from prison and that they should endeavour to get the NC rank and file on their side as it would help the state to thwart nefarious Pakistani designs. Sheikh Abdullah had been jailed a few months earlier for leading a 'Civil Disobedience Movement' against the Maharaja. Sheikh Abdullah and a few other NC leaders were subsequently released after Nehru and Sardar Patel's advice.

The ensuing period from September to October 1947 witnessed heightened communal tensions in the country, state and surrounding areas of Pakistan. Meanwhile, by the first week of October, even Maharaja Hari Singh had lost control of the western districts of the state.

This period also witnessed a rare mutiny in which the call of religion transcended customary soldiering values. The 4th Battalion Kashmir State Forces, the oldest unit in the State Forces, under the command of the Burma-hardened and decorated Lieutenant Colonel Narain Singh, OBE, was deployed in Domel. This battalion had two companies each of Dogras and Muslims. Despite reports by military intelligence suggesting him to disarm his Muslim troops owing to growing disaffection among them, Colonel Narain Singh laughed away this suggestion exclaiming that 'he knew each man in his battalion, who were his children'. The faith of this brave and trusting commanding officer, however, was razed to the ground when his own Muslim troops brutally murdered him and several Dogra officers and soldiers of their unit and joined the raiders who were reassembling to march towards Srinagar from Domel.

As on 1 October 1947, the Kashmir State Forces, comprising over 16,000 troops, was under the command of another seasoned soldier, Brigadier Rajendra Singh. These well-trained troops were organized in four brigades and prudently deployed in Jammu, Mirpur, Poonch and the Kashmir Valley. However, in the days preceding the Pakistan-led tribal invasion, over 3,000 Muslim troops of the State Forces had defected along with their arms and ammunition, which resulted in the remainder troops getting over-stretched in their deployment.

PAKISTAN INVADES KASHMIR

On the night of 22 October 1947, Pakistan precipitated the first India–Pakistan war on Kashmir by launching a well-deliberated tribal lashkar comprising Pashtuns, Afridis, Wazirs, Swatis and Mashud tribals from NWFP and Waziristan. Masquerading as 'Razakars' (religiously motivated volunteers), covertly led by Pakistani Army officers, this over 5,000-member, well-armed force met with rapid success with no worthwhile opposition at the border outposts to confront them.

These tribals looted, plundered and raped all along as they advanced into Poonch and Baramulla on their way to Srinagar, the state capital. Meanwhile, on the Uri–Srinagar axis, alarming reports of the tribal advance prompted the Maharaja to dispatch Brigadier Rajendra Singh to personally control the situation at Uri and stem the advance of the invaders. The next 72 hours saw the Brigadier gallantly delay the advancing and overwhelmingly strong hordes along this axis which, in the long run, perhaps turned the tide in favour of Indian Army's operations to follow. Ultimately, the courageous Brigadier made the supreme sacrifice at Buniyar and was awarded free India's second highest gallantry award, the Maha Vir Chakra.

The tribal forces had entered Baramulla in the early hours of 26 October and unleashed an orgy of violence. During the next few days, the tribals also killed the British commandant of the Sikh Regimental Centre at Naushera, and his wife and daughter. The Mission Hospital at Baramulla was also razed to the ground, its staff and patients killed and the nurses raped. In the nearby Convent of St Joseph, the Mother Superior and her Sisters of Mercy met the same fate—all raped and murdered. According to most analysts, the lust, cruelty and greed of these tribals was the tipping point leading to the ultimate defeat of the Pakistani invasion of Kashmir.

The self-imposed delay by the rapacious invaders in order to gratify their animal instincts, gave Indian forces the breather needed to land at Srinagar airport just in time to turn the tide in the First Kashmir War.

J&K ACCEDES TO THE UNION OF INDIA

Analysing the overall deteriorating security situation in J&K as a result of Pakistani perfidy, Maharaja Hari Singh immediately sought India's assistance and thus signed the Instrument of Accession on 26 October 1947. The document was handed over to India's Secretary of the States Ministry, the brilliant V.P. Menon, who rushed back to Delhi. Incidentally, Menon was also earlier involved in many sensitive parleys between the princes and the Government of India for their integration to the Indian Union in the earlier months.

Within 24 hours of the signing of this historic document and the resultant accession of J&K to the Union of India, Indian troops landed at the Srinagar airfield. The rest was history in the making.

Indian Air Force pilots in Dakotas, led by legendary Group Captain Mehar Singh, worked arduously night and day to land, at Srinagar, troops and the much-needed equipment of one of Indian Army's finest and battle-renowned battalions, 1 Sikh, commanded by the valiant Lieutenant Colonel Dewan Ranjit Rai. The airport had no night-landing facilities, yet Mehar Singh and his team braved all odds to carry out their mission. Lord Mountbatten, commenting on this magnificent airlift, expressed that, 'In all my war experience, I have never heard of an airlift of this nature put into operation at such notice.'

Immediately on landing, 1 Sikh took up defence of the airfield and sent out some troops to organize the perimeter defence of the capital city. Badgam, in the vicinity of Srinagar, was fortified and held out against all odds. Colonel Rai marshalled the remnants of the State Forces with troops under his command to fortify Srinagar against the advancing hordes. Meanwhile, in a brilliant outflanking manoeuvre, armoured cars under the unassuming Lieutenant Noel David of the battle-renowned 7th Light Cavalry created havoc among

Pakistani tribals in the Battle of Shalateng. Subsequently, these tribal forces were pursued as far as Baramulla and Uri and the two towns were recaptured by the Indian Army's 161 Infantry Brigade under the command of Brigadier L.P. Sen, who has written comprehensively about these operations in his book aptly titled, *Slender Was the Thread*.

Two significant events of this period also merit mention. On 24 October, a provisional government of 'Azad Kashmir' was established in Palandri under Sardar Ibrahim, who was originally from the radical-oriented Muslim Conference. On 31 October, Major Brown of the Gilgit Scouts broke his oath of loyalty to his ruler, imprisoned Brigadier Ghansara Singh, the Governor of Gilgit, and hoisted the Pakistani flag in the Gilgit Agency. He subsequently influenced the locals to establish a provisional government loyal to Pakistan in Gilgit. He was also assisted by troops from the tiny Chitral state, which had acceded to Pakistan.

After recapturing Uri and Baramulla, Indian forces ceased the pursuit of the raiders, but seriously attempted, initially unsuccessfully, to relieve Poonch. On 25 November, tribal forces captured Mirpur and many local Hindu women were abducted and taken into Pakistan—some of them were, reportedly, sold in the brothels of Rawalpindi. Around 400 women killed themselves by jumping into wells in Mirpur to escape abduction.

THE INDIAN SUMMER OFFENSIVE

By the end of November and weeks thereafter, the tribals attacked and captured Jhanger, but their attacks on Naushera and Uri were rendered unsuccessful. Meanwhile, Indian troops captured Chamb in the south. As more troops became available, the Indian Army launched Operation Vijay in February 1948 onwards, and in a successful counterattack, recaptured Jhanger and Rajouri. However, in the Kashmir Valley, tribal forces continued attacking the Uri garrison, while Gilgit Scouts laid a successful siege at Skardu in the upper northern reaches of Kashmir.

With the Indian Army succeeding in stabilizing the overall situation in J&K by mid-1948, regular units of the Pakistan Army openly joined the battle to prevent the collapse of the 'Azad Forces'. Their British Commander in Chief (C-in-C), General Douglas David Gracey, continually in touch with his Governor General, Mohammad Ali Jinnah and Liaquat Ali Khan, instructed the Pakistan Army that 'the Indian Army was not to be allowed beyond the general line, Uri-Poonch-Naushera'. They were to avoid, as far as possible, direct clashes with the Indian Army. By May–June 1948, the Pakistan Army had taken over formal control of the war in Kashmir.

On 1 May 1948, the Indian Army launched Operations Eraze and Gulab in the Kashmir Valley to capture Keran and Gurez, respectively, in the north. Indian forces also repelled a counter-attack directed at Tithwal. In the Jammu region, State Forces' troops besieged in Poonch broke out and linked up again with the Indian troops. However, according to some Pakistani accounts, 'The Indian summer offensive had failed to achieve a major breakthrough.' Meanwhile, detachments of the Kashmir State Forces continued to defend Skardu from the Gilgit Scouts and considerably delayed their advance down the Indus Valley towards Leh. However, this was a short-term success for the State Forces as the Chitral Scouts successfully besieged Skardu and, with the help of artillery, were able to recapture Skardu and free the Gilgit Scouts to advance further towards Ladakh.

Owing to international pressure, primarily from the US and the UK, the UN sent a special team to investigate the situation in J&K in an endeavour to prevent further hostilities. Accordingly, General Maurice Delvoie led the United Nations Commission for India and Pakistan (UNCIP) to assess the situation and suggest measures for a ceasefire between the two nations.

The period between 15 August 1948 and the end of that year witnessed the launch of a few actions by the Indian Army to stabilize the overall operational situation. After 77 Parachute Brigade had earlier failed to capture the vital Zojila Pass that links Kashmir with Ladakh in mid-1948 (Operation Duck), Lieutenant General (later Field Marshal) K.M. Cariappa launched Operation Bison to capture this tactically significant pass. The overall commander for this operation was the dynamic Major General K.S. Thimayya, who conceived the capture of this pass. In a daring move on 1 November 1948, Stuart tanks of 7th Light Cavalry along with 77 Parachute Brigade supported by adequate artillery and a company of the Madras Sappers attacked the enemy positions. Pakistani troops holding the pass were totally surprised and fled, and the pass was captured. Tanks of 7th Light Cavalry operated at a height of approximately 11,500 feet—never ever had tanks anywhere operated at this altitude before. Pakistani forces were pushed eastwards towards Matayan and Dras. Meanwhile, this brigade linked up with Indian troops advancing from Leh at Kargil and the Pakistani troops had to move northwards towards Gilgit and Skardu to escape being eliminated in this pincer movement. Having regrouped north of the Zojila-Dras-Kargil axis, Pakistani troops and the raiders attacked the besieged Kashmiri State troops at Skardu. Colonel Sher Jung Thapa had held the Skardu garrison for six months without any reinforcements or replenishment. Ultimately, after a year-long siege, Sher Jung surrendered to the Pakistani Army.

In the two months preceding the UN-brokered ceasefire in January 1949, the Pakistani government was keen to terminate hostilities in the state and prevent an all-out war with India, even as it concentrated on building international opinion in its favour as also in the UN. However, some senior Pakistani Army officers, including Major General Akbar Khan and Major General Sher Ali Khan Pataudi, believed, unrealistically, that getting on to the offensive would give them better dividends on the battlefield. As the years that followed and battles between the two nations would prove time and again, bravado was endemic to Pakistani Army officers than military prudence or clear-cut professional judgement.

UN-BROKERED CEASEFIRE

By late November and early December 1948, with the onset of the snows and the battle situation all over J&K getting more or less stabilized, a ceasefire was agreed to by both countries after protracted negotiations. The terms of the ceasefire, as enunciated in a UN resolution of 13 August 1948, were adopted by the world body on

5 January 1949. This Resolution clearly states that it requires Pakistan to withdraw its forces, both regular and irregular, from the entire state of J&K while allowing India to maintain minimum strength in the state to preserve law and order. After the implementation of these conditions, a plebiscite was to be held under the aegis of the UN to determine the future of the state.

REPERCUSSIONS OF THE UNFINISHED WAR

The First Kashmir War saw India emerge clearly with an upper hand. Had military operations not been called off by India followed by its protest with the UN prompted by Lord Mountbatten's advice, perhaps India could have militarily pushed back all Pakistani troops and raiders from the geographical limits of the erstwhile princely state. Around 1,500 Indians were killed and 3,500 wounded, whereas Pakistan lost 6,000 men and over 14,000 were wounded. India gained control of roughly two-thirds of J&K while Pakistan gained one-third of the state. However, the First Kashmir War sowed the seeds of many conflicts between India and Pakistan in the future.

Punjab's Chief Minister, Captain Amarinder Singh, in his highly readable book, *Lest We Forget*, has very candidly commented on the outcome of the First Kashmir War. He insists, 'The acceptance of the ceasefire was the proverbial last straw for the Army. A further six months hard campaigning would have seen the end of the Pakistani presence in Kashmir. The troops in Kashmir were already gearing for their summer offensive and were confident of success. When General Thimayya heard the news of the ceasefire, he at once took leave and left the Valley in disgust, reflecting the general feeling of all those under his command.'

It is the professional view of a large number of senior army officers of that era that with a slight accretion of troops from the hinterland (and some uncommitted formations were available), Indian troops had the ability to wrest the entire state of J&K from Pakistani invaders. History would have then altered in India's favour. Perhaps Mountbatten, discreetly pursuing the overall British designs for the Indian subcontinent, influenced the minds of Nehru and

Patel to go in for a ceasefire and to the UN for resolution of the Kashmir dispute.

Eminent Pakistani author and journalist Shuja Nawaz, in *Crossed Swords: Pakistan, its Army and the Wars Within*, has succinctly summed up the effects of the First Kashmir War on the Pakistan Army. He opines that, 'The end result was an unfinished war that contributed to the political instability of Pakistan. The unhappiness with the ponderous and meandering decision-making of the politicians led to tensions—some overt, others hidden—between the military and politicians. This internal conflict fuelled the eventual expansion of military influence in Pakistan and created a serious imbalance between military and political decision-making in the fledgling nation. Kashmir became both a reason for not allowing a democratic polity to emerge and a massive financial hemorrhage for the new nation state. It was to become the cornerstone of Pakistan's foreign policy and domestic politics for decades, as civilian and military leaders struggled to keep the issue alive enough to further their own careers.'

Though Pakistan could not achieve the capture of the whole of J&K, as it had set out to do, it did achieve some of its goals for Kashmir. Firstly, though it had no locus standi as the ruler had acceded to India, by invading Kashmir and by the time the ceasefire was enforced, it had one-third of the state's territory in its possession. Importantly, with internationalization of the Kashmir problem, a 'disputed territory' status got indelibly clamped on to the state.

The First Kashmir War was also unique in a number of ways, as felt by professionals in both the armies. For decades, units of the British Indian Army, comprising all classes, castes and religion, had fought together successfully and valiantly against the enemies of the Raj in both the world wars and various theatres of operations between these wars. Yet, in just a few weeks, the former comrades in arms were fighting each other. A distinct difference between the soldiers of the two dominions was visible. All throughout the Kashmir operations, the Indian Army soldiers doggedly endeavoured to adhere to their strongly imbibed virtues of honour, chivalry and magnanimity in victory. While in a matter of a few weeks, the

Pakistan Army, provoked by religious nationalism and misplaced ambitions, showed its fangs by indulging in medieval savagery and inhuman acts against innocent civilians who were part of the same nation till a few months earlier. This brutality and unsoldierly behaviour by the Pakistan Army would gravely impact the integrity of their nation in the years to come.

3

Inside Pakistan's Armed Forces

There are armies that guard their nation's borders, there are those that are concerned with protecting their own position in society and there are those who defend a cause or an idea. The Pakistan Army does all three.

—Stephen Cohen, expert on Indo–Pak affairs

The Pakistan armed forces, referred to in the native Urdu language as Musallah-e-Afwaj-e-Pakistan, are the seventh largest armed forces in the world and the largest in the Islamic world. In addition, Pakistan is the sole nuclear weapon power among Muslim nations with Islamic Iran still considered a developing nuclear weapon state. The Pakistan Army, de facto and more than substantially, represents the ambitions, psyche, power and equally the failings of its nation since 14 August 1947. Therefore, a thorough examination of its strengths and foibles, its diverse motivations, vaulting ambitions and geostrategic compulsions is necessary to anticipate its likely actions in a region wrecked by increasing instability and violence. Most in the world, including Pakistan's former mentors, will wonder how, since its birth, the Pakistan Army, steeped in the traditions of the British Army, graduated to become the cause célèbre of most terror-driven problems in the region, and even other parts of the globe.

Across the world, there exist two oft-quoted truisms about the Pakistan Army. First, that generally countries have armies but in Pakistan's case, the army has a country. And, secondly that Pakistan owes its existence to the three As—Allah, America and the Army. That the Pakistan Army is the most powerful in this trinity brooks no elaboration.

AT PARTITION

India's partition gave Pakistan 21 per cent of British India's population, 17 per cent of its revenue but as much as one-third manpower from the huge Indian armed forces that had been raised by the British during the Second World War. The British policy of classifying certain ethnic groups in India as 'martial races' had favoured recruitment of Punjabi Muslims and Pashtuns, who were now part of Pakistan. Under the terms of the Partition, Pakistan received 30 per cent of British India's army, 40 per cent of its navy and 20 per cent of its air force. Accordingly, Pakistan's first prime minister was forced in 1948 to allocate 75 per cent of Pakistan's first budget, hampered grievously with meagre resources, just to cover the salaries and maintenance of this large force.

India's share from the undivided armed forces was twice that of Pakistan in keeping with India's size and revenue base, but importantly, because India faced multiple threats to its security. However, Pakistan faced a threat, mostly self-assumed and later self-cultivated, to justify maintaining a large army. Husain Haqqani expresses succinctly that, 'Pakistan was not like other countries that raise an army to deal with threats they face, it had inherited a large army that needed a threat if it was to be maintained.' He further clarifies on his view that, '...in Pakistan's case, the only threat that could be invoked to retain the legions inherited from the Raj was from India.' Shuja Nawaz, however, has stated somewhat differently that on '14 August 1947, Pakistan not only came into being as a "moth-eaten" political entity, but it also came with a "moth-eaten" military which was under the firm command and control of British officers who chose to remain ostensibly under Pakistan control, (notwithstanding the secret "stand down" order of the supreme commander).'

At the time of the Partition, the British government had designated Sir Claude Auchinleck as the Supreme Commander of the armies of both dominions. 'Auk', as he was fondly known by many of his contemporaries, had a reputation for fair play, which he faithfully displayed all along those difficult days as regards the division of the armed forces between the two emerging nations. However, both the first and second British C-in-Cs of the Pakistan Army, Generals Sir Frank Messervy and Sir Douglas Gracey (who took over from Messervy in February 1948) cannot be clubbed with 'Auk' in matters of even-handedness. Both these generals, while in office, went subtly against the official dictates of the Viceroy and their Supreme Commander, Lord Mountbatten, and did nothing much to rein in the military operations of the Pakistan Army in J&K during that period.

The formula for division of military assets, as dictated by Britain, was also a bone of contention felt by the Pakistani leadership of the day. The Pakistan Army was allotted roughly 1,50,000 troops, comprising 508 units of various sizes and composition. It received six out of fourteen armoured regiments, eight out of the forty artillery regiments and eight out of the fifteen infantry regiments. The Gurkha regiments of the undivided British Indian Army were not given any option, but to join the Indian Army. Thus, Pakistan got thirty-three infantry battalions to India's eighty-eight. Geography too, at the time of the division, was not in favour of Pakistan, for out of the forty-six training establishments, only seven were located in what then became Pakistan. Even the munitions industry, which had been substantially expanded to cater for World War II demands, had only three ordnance factories in Pakistan out of the seventeen, with the rest in India. With units and their officers moving to Pakistan from different military outposts in India, General Messervy set up the Pakistan Army General Headquarters (GHQ) at Rawalpindi on the same lines as the GHQ in New Delhi. The capital of the newly created Pakistan was some distance away in Karachi and, thus, the military leadership at Rawalpindi, right from the very start, was not under close and direct supervision of the country's political leadership. Rawalpindi was destined to play a more than significant role in the polity of Pakistan in the years to follow.

NOT A 'MOTH-EATEN' MILITARY

The Pakistan Army, one of the largest and most professional armies in South Asia, has an overall strength of 5,50,000 personnel spread over nine corps (four for offensive and five for defensive roles—though these are all interchangeable as required), two armoured divisions, seven independent armoured brigades, two mechanized divisions, nineteen infantry divisions including Force Command Northern Areas, six independent infantry brigades, two artillery divisions, two air defence divisions, one engineer division and five logistics areas. A relatively newer feature in the army structure has been the creation of two regional commands, both for offensive operations and as army reserves. The Central Command consists of 1 Corps and 11 Corps, while the Southern Command has 2 Corps and 41 Infantry Division on its order of battle (ORBAT). Pakistan's nuclear weapons are placed under the command of its prestigious Army Strategic Forces Command (ASFC), which has approximately 15,000 personnel deployed under the operational control of the National Command Authority (NCA).

In addition to the above, Pakistan has over 2.05 lakh paramilitary personnel in its Frontier Corps (FC), Pakistan Rangers (PR) and Mujahid and Ansar battalions. These paramilitary personnel are spread over fifty-five Mujahid battalions while the FC comprises fifty-nine wings in Khyber Pakhtunkhwa (KPK), fifty-six wings in Balochistan and three wings in the Gilgit–Baltistan region. The PR has twenty-five wings each in Punjab and Sindh.

The bulk of Pakistan's military equipment comes from the US and China, though earlier some equipment was also procured from France. However, in the past twenty years or so, Pakistan's excessive dependence on the US has gone down and centred mainly on Chinese weaponry. The country's defence forces are swiftly aligning themselves with the Chinese military, which is also understandably liberal with their Pakistani counterparts, owing to the common anti-India factor.

The ASFC has an estimated strength of 12,000-15,000 personnel. Deployed assets include 105 Hatf I missiles, unspecified number of Abdali/Hatf II missiles, fifty Hatf III missiles (M-11s from China), up to ten Shaheen-I/Hatf IV missiles and up to twenty-five Hatf V/Ghauri-II missiles. The total surface-to-surface missiles are estimated to be about 200 in number.

Of the total of sixty-nine infantry brigades, approximately twenty-four are currently deployed in the FATA (Federally Administered Tribal Areas) and KPK regions. Sixteen infantry brigades are deployed along the Line of Control (LoC) by Pakistan and this leaves only around twenty-nine infantry brigades for deployment from the J&K border right down to Sir Creek. This poses a dilemma for the Pakistan Army, whether to have a strong forward posture in defence or hold the rear areas in strength. Even with some redeployment from the western to its eastern border, losing territory to major Indian offensives is more than likely, which has thus resulted in Pakistan's obsessive reliance on tactical nuclear weapons (TNWs) to contain Indian offensives.

SOCIAL BACKGROUND

Since its inception, the Pakistan Army has been overly Punjabi-dominated, which stems from primarily two factors. Firstly, the population composition of the nation has been predominantly Punjabi. Secondly, it was a legacy of the British form of recruitment of soldiers from certain races from those regions, which according to them, produced better soldiers. This was the concept of preferential selection towards the Pathans, as also among the Punjabi Mohammadans, Gurkhas, Rajputs, Jats, Marathas, Dogras and Jat Sikhs, considered as martial classes resulting in preferred recruitment in larger numbers from these castes. After the 1857 Sepoy Mutiny, the British, shaken by the widespread support of people and soldiers from the United Provinces and areas around Delhi (both Muslims and non-Muslims), carried out extensive surveys to recruit only those whose moral, mental and physical attributes suited the armies of the Raj. The British subsequently ensured that Muslims were not grouped together in pure Muslim units, unlike Sikhs and Hindus in pure Sikh and Hindu units, respectively. Over the years, the British also successfully experimented with the practice of granting arable land to the Punjab peasantry from whom they were also recruiting soldiers especially in the Potohar belt, namely the districts of Chakwal, Rawalpindi, Attock, Jhelum and Gujarat.

The Pakistan Army continues with the above-mentioned system notwithstanding the resentment for this outdated practice in its restive regions like Balochistan and Sindh. At Independence, though East Pakistan had 50 per cent of the total population of the new state, it barely had 1 per cent representation in the nation's armed forces. General Ayub Khan did endeavour to recruit more Bengalis into the armed forces by lowering the physical standards for recruitment. But on the ground, the situation did not improve vastly and was one of the many reasons for the resurgence of Bengali nationalism in later years. By the time the radical Islam-oriented General Zia-ul-Haq took over the reins of Pakistan, he encouraged more home-bred Punjabis and not necessarily better English-speaking second or third generation sons of army officers. Islamic practices of sporting beards, regular prayers, keeping of rozas (fasting during the holy month of Ramazan) and not drinking at public places were encouraged within the army. Junior Commissioned Officers (JCOs) and other ranks (ORs) with madrasa (religious schools) background were encouraged for recruitment.

In his book, *The Pakistan Army*, Stephen Cohen, taking 1979 as the sample year, reveals the predominant bias towards Punjabis, both among officers and ORs. Among the soldiers, 77 per cent were from Punjab, 19.5 per cent were Pathans, 2.2 per cent were from Sindh and only 0.06 per cent from Balochistan. In the officer class, Punjabis accounted for 70 per cent, Pathans 14 per cent, Sindhis 9 per cent and Baloch 3 per cent. Kashmiris from Pakistan Occupied Kashmir (POK) rose to 1.3 per cent after they commenced getting into the Northern Light Infantry (NLI) and Mujahid battalions. The opening of the Pano Aqil cantonment in Hyderabad, Sindh, helped to give some impetus to the recruitment of Sindhis, but the Baloch still preferred to ignore these recruitment drives. Though Mohajirs (Muslims who migrated at Independence from northern India to Pakistan) were doing well in other professions, their eagerness to join the armed forces was not compatible with their population strength. Notable among the few Mohajirs who have made their mark in the Pakistan Army have been General Aslam Beg (from Azamgarh, Uttar Pradesh) and former President General Pervez Musharraf (from Daryaganj, Delhi).

Learning to some extent from their mistakes in erstwhile East Pakistan, successive governments have tried to address the wide disparity in the recruitment patterns among the various regions of the country. Statistics released in 2010 indicate that as a result of various measures undertaken by the establishment, the percentage of Punjabis in the army dropped to nearly 56 per cent, while all others grew, with the Pashtuns now marginally at 15.5 per cent, Sindhis to slightly over 15 per cent, Baloch to 2.35 per cent and entry from the erstwhile Northern Areas to 8.5 per cent. General Ashfaq Parvez Kayani, a Musharraf favourite, during his tenure as the Chief of Army Staff (COAS) from 2004–07, is also noted for his efforts to redress the regional imbalance in recruitment in the army. Though some official figures released by the Pakistani establishment may not be necessarily accurate, it is the opinion of many that the Punjabis still have a disproportionate representation both among the officers and the ORs. However, for the promotion to the most powerful appointment in the structure, namely the post of the Army Chief, many non-Punjabis have been promoted. One reason ascribed to this benevolence has been successive Pakistan prime ministers preferring non-Punjabis to command an overly Punjabi predominant army.

ISLAMIC CRUTCH FOR THE DEFENDERS OF THE FAITH

Since the raison d'être for Pakistan's birth was religion, it was but natural that the Islamization of its army commenced in 1947 itself. The religious identity of the army was emphasized upon to make its soldiers feel distinct to their erstwhile Hindu and Sikh compatriots.

However, in the first few years after Partition, the Pakistan Army retained its British orientation and remained more professional than merely religious. Shuja Nawaz explains the early nod to Islam of the Army, 'The largely Muslim rump of the British Indian Army was also saddled at birth with this paradoxical identity: the symbols of Islam but the substance of a colonial force, quite distant from the body politic of the fledgling state. It adopted, for instance, the numbers 786 for the identification of its General Headquarters in Rawalpindi. In Islamic numerology, 786 represents the Arabic "Bismillah ir-Rahman ir-Rahim", the invocation that Muslims intone at the start of any action or venture of note. This numerical code was emblazoned on all gateposts and vehicles as a reminder that this was the Army of a Muslim country. The senior echelons of the Pakistan Army at its birth were still British officers who had adopted to stay on and they were succeeded by their native clones: men who saw the army as a unique institution, separate and apart from the rest of civil society and authority. With time, this schism between the cantonment and the city pervaded the army's thought processes and seemed to guide, as well as bedevil, the military's relationship with the civilian sector. The army initially retained its largely moderate and secular nature.'

It is also a matter of fact that right from the start, Pakistan has unfailingly utilized militant Islamists as a weapon. During the First Kashmir War, thousands of Pashtuns and other tribesmen from the FATA region were employed to invade J&K by appealing to their Islamic loyalties to the new state. Subsequently, even Pakistan's first military dictator, the British-leaning General Ayub Khan, employed the Muslim card to keep the Pakistan People's Party (PPP) in West Pakistan and the popular Awami League (AL) in East Pakistan in check and ensure support to his own domestic constituency. The Pakistan Army's senior hierarchy's aversion towards civil governmental control of them has been consistent as once remarked by Ayub himself. On capturing power after ousting President Iskander Mirza in 1958, when asked: 'After Ayub who?' General Ayub Khan in a nonchalant manner had replied: 'Simple, after me another general, after that another general and then another general.' In the 1965 operations against India, Ayub Khan once again tried to use the Muslim card, though unsuccessfully, when he felt that local Kashmiris, being Muslims, would rise against India. During 1970–71, in East Pakistan, where West Pakistanis felt the Bengalis were lesser Muslims, General Yahya Khan employed hard-line Deobandi 'mujahideen' against his own Bengali citizens.

After Pakistan's debacle in 1971, even the Western-educated Zulfikar Ali Bhutto employed the Islamic discourse extensively to maintain a hold over his nation. He coined the term 'Islamic Socialism' as the cardinal of his policy. Most unfairly, he amended Pakistan's Constitution to declare the Ahmadiyya sect of the Qadiani people as non-Muslims.

When General Zia-ul-Haq ousted Bhutto and assumed power, he stepped up efforts to strengthen Islamization of the Pakistan Army which had commenced in right earnest in General Yahya Khan's rule. Thus, recourse to employing Islamization to appease clerics and fundamentalists has been more than a rule and, surprisingly, even zealously practised by its army rulers.

The Soviet occupation of neighbouring Afghanistan triggered a widespread Islamic resurgence in the region, which Zia fully capitalized upon, with the assistance of the US and other Islamic nations. In March 1976, immediately after he took over as the Army Chief, Zia replaced Jinnah's motto of 'Faith, Unity, Discipline' with 'Iman, Taqwa, Jihad-fi-Sabilillah (Faith, Piety, Holy War [or struggle] in the name of God). The General who is referred to by some in Pakistan as the 'father of the new military mind' had laid down the law in 1979: 'Our present political edifice is based on the secular democratic system of the West, which has no place in Islam. In Pakistan, neither anarchy nor Westernism will work. This country was created in the name of Islam and in Islam there is no provision for Western-type elections.'

Christine Fair, in her book on the Pakistani Army, entitled *Fighting to the End: The Pakistan Army's Way of War*, tersely observes that when Zia '…[became] army chief, he set a qualitative new tone for the military and the role of religion in it. He was particularly sympathetic to Jamaat-e-Islami (JI) and used his authority to allow the party to distribute literature among officers and enlisted men.

This allowed JI to make inroads into the army and other services, and many officers began to overly affiliate with JI and its founder, Maulana Abul A'la Maududi. Zia also permitted other Islamic groups, such as the Tablighi Jamaat, to expand their presence among army personnel.' (Tablighi Jamaat is a revivalist group, dedicated to proselytization, which claims to eschew political activity). Such freedom would have been anathema to previous army chiefs. Zia was the first head of state to attend Tablighi Jamaat's annual meeting in Raiwind, near Lahore, which encouraged several officers to openly associate with the group to demonstrate their piety. Bhutto was reportedly dismayed by Zia's pro-JI activities, even summoning him before the cabinet to explain himself. During his trial before the Supreme Court, Bhutto remarked, 'I appointed a Chief of Staff belonging to the JI and the result is before all of us.' Thus under Zia, the Islamization of the Pakistan Army was complete. Meanwhile, the notorious ISI continued to employ the bevy of Sunni Islamist groups being trained, equipped, funded and nurtured by it for terror activities in Afghanistan and J&K.

In the autumn of 1999, after General Pervez Musharraf ousted Nawaz Sharif and took over the reins of power in Pakistan, he touted his inspiration to be the moderate Turkish Islamic leader, Mustafa Kemal Attatürk. He frequently stated his desire for Pakistan to follow the example of Turkey of the late 1930s and '40s. He proclaimed the adoption of a policy of 'enlightened moderation', and even outlawed some militant groups.

After the 9/11 terror attacks in the US and the deployment of US troops in neighbouring Afghanistan, on US insistence, Musharraf expressed his willingness to take appropriate action against the al-Qaeda, the Afghan Taliban and the Haqqani and Hekmatyar networks in Afghanistan.

After Musharraf's resignation in 2007, Asif Ali Zardari rose to power post his electoral victory. Zardari did make some noise but hardly launched any action to take on terrorists both in Afghanistan and inside Pakistan. This was primarily to assuage the apprehensions of the Americans, who were by then fully engaged in stabilizing Afghanistan. After Zardari finished his tenure as president, he was succeeded by the wily Punjabi politician Nawaz Sharif, in his second avatar as the prime minister. Sharif, despite giving misleading statements regarding reinforcing the war on terror, maintained strong links with most Sunni-oriented militant groups, especially in Punjab. Nawaz Sharif practised with finesse the long perfected Pakistani stratagem of 'running with the hares and hunting with the hounds'.

ABORTIVE COUP ATTEMPT

Rana Banerji, senior Research and Analysis Wing (R&AW) officer, in his monograph, *The Pakistan Army: Composition, Character and Compulsions*, has recounted an interesting episode of a failed coup attempt by some radicalized Pakistani Army officers. In September 1994, Pakistan Army intelligence uncovered a plot led by Major General Zaheer-ul-Islam Abbasi with forty other officers to overthrow the Benazir Bhutto government and establish an orthodox Islamic state. This group had been under the influence of a radical cleric, Sufi Iqbal from Taxila. Banerji recounts, 'The then Corps Commander of Rawalpindi, Lt General GM Malik was impressed by his teachings and was running a character building course in the forces under him based on Sufi Iqbal's teachings.' It is worth recounting that in the late eighties, while serving as Colonel Foreign Division at the Military Intelligence Directorate at the army headquarters in New Delhi, I had the opportunity to meet (then) Brigadier Abbasi who was posted as the Pakistani Defence Attaché. Brigadier Abbasi was caught red-handed while interacting with an Indian informer at Hotel Ranjit and declared persona non grata for his botched-up intelligence gathering operation. He must have returned to Pakistan even more pronouncedly anti-India than he would have been prior to assuming his assignment in New Delhi.

At the time of the coup attempt, General Abbasi was supposed to storm an important meeting at the GHQ in Rawalpindi, assassinate the senior officers present there and announce the Pakistani caliphate. However, the Pakistani Army had got wind of it and before any damage could be done, Abbasi and his co-conspirators were caught.

Subsequently, the senior hierarchy of the Pakistan Army has been conscious of similar attempts likely being undertaken in the future and have been keeping a close surveillance on such overly-radicalized elements in their organization. Notably, General Musharraf in his nine years of power (1999–2008) did manage to weed out a few senior officers with fundamentalist leanings.

The Pakistani armed forces maintain a strong and undying orientation towards Islam as a unifying force for itself and the nation. Overall, Islamization of the armed forces continues unabated, especially among the lower ranks. This adherence to the tenets of Islam is not likely to ever change and with the resurgence of extremism in global Islam, the country is likely to become far more radicalized than in its earlier years. Former Army Chief, General Aslam Beg, recently stated that, '…unfortunately democracy in Pakistan has been preferred over the principles of Quran and Sunnah. No government in the past or the present one, nor the conglomeration of over two dozen religious parties, ever made any serious attempt to fortify our ideological identity. We have failed to give our children their Muslim identity, because our education system is devoid of teachings of the principles of Quran and Sunnah.' When even senior army officers get so gravely affected, it is not very difficult to imagine the impact of religious obsessions.

That some of these armed forces personnel would be gravely affected and develop sympathy for some of the radical elements and countless terror groups roaming all over country is a development which cannot be ruled out. As a matter of fact, some of the serious attacks on various military and intelligence establishments in the last few years, including the attack on Mehran naval base near Karachi and the ISI headquarters in Islamabad, have been suspected by Pakistani authorities as 'inside jobs'. Thus, Pakistan has to be doubly careful of its nuclear assets/fissile materials falling into the wrong hands which could have catastrophic consequences for both the nation and the region.

The US has generously supported Pakistan financially and militarily for the last sixty years and looked the other way even when Pakistan has itself fostered terrorist acts against US-friendly assets in the region. Some analysts also feel that the increase in radicalism and Islamism in Pakistan and its institutions is directly linked to the levels of anti-Americanism prevalent in the Pakistani society.

STRATEGIC IMPERATIVES AND MILITARY DOCTRINES

Strategic imperatives for a nation stem from the geopolitical environment it is a part of—the internal and external security challenges, overall economic situation, its social fabric and cohesion, the natural resources it commands and its technological prowess. All these factors ultimately contribute to the development of its strategic culture. Consequently, the nation's military doctrines flow from these imperatives. Even though Pakistan does not conform to many universally accepted norms, it still has to confront the vagaries and demands of diverse factors to arrive at the best possible solutions for its myriad security and economic problems. Before the canons of Pakistan's strategic culture are enumerated, it is essential that all those factors which have contributed, in Pakistan's understanding or otherwise, to its strategic imperatives are understood.

Since its independence and unanimously fostered by all sections of Pakistani society till date, India is at the core of all of Pakistan's politico-strategic formulations, bordering upon paranoia and defying all logic. Even seventy years after being born, Pakistan's search for its own identity continues and emerges into an abiding hatred for a 'Hindu India' (it forgets conveniently that India has more Muslims than itself).

Firstly, terrain imperatives, which have contributed to Pakistan's strategic thought, include, geographically speaking, the lack of strategic depth which is the main driver for its insecurity vis-à-vis India. Pakistan's eternal quest for strategic depth, outdated now by the reach of modern weaponry, does not sound logical. General Zia-ul-Haq believed that the strategic depth his nation 'needed in its confrontation with India was best achieved by building an Islamic bloc between the Arabian Sea and the Urals'. But former Pakistani Army Chief General Ashfaq Kayani's statement that replaced the outdated military point of view—that the quest is now more political, and seeks to have a Pakistan pliant regime in Kabul—is an extension of the same objective.

Strategic Indian military assets can be located well in depth and widely dispersed in the Indian hinterland and staged forward as required for offensive action against Pakistan and then redeployed as militarily desired. This military flexibility is not available to Pakistan, and thus prompts it to seek strategic depth—earlier it sought it in Iran and thence continually in Afghanistan. Hence, Pakistan's consistent endeavours to keep India's influence out of Afghanistan, an objective it has been pursuing relentlessly since decades.

Secondly, a large number of value objectives in Pakistan are situated close to the international boundary and hence vulnerable to capture consequent to any swift offensive by Indian forces. Major towns of Lahore, Sialkot, Shakargarh, among others, are situated barely 20–35 kilometres from the international boundary. In a short-duration conflict, capture of even smaller townships confers significant psychological dividends. Thirdly, since India controls all waters in the rivers that flow into Pakistan, it could use water as a weapon in diverse ways to pressurize Pakistan, in both peace and war. While the international boundary between India and Pakistan is 2,900 km long, the large 740 km long mountainous/hilly sector along the LoC/Actual Ground Position Line (AGPL) lends itself to merely shorter objectives and more of a war of attrition which will necessitate very large and well-equipped forces required to achieve any strategic or worthwhile gains in the mountains. In the vast desert sectors bordering both the nations, sufficiently strong and modern mechanized forces are required to achieve military gains by an amalgam of manoeuvre and fire power, including air power. The fact that the country's main ports of Karachi, Ormara, Gwadar and Pasni lend themselves to being easily blockaded by the Indian Navy also plays a significant part in Pakistan's insecurity in the maritime domain. Pakistan, with ongoing Chinese assistance, endeavours to lessen its naval vulnerabilities by developing the Gwadar deep sea port, where even in the near future, the Chinese Navy is certain to deploy some of its maritime assets, including nuclear-capable submarines.

An overall force analysis of the Pakistan Army indicates that it has a force structure responsive to its strategy of 'offensive defence'. It is capable of developing its major offensive missions based on the availability of two strike corps, namely 1 and 2 Corps augmented by elements of 11 and 12 Corps, when required.

In the last few years, to counter India's so-called Cold Start doctrine, now referred to as a 'Proactive Strategy', Pakistan has been working on a revised strategy called the 'New Capability of War Fighting' (NCWF). It has carried out various war games to consolidate NCWF in the current operational environment prevailing in the subcontinent. Further, the NCWF aims to achieve an effective interface between Pakistan's nuclear and conventional capabilities. The army opines that its NCWF will deter war and, more importantly, keep the duration of war to the minimum possible duration. Pakistan also aims to reduce the conventional asymmetry between itself and India by various measures, including sub-conventional means. In its proposed concept, at the national level, it strives to achieve war deterrence through a combination of conventional and non-conventional means adopting a 'whole of nation approach'. It will endeavour to reinforce deterrence through communications, capability and credibility (CCC), which gives weight to the notion of nuclear deterrence/threshold. In addition, the Pakistan Army will 'develop disincentives for India at the sub-conventional level'. Interestingly, some Indian think tanks opine that the Pakistan Army is pursuing a deliberate policy of 'cultivated irrationality' in its nuclear grammar, and its nuclear threshold is not as low as they would like India to believe.

After the loss of East Pakistan in 1971 and India's experiment with a nuclear device in 1974, Pakistan has been hell-bent to develop its nuclear programme by cleverly branding an India-specific weapon as an 'Islamic bomb'. That today Pakistan has the fastest growing nuclear arsenal in the world with reportedly over 130 nukes in the basement, should be a cause of concern for the global community. Further, to deter India's conventional arms predominance and the Cold Start doctrine, it has developed TNWs, like the 60–75 km range Al Nasr. The development of TNWs has brought down Pakistan's nuclear threshold. Unlike India, Pakistan has ruled out adopting the No First Use (NFU) doctrine.

Notwithstanding its overall weak economy, for many years, the Pakistani armed forces have been allocated budgets far beyond affordability, disregarding essential expenditures required in the country for augmenting agriculture production, infrastructure, education, healthcare and poverty alleviation programmes. Pakistan's defence budget for 2016–17 was $8.2 billion as compared to India's defence budget of $53.5 billion for the same period. This gap between India and Pakistan is likely to increase in the coming years, despite assistance for Pakistan from nations like China, Saudi Arabia and the US.

J&K: AN INTENSE OBSESSION

Pakistan terms J&K as its 'jugular vein' and an unfinished agenda of the Partition. For India, the accession of J&K is complete and it considers the entire erstwhile princely state an integral part of itself. However, one of the most significant aspects of Pakistan's strategies is to constantly rally its people on the Kashmir issue, keep the pot boiling in J&K by its terrorist proxies and make all efforts to internationalize the dispute despite two agreements with India (the Simla and Lahore agreements) to resolve all such issues bilaterally.

STRENGTHS AND WEAKNESSES

The Pakistan Army has several strengths. Firstly, in public perception inside the country, it is considered as the saviour of the nation. In addition, it has control over its nuclear assets, has an efficient and active intelligence set-up, namely ISI, apart from its military intelligence branch. For its agendas, no matter how notorious, the army nurtures and controls diverse militant groups as strategic assets. They are active even during peacetime and have kept both the Indian and Afghan security establishments occupied with the latter having to divert substantial resources to checkmate the crafty and violence-driven ISI. The army also dictates its nation's foreign and defence policies far more than its elected governments. By establishing cantonments closer to the international boundary since Independence, Pakistan has prudently shortened its lines of communication and successfully reduced its operational response timings.

Apart from the much-vaunted lack of strategic depth, the other important glaring shortcomings and challenges for the army include the conventional force asymmetry with India, its operational commitments in the FATA region, limited logistics stamina, inadequate air defence capabilities against India's state-of-the-art aircraft and shortages in Armoured Personnel Carriers (APC). More importantly, its over-dependence on China and the US for military hardware could hamper its overall performance during a battle, especially in prolonged conflicts if these nations ever impose sanctions. Radicalization among junior ranks and the overall internal security situation in Pakistan itself may weaken its operational worthiness in times of conflict. By conservative estimates, even during peacetime, nearly 65 per cent of its total manpower is operationally committed.

Based on the experiences of the 1965, 1971 and Kargil operations, Pakistan has fine-tuned its propaganda and psychological warfare operations to mislead its own public and, not so successfully, world opinion regarding the outcome of any conflict situation. In full knowledge that it cannot achieve any significant military victory over India, Pakistan is likely to desperately endeavour to capitalize on the psychological fallout of even the small gains they make anywhere, and at the same time, order a blackout on significant losses to itself from India. Pakistan is of a strong belief that the notion of victory or defeat is in the abstract domain, more notional than factual, and will effectively utilize information operations and perception dominance as a major tool. If not with the world, but with its own simple, ill-informed people, it has successfully managed to hide the bitter truth, which speaks volumes of Pakistan's media and truth management.

In the near future, it does not appear that the Pakistani armed forces will change their basic strategic culture of dominating their nation and influencing its internal and external policies—something which has been adopted by them since Pakistan's birth and perfected in later years. More than Pakistan's successive governments, its military has crystallized an enduring rivalry with India. Despite many abortive attempts to destabilize India, the Pakistan military will continue its efforts to do so by employing non-state actors under the security of its ever-expanding nuclear umbrella. These so-called non-state actors will be more formidable, radicalized and professional than in the years past. Kashmir will continue to remain the army's main focus to keep India on the boil. In addition, the Pakistani armed forces will continue to seek better synergy in their strategic and operational planning with the Chinese People's Liberation Army (PLA) to counter India's conventional forces' superiority and keep India occupied on two fronts.

4
ISI: Symbol of the Deep State

We are confident of our information that your intelligence service, the Inter Services Intelligence Directorate, and elements of the Army are supporting Kashmiri and Sikh militants who carry out acts of terrorism... This support takes the form of providing weapons, training and assistance in infiltration... We're talking about direct, covert support from the Government of Pakistan...our information is certain. It does not come from the Indian government... If the situation persists, the secretary of state may find himself required by law to place Pakistan in the USG (United States Government) State sponsors of terrorism list... You must take concrete steps to curtail assistance to militants and not allow their training camps to operate in Pakistan or Azad Kashmir.

—James Baker, US Secretary of State, May 1992

Given the Taliban's intimate knowledge of the plan for the 9/11 attacks—the debate within the top ranks of the Taliban and the Al Qaeda, a shura council meeting, and the suggestion that Pakistan was pressuring Omar to keep Al Qaeda inside Afghanistan–it seems evident that the ISI must have known what was about to happen. In a so-called ally, this is treachery of the highest order.

—James Ridgeway in *The Five Unanswered Questions about 9/11: What the 9/11 Commission Report Failed to Tell Us*

Among the intelligence agencies in the last four decades that truly reflect a 'state within a state', Pakistan's ISI would easily be the most powerful among all. That the notorious ISI is more than a pillar of the Pakistani Deep State—to nations in the neighbourhood and its own people—would be merely stating the stark truth. It is a universally accepted truism that since decades, no political force has driven Pakistan's domestic and external agenda more than the ISI. Many, over the years, have dubbed the ISI as the 'invisible government'.

From relatively humble beginnings after the First Kashmir War in 1948, the ISI has not only outgrown the role and charter ascribed to it by Pakistan's founding fathers, but its notoriety, diabolical orchestration of terrorists of myriad hues inside Pakistan and in its neighbourhood—indeed its devious professionalism—make it a force to reckon with. Since its inception, the ISI has symbolized and worked cleverly for Pakistan's core philosophy of associating with radical Islamists whenever required, while also maintaining close contacts with Western powers as mandatory, politically. From its headquarters on Khayaban-e-Suhrawardy street in Islamabad, the ISI has worked passionately to suppress political opposition to the many military regimes it has serviced in Pakistan.

Australia-born British Army officer, Major General Walter Joseph Cawthorne, who had opted to serve the Pakistan Army immediately after Partition, was Pakistan Army's deputy chief. At Partition, Pakistan had inherited some Muslim elements of the Intelligence Bureau (IB) for its intelligence work, whose performance was found inadequate during the Kashmir hostilities initiated by Pakistan. Having gained the confidence of Pakistan's first C-in-C, General Ayub Khan, and Defence Secretary Major General Iskander Mirza (later President of Pakistan), Major General Cawthorne was asked to raise an organization to cater to the intelligence requirements of Pakistan's fledgling armed forces.

General Cawthorne, a World War I veteran, also had vast experience in intelligence work, having held many important intelligence appointments in his service with the British Army in the Middle East, India and South East Asia. After his pioneering work, Cawthorne retired in 1951 from active service. He was later posted as Australia's High Commissioner in Karachi (1954–58). Thus, the ISI, in its formative years, owing to Cawthorne and his legacy, established close and useful links with intelligence agencies of Western nations which stood them in good stead in the future.

The ISI drew its personnel from Pakistan's three services and a few civilians from their IB (Pakistan's share out of the original IB set-up of undivided India). It was chartered to collect, coordinate and disseminate military related intelligence for the three services, focusing mainly on India. Though the three services had their own service-specific intelligence directorates, the ISI was designated as the nodal agency for all strategic military related intelligence.

America's Central Intelligence Agency (CIA) and the French Service de Documentation Extérieure et de Contre-Espionnage (SDECE) also reportedly trained the ISI in the nuances and craft of intelligence. In addition, the UK's MI6 also provided training and equipment to the ISI in its initial years. The ISI was given no domestic intelligence responsibilities except in POK and the Northern Areas (now Gilgit–Baltistan). It was just a matter of time before it was destined to play a larger-than-life role in Pakistan's polity.

General Ayub Khan, like most of his West Pakistani kinsmen, never fully trusted the loyalties and professional competence of the Bengali officers in the Subsidiary Intelligence Bureau (SIB) of the IB based in East Pakistan's capital city of Dacca. He thus directed the ISI to maintain a close watch on these Bengali army officers and senior government officials. He even admitted to keeping tabs on Prime Minister Feroz Khan Noon through the ISI.

Years later, Zulfikar Ali Bhutto also, similarly, suspected Baloch personnel in the police force in Balochistan and in Pakistan's intelligence agencies. Thus, he gave sweeping powers to the ISI to keep the Baloch personnel under surveillance, and in check. During his tenure, General Zia-ul-Haq also expanded the internal intelligence responsibilities of the ISI to monitor the activities of Sindh nationalists and those in Bhutto's Pakistan's People Party (PPP). In addition, Zia had also put the ISI in charge of monitoring Shia organizations in Pakistan, particularly after the success of the Iranian

Revolution in 1979. Accordingly, the footprint of the ISI gradually expanded over most of the country's political and security landscape.

1950–1971: THE FORMATIVE YEARS

In the initial years after Pakistan's formation, the IB looked after domestic intelligence and reported to the Ministry of Interior. On the other hand, though the ISI came under the Ministry of Defence, it reported to the head of the government. The factual position was that the Army C-in-C usually decided on the kind and volume of information from the ISI to be forwarded to the political leadership.

Pakistan's last Governor General and first President, Iskander Ali Mirza, with the assistance of his C-in-C, General Ayub Khan, suspended the 1956 Constitution, imposed martial law in October 1958 and appointed Ayub Khan as the Chief Martial Law Administrator (CMLA). However, the overambitious Ayub Khan came to know from his intelligence personnel that President Mirza had endeavoured to establish contacts with eminent Pakistanis in various walks of life to strengthen his own position. Thus, barely three weeks into martial law, Ayub Khan threw out President Mirza and sent him unceremoniously to London. Reportedly, General Cawthorne prevailed upon Ayub Khan to ensure that no bodily harm comes to Iskander Mirza. Years later, Mirza's son, Humayun, wrote that had it not been for Cawthorne, 'It is quite possible that the generals would have arranged a convenient accident to kill the unfortunate President.'

General Ayub Khan also ordered the establishment of a covert action division in the ISI structure. In addition, he directed the military intelligence to report directly to the Chief of the General Staff (CGS) and both the ISI and IB to the CMLA. From thence onwards, the ISI also started focusing on internal political intelligence, monitoring important politicians and was called upon to deliver warnings and threats if they were getting too much in the way of the military. Meanwhile, in the 1960s, the ISI commenced, in right earnest, their activities in India's restive Northeastern states and in the '70s to stoke fires in Indian Punjab.

In May 1967, however, Ayub Khan pulled up the ISI and naval intelligence as the Karachi police uncovered an assassination plot being hatched against him, stating that, '...[the] naval intelligence and the ISI were nearly asleep...it just shows that we are babes in intelligence network'.

INTELLIGENCE FIASCO: THE 1965 WAR

One of the major failures of Pakistan's intelligence community, especially the ISI and military intelligence, were the intelligence lapses born out of totally wrong analyses of India's likely reactions in 1965 to Pakistani perfidy based on the leadership's ignorant ambitions. This was only a precursor of many such events to follow in the years ahead.

In early 1965, the ISI became an enthusiastic partner with the Kashmir Cell in Pakistan's Foreign Office in a plan to destabilize Kashmir. The mission, dubbed Operation Gibraltar, was to infiltrate armed groups into the Kashmir Valley, merge with the locals and create an uprising against the Indian state. This was to be followed up by military action in J&K against a supposedly beleaguered Indian Army. The ISI-sponsored plan, when first presented to General Ayub Khan, was outrightly rejected by him. However, in May 1965, the General succumbed to the convincing presentation of his GOC XII Corps, Lieutenant General Akhtar Malik, for a larger guerrilla-cum-military mission against J&K, dubbed Operation Grand Slam. Thus, by July end and early August, thousands of infiltrators were smuggled across J&K to create an uprising inside the state. On 1 September, the Pakistanis struck across the Akhnoor sector with an infantry division and adequate armour to cut off the Rajouri-Srinagar road and capture the vital Akhnoor Bridge on the Jammu-Srinagar highway. The Indian Army successfully thwarted the incursion of the Pakistani Army in Akhnoor sector, though losing Chamb. A few days later, the Indian Army surprised the Pakistanis by launching a major offensive across the international boundary in J&K and Punjab and radically altering the conflict grammar. The infiltrators who had crossed the ceasefire line (CFL) were caught, killed or pushed back to their side of the border. Ayub's grandiose plans based on his intelligence community's gravely wrong analyses and prodding by his young, over-ambitious foreign minister, Zulfikar Ali Bhutto, were a dismal failure. Pakistan tasted grave ignominy at the hands of its major adversary—the Indians. Some of the captured Pakistan Army personnel, who had masqueraded as local mujahideen, were made to testify the details of their plan inside the Valley on All India Radio. When Pakistan's military intelligence chief, Brigadier Muhammad Irshad, was informed, he reportedly expressed his anguish with the words, 'Oh my God, the bastards have spilt the beans'. The abysmal performance of Pakistani intelligence in this conflict led the then ISI director, Brigadier Riaz Hussain, to express his opinion to General Ayub Khan that, '…all these years, we were not doing our real work of counterintelligence, because we were too busy chasing your domestic political opponents.'

Many intelligence analysts have compared this Bhutto-driven botched-up operation in J&K to the disastrous Bay of Pigs invasion of Cuba, conducted a few years earlier during US President John Kennedy's tenure.

1969-1971: ISI AND GENERAL YAHYA KHAN

Pakistan's unsatisfactory performance in the 1965 operations followed by the Tashkent Declaration in 1966 took a toll on Field Marshal Ayub Khan's prestige in his country. With his health also failing, he handed over powers of the CMLA to his C-in-C, General Yahya Khan. In Pakistan's history, this was the second time when the military had assumed power. Yahya Khan created a National Security Council to which all intelligence agencies would report. Emphasis was also accorded to the restive province of East Pakistan and the ISI was further strengthened there under Major General Ghulam Umar to keep a watch on the internal security situation. Many sub-offices of the ISI were set up in the East but were manned exclusively by West Pakistanis. The worst was yet to follow.

To dilute the faith of secular-minded Bengalis who anyway outnumbered the Islamic fundamentalists in their province, the ISI set about establishing close links and supporting the Islamist JI. The ISI, however, misread the overall situation and glibly cabled this to their headquarters in Rawalpindi: '...massive show on Shaukat-e-Islam Day by Muslims indicate[s] their unflinching faith in Islamic cum Pakistan ideology.' There was nothing farther than the actual truth.

The results of the general elections soon after were more than a rude shock for the Pakistani establishment and more importantly for the ISI, whose surveys had conveyed a totally different picture. The ISI grossly misread the overall political situation in both the provinces, especially in East Pakistan. Yet militarily, the ISI claims of having pinched a copy of the Indian Army Chief's operational directives to his commanders for the ensuing invasion of East Pakistan. The Indian Army, however, has never confirmed that this leak ever took place. General Zia's former chief of staff, K.M. Arif, some years later also expressed that, '...notwithstanding the timely availability of strategic- and technical-level intelligence, there was something lacking in putting together of the Pakistani act.'

The loss of East Pakistan in December 1971 led to the end of the heavy drinker, unabashed womanizer, General Yahya Khan, as Pakistan's president. As a young squadron commander moving to battle locations opposite the Shakargarh Bulge, I vividly recall General Yahya Khan's speech on Pakistan Radio to his troops, in which the General spoke of Pakistan and the glory of Islam in a drunken stupor.

1971-1977: ZULFIKAR ALI BHUTTO

Immediately after General Yahya Khan's resignation and the loss of East Pakistan, Zulfikar Ali Bhutto was sworn in as Pakistan's Prime Minister. Though Bhutto was also guilty of contributing to the circumstances leading to the emergence of Bangladesh, he was now the beneficiary of the situation. Bhutto was never overly enamoured of the army or the ISI, but one of his first acts after assuming office was to grant a 'three-star general' status to the ISI director from the rank of brigadier. This sop was awarded to the ISI for ostensibly raising their morale after Pakistan's capitulation at the hands of India in the 1971 War.

With the Soviet occupation of Afghanistan having fully established by the early 1980s, Pakistan felt that the Soviets may invade the northern parts of their country, namely the NWFP and FATA regions. In addition, their military analysis contended that Pakistan would not be able to resist the Soviets conventionally and hence they prepared themselves to wage guerrilla actions against the Soviets. Accordingly, with the wholehearted approval of the US, a Special Forces School was set up in Cherat, near Peshawar, for training in guerrilla tactics. The school in Cherat became the institution to train Pakistan's elite Special Services Group (SSG) brigade with US instructors and equipment provided in generous measure. The CIA also pitched in and many Pakistanis were sent to Fort Benning and Fort Bragg in the US for specialized training. One of the prominent trainees in this establishment was Colonel Pervez Musharraf (later to be Pakistan's military ruler). This collaboration further cemented the ties between the US and Pakistan armies, and the CIA and ISI.

The early 1970s had also seen unrest and the winds of separatism blowing in Pakistan's largest province of Balochistan. Bhutto placed additional ISI personnel in Quetta and other parts of the province to monitor the internal security situation as he did not trust the local police or politicians there. There was internecine rivalry between the Bugti, Zehri, Jamoto tribes, considered pro-Centre and the Marri, Bizenjo and Mengal tribes who mostly constituted the provincial government. In addition, Baloch separatists also committed arson on the property of non-Baloch settlers. A large cache of arms was also found within the premises of the Iraqi embassy, ostensibly meant for the Marri tribe. Bhutto then dissolved the Balochistan provincial assembly and appointed Nawab Akbar Bugti as the Governor of the province. This also led to the NWFP provincial government resigning in protest against Bhutto's decision. All along, the ISI played a vital role in keeping Bhutto's government well-informed.

Meanwhile, neighbouring Afghanistan was also following the Balochistan unrest with concern. As is known, no government in Afghanistan to date has ever recognized the legality of the Durand Line. Many Pashtuns have dreamt of a larger Pakhtunistan embracing the Pathan-dominated areas in Pakistan, like the NWFP (now officially renamed as KPK). The then Soviet-influenced government in Kabul commenced the provision of training and arms to some Baloch separatists, especially of the Marri tribe. The Soviet intelligence agency, the redoubtable KGB, and Afghanistan's secret service, Khadamat-e Aetla'at-e Dawlati (KHAD), joined hands to equip and train these rebels for targeting Pakistani governmental assets in their own province of Balochistan. Both the Baloch and Pashtuns felt deprived by the dominance of Punjabis in their province who, they felt, were economically milking their resource-rich state without them getting anything in return.

Sensing Baloch unrest in the offing, Bhutto immediately swung into action. He requested for assistance from the Iranian ruler, Shah Reza Pahlevi, and the US to quell the rebels in Balochistan. The Shah was himself concerned about the political loyalties of the Baloch people settled in the eastern part of Iran and did not wish them to join the movement gathering strength in neighbouring Balochistan. Accordingly, his dreaded secret service, Sāzemān-e Ettelā'āt va Amniyat-e Keshvar (SAVAK) joined hands with the CIA and ISI to synergize their efforts to suppress the rebellious Baloch elements. The operations at that time were a success and thousands of Baloch rebels fled to neighbouring Afghanistan and into the arms of the waiting KGB and KHAD. Not satisfied with the state of preparedness against any misadventure from Afghanistan, Bhutto set up an Afghan desk in the ISI. Importantly, on the advice of his Frontier Constabulary chief, Major General Naseerullah Khan Babar, Bhutto gave orders to raise a 5,000-strong Afghan force to deal with rebels from across the Durand Line. This ambitious undertaking, successful in the initial years, had many renowned Afghan warlords and leaders of various ethnic hues like Gulbuddin Hekmatyar, Ahmad Shah Massoud and Burhanuddin Rabbani—all were destined to play an important role in Afghanistan in the years ahead.

The ISI, with Bhutto's full patronage, directed many hit-and-run acts employing their local insurgents inside Afghanistan besides initiating a few uprisings against the Kabul government. These pressure tactics led to Afghan PM Mohammad Daoud calling off his special operations against Pakistan and initiating peace talks with his Pakistani counterparts.

Bhutto also enhanced ISI's political role in his government far more than what the IB was allotted. An Internal Security Wing was created in the ISI and it was reputed to be monitoring his political opponents. One official of that time confirmed this, saying, '…even his minister's phones and offices were bugged and their personal lives monitored, since Bhutto trusted no one and relished replaying tapes in front of those who had fallen from grace.'

One of the major decisions taken by Bhutto in his tenure was redesignating the Army C-in-C as the Chief of Army Staff (COAS), taking a cue from India. In February 1976, General Tikka Khan, also known as the 'Butcher of Balochistan', retired as the Army Chief and was replaced by the unknown General Zia-ul-Haq, superseding a few senior lieutenant generals. Years later, one of Zia's close friends commented that Zia was 'the best sycophant to win over Mr Bhutto'. Not many in the army thought highly of Zia and most felt that his limit for upward mobility was not more than of a brigadier. Reportedly, King Hussein of Jordan, where Zia had served as a Brigadier, had put in a word for him to which Bhutto had demurred and Zia was then unstoppable. But most Pakistani analysts who have written about that era opine that though Zia was eighth in the order of seniority among the serving lieutenant generals, it was, in reality, the overly clever and self-serving director general of ISI, Lieutenant General Ghulam Jilani Khan, who prevailed upon an unsuspecting but flattery-prone Bhutto to appoint Zia as the COAS. How Zia changed Pakistan's future course amazingly, for better or worse, has still not been fully analysed.

After taking over as COAS, General Zia, though appearing rather subservient to Bhutto publically (as stated by his daughter Benazir Bhutto many times), was already plotting his and his nation's future. Pakistan's then Chairman of Joint Chief of Staff Committee (CJCSC), General Muhammad Sharif, got wind of something and duly warned Bhutto that Zia 'was up to no good, and might be planning some kind of coup'. When Bhutto inquired from his ISI chief, Ghulam Jilani Khan, about the authenticity of the disturbing news going around the capital, he feigned ignorance and attributed it to General Sharif spreading disinformation as he was jealous of General Zia. Bhutto at that time was seriously considering sacking his COAS; presumably Jilani had warned Zia that he may be sacked. The plot was thus finalized. Zia and Jilani were in this together right from the time Jilani had impressed upon Bhutto to appoint Zia as the next COAS. General Zia then moved swiftly and subsequently ousted Bhutto on the night of 4 July 1977, assuming total power in Pakistan.

Bhutto was jailed, treated rather shabbily and had false cases framed against him by Zia's military government. Notwithstanding clemency pleas by many foreign heads of state, including those who were traditionally friendly to Pakistan like the US, Saudi Arabia and Iran, Bhutto was hanged on 4 April 1979. General Jilani was, by then, comfortably ensconced as the Governor of Punjab. He left no doubt in anyone's mind that the ultimate loyalty of the uniformed community in Pakistan was to themselves and not to those elected. This indelible facet of the country's political destiny has come to the fore many a time!

1977–1988: GENERAL ZIA-UL-HAQ

Upon taking over the reins of Pakistan, General Zia knew that he was not well-versed with the intricacies and intrigues of the country's turbulent politics. However, he had to overcome his aversion for politicians, which he did with the help of the ISI and some of his trusted lieutenants like General Jilani. The latter is reported to have even spotted the young and promising Nawaz Sharif of the Pakistan Muslim League (PML), subsequently to be groomed for a larger political role in consonance with the military's vision for their nation.

General Zia directed the ISI to keep a strict watch on the PPP and its allies, led by Benazir Bhutto, which had started the Movement for the Restoration of Democracy (MRD) in the early 1980s with other political forces. A senior R&AW officer, the late B. Raman, recalls that the 'ISI's Internal Political Division had Shah Nawaz Bhutto, one of the two brothers of Benazir Bhutto, assassinated through poisoning in the French Riviera in the middle of 1985, in an attempt to intimidate her into not returning to Pakistan for directing the movement against Zia. But she refused to be intimidated and returned to Pakistan.'

Meanwhile, the relationship between US President Jimmy Carter's administration and Zia's government was deteriorating owing to Carter's disapproval of Pakistan's secret nuclear programme, which the latter pursued relentlessly with Chinese assistance and subterfuge. The attempt by some radical elements to set the US embassy in Islamabad on fire in November 1979 also soured the relationship. However, the onset of the Iranian Revolution, which led to the Shah's downfall, forced the CIA to elicit Pakistani help in setting up electronic equipment for the CIA's listening posts to monitor elements of the Soviet Union present in Iran during the Shah's rule. President Carter also endeavoured to mend fences with Pakistan by increasing assistance for the resistance fighters in Afghanistan battling the occupying Soviet troops. Accordingly, Carter offered a $400 million package which Zia famously dismissed as 'peanuts'.

After the visit of Carter's national security adviser, Zbigniew Brzezinski, to Pakistan in 1980, the US took a decision to vastly enhance its economic and military aid to it. At Brzezinski's suggestion, the US approved a $500 million package, dubbed Operation Cyclone, whose major aim was to destabilize the Soviet Union by promoting Islam in the CARs. Brzezinski wrote to his president, 'We now have the opportunity to give the USSR their Vietnam War.' Using religion as a weapon of war has thus not been the prerogative of Islamists alone.

Ronald Reagan, the new US president, raised the aid package to $3 billion and sent in a substantial amount of modern military equipment to Pakistan. The ISI also managed to convince the US regarding them being the sole agency to oversee the receipt and distribution of all arms, equipment and money for the Afghan resistance. The ISI's Afghanistan Bureau reportedly had sixty officers, 100 JCOs and 300 non-commissioned officers with its headquarters located at Ojhri Camp, in the northern outskirts of Rawalpindi. Reportedly, nearly 40 per cent of US aid was clandestinely kept by

Pakistan for its own utilization. During this time, the ISI raised, funded, trained and nurtured diverse elements of the Afghan mujahideen for employment to further Pakistani interests in Afghanistan in the coming years.

During all these years, the ISI scored many a success against the Soviet Occupation Forces. Much of the credit, apart from generous all-round assistance of the US, has to be also given to the ISI chief, Lieutenant General Akhtar Abdul Rehman, who was at the helm of the agency for seven years at a stretch. Though a favourite of Zia, General Akhtar had developed close relations with Afghan warlords of the likes of Hekmatyar and others, some of whom the Americans, especially the CIA, distrusted. Even Zia felt that Akhtar had outlived his usefulness and had amassed wealth dubiously during the Afghan conflict. Zia also felt the need to move Abdul Rehman out before the final triumph in Kabul, as he believed that the General would become a greater hero than him in the eyes of the Pakistani public. Accordingly, General Akhtar was awarded his 'fourth star' and kicked upwards by promoting him as CJCSC. Prime Minister Muhammad Khan Junejo, with the tacit approval of Zia, then appointed Major General Hamid Gul as ISI's new director general. Hamid Gul was also destined to play a major sinister role for the next two years as the chief and even for decades after his retirement.

Prior to his appointment, Hamid Gul had developed adequate contacts with leading figures of the US establishment in Pakistan and many of the Afghan warlords and other Pashtun leaders in Afghanistan—him being a Pashtun also helped. Meanwhile, the Najibullah regime in Kabul was fast losing power and the US dreaded the prospect of either of the radical Afghan leaders, wedded to their violent ways, assuming leadership roles. The US wanted the previous monarch, King Zahir Shah, to return to Kabul from his exile in Rome and head the reconciliation government. It was a plan which met with vehement rejection from the mujahideen commanders. The fact that both the Pakistani political and military leaders were of the same opinion as the mujahideen leaders is one of Afghanistan's tragedies.

MONUMENTAL CATASTROPHES: HAMID GUL'S TENURE

To the radical Islamists both among the Pakistani population and its numerous 'terror tanzeems', Hamid Gul has a larger-than-life image and following. But in his grandiose ambitions, Gul did more damage to his nation and its cause than generally perceived.

In April 1988, the Ojhri Camp which housed a diverse quantity of weaponry, including small arms ammunition, grenades, anti-tank mines, Stinger missiles, mortars and rockets meant for Afghan resistance fighters, and received primarily from the US, Egypt and Iran, went up in flames. The intensity of the fire and explosions had never been heard or seen before in Pakistan. The conflagration went on for three days before the blaze was finally doused. This unprecedented event shook the entire establishment and, till date, despite many courts of inquiries and investigations including those by the CIA and ISI, no one has been able to pinpoint the exact cause of this catastrophic event. Apart from poor storage conditions of this highly inflammable ammunition and equally inadequate firefighting systems in place, the blame game also involved the KGB, KHAD, India's R&AW and the corrupt elements inside the ISI. Nevertheless, the ISI's reputation did take a severe beating as it was directly managing this facility.

Another event which affected the ISI's professional reputation was the attack on Jalalabad in Afghanistan. This operation turned out to be very costly in terms of casualties to the Afghan resistance as the ISI did not fully appreciate the resilience of the Afghan defenders in Jalalabad and mistimed the launch by ISI-sponsored Hekmatyar's force. This action has, perhaps, been mostly forgotten in the overall narrative of the Afghan fight against the Soviets in the last stages of the Soviet occupation.

In 1988, the event—perhaps the most catastrophic—which shook Pakistan, and the standing of its entire Deep State, was the crash of the Presidential plane, Pakistan I, on 17 August. On board were General Zia, CJCSC General Akhtar, US Ambassador Arnold Raphel, chief American defence attaché to Pakistan Brigadier General Herbert M. Wassom and eight Pakistani generals. They were all returning to Islamabad after watching the live demonstration of the latest American tank, Abrams, at the firing ranges near Bahawalpur. This yet unsolved accident points to many conspiracy theories. The sabotage theory remains uppermost with fingers being pointed at the KGB, KHAD, R&AW and even US and Pakistani perpetrators. General Zia's accidental death impacted not only Pakistani politics, but also the region and the vexed Indo–Pak relations. General Zia had reportedly built up a reasonably friendly relationship with India's Prime Minister Rajiv Gandhi, and both were working to resolve some of the problems afflicting bilateral relations.

As regards the redoubtable Hamid Gul, some in Pakistan feel that though he kept himself busy with various terrorist tanzeems in Pakistan and Afghanistan even after his retirement, he was more sinned against than sinning. The fact, however, remains that Hamid Gul, till his last breath in August 2015, unquestionably symbolized the deviousness, violence and self-aggrandizement of the ISI. That he remained passionately anti-Afghanistan and anti-India till his end, despite being a Pashtun, remains a surprise to many.

POST ZIA'S DEATH

One of the significant developments during Zia's rule was the mounting involvement of intelligence agencies in the country's internal politics. The ISI played a significant part in cobbling together a major political alliance—the Islami Jamhoori Ittehad (IJI) which opposed the PPP in the 1988 general elections. Benazir Bhutto had become aware of the ISI's devious role of trying to manipulate results in these elections. After Bhutto's unexpected electoral victory and due to her not-so-cordial relations with President Ghulam Ishaq Khan, the latter took ten days to call her to take the oath as the next prime minister of Pakistan. In the 1990 general elections, the ISI also funded a few political leaders of their choice leading to Benazir's growing antagonism against them. As the Prime Minister, Benazir was uncomfortable with Hamid Gul and had him removed from his post as the ISI chief.

After sacking Hamid Gul, Benazir endeavoured to bring reforms in the ISI. She formed a committee under Air Chief Marshal Zulfiqar Ali Khan to review the role of all intelligence agencies in a democratic system of governance. Ironically, it was her father Zulfikar Ali Bhutto who had introduced military-dominated intelligence agencies to look into the internal politics of the nation beyond their normal charter, which led the ISI to assume widespread powers in the country's polity. It was then just a matter of time before the ISI spread its wings and became a potent force which no prime minister or even army chief could ignore. The ISI, as a matter of routine functioning, reportedly, normally 'bugged' their prime ministers and foreign dignitaries visiting Pakistan. It is common knowledge that Benazir Bhutto had even cautioned Indian PM Rajiv Gandhi to be careful in his conversations with her during his visit to Pakistan in December 1988 as the ISI had 'bugged' her office and residence.

As the prime minister in her first tenure in 1988, Benazir had, though in vain, tried to control the ISI, which functioned under the CJCSC, by appointing retired Lieutenant General Shamsur Rahman Kallue as the director general of ISI. This move further accentuated the differences between her and the senior military hierarchy. The Military Intelligence Directorate also stopped cooperating with the ISI and became the 'eyes and ears' of the COAS, General Mirza Aslam Beg. The handling of the unrest in Sindh during this time by General Kallue came in for much criticism by the Pakistani elite. Meanwhile, General Beg also received adverse attention for diverting the money paid by a businessman (Yubus Habib) meant for the IJI into his own private think tank called 'Friends', as exposed in the Mehrangate scandal. Pakistan's Chief Justice Iftikhar Chaudhry had reopened this old case and passed adverse comments against General Beg and the ISI chief, General Asad Durrani, on their mishandling of accounts.

Lieutenant General Asad Durrani, unlike his predecessors, had managed to develop good relations with Benazir Bhutto, despite disapproval of the senior military hierarchy. General Durrani was duly awarded by Benazir, in her second tenure as PM, with the appointment as the country's ambassador to Germany. Even General Musharraf during his tenure had sent him to Saudi Arabia as Pakistan's envoy.

After General Durrani retired in March 1992, the then PM Nawaz Sharif appointed his 'father's Tablighi Jamaat acolyte, Lieutenant General Javed Nasir, as his replacement.' General Nasir was known for his strong radical views and the military hierarchy was not pleased with this appointment. They rightly saw it as a political ploy by the Sharif family to appease their hard-line political constituency.

Rana Banerji, in his monograph on the Pakistan Army, has expressed his views in detail on the near fanatical Islamist leanings of a flowing beard-sporting General Nasir. He states that Nasir, '...as ISI chief was keen to find ways of supporting Islamic causes worldwide. He set up arrangements to arm and support Bosnian Muslims in collaboration with Iran. He saw opportunities to hurt India not only in Kashmir, but [in] other regions as well. He is reported to have established contact with Tamil extremists (LTTE) and set up a gun running operation with links to LTTE in Bangkok. He funded Arakanese Muslims (Rohingiyas)—who inhabit the area bordering Myanmar's frontier with Bangladesh—to help their fight for an independent enclave.' Rana further adds that, 'A strange, almost non-military atmosphere prevailed at ISI during General Javed Nasir's tenure. Bearded officers in the local dress, shalwar kameez, many of them hitched up to their ankles (a signature practice of the Tablighi Jamaat) kept strolling about in the office corridors. The 'strong room' which had currency stacked to the brim during the heyday of Afghan operations was now empty, as 'adventurist' ISI officers had been allowed to take away suitcases filled with cash to the field ostensibly for operations in the Central Asian countries. Discipline had gone down in the ISI and a large number of junior functionaries would miss their normal duties on the pretext of attending mosques.'

Rana also states that '...the Americans were aware of some of these hair-brained operational initiatives and complained about the same to Nawaz Sharif, but he initially disregarded these reports. A US TV channel investigated ISI's links during Javed Nasir's tenure in funding activities of the Jamaat-ul-Faqra, a militant Islamic outfit in USA. One of its operatives, Mubarak Shah Gilani was later found involved in the Daniel Pearl kidnapping (and subsequent murder) from Lahore.'

In May 1993, General Abdul Waheed Kakar took over as the COAS after General Asif Nawaz's untimely demise while in office. The new COAS managed to persuade the PM to remove Javed Nasir and had him replaced with Lieutenant General Javed Ashraf Qazi, the director general of the military intelligence. Interestingly, General Kakar was the choice of President Ghulam Ishaq Khan and not Nawaz Sharif. Relations between the president and prime minister gradually deteriorated and General Kakar unsuccessfully tried to mediate between the two. The general elections of October 1993 brought back Benazir Bhutto for her second stint as the prime minister. She had a cordial and smooth working relationship with her COAS. Her offer of an extension to General Kakar was politely refused by him.

The suave General Jehangir Karamat, an Armoured Corps officer, became the COAS in January 1996 after reports of initial differences of opinion between Bhutto and President Farooq Leghari on the choice of the next COAS. Apparently, Bhutto's first preference was Lieutenant General Javed Ashraf Qazi, former director general of ISI, while her husband Asif Zardari supported the then Karachi Corps Commander, Lieutenant General Mohammad Aslam, but he was deemed too junior. Ultimately, Karamat was selected on Kakar's recommendation. Differences soon surfaced over political demands for the use of army in non-military functions. Lieutenant General Khawaja Ziauddin Butt was brought in as the new director general of ISI, again without the approval of the Army Chief. Karamat criticized the profligacy of certain grandiose civilian government schemes and demanded setting up of a National Security Council (NSC) in a speech at the Naval Staff College, Lahore, in October 1998. This incensed PM Nawaz Sharif and he called in the Chief to remonstrate. But like many of his breed in the Armoured Corps, considered in armies the world over as the 'corps-de-elite', the self-respecting Karamat decided to quit instead.

Pakistan's Kargil fiasco, masterminded by the then Pak COAS, General Pervez Musharraf, led to tremendous discomfiture for Pakistan and PM Nawaz Sharif. Rana Banerji, says that as 'differences between General Musharraf and Nawaz Sharif widened and with the international disclosure of Pakistan Army's direct complicity in the Kargil misadventure, through Musharraf—General Aziz tapes, a strange spectacle was witnessed—that of the DG MI tapping the conversations between the DG ISI and the PM and reporting to the Army Chief. This also led to the unprecedented sacking of Lieutenant General Tariq Pervaiz, GOC XII Corps, at Quetta by General Musharraf, on grounds of leaking of minutes of a Corps Commanders meeting with the prime minister. Developments soon came to a head, with Nawaz Sharif appointing General Ziauddin as his new Army Chief even while General Musharraf was on a tour abroad (Sri Lanka and Maldives), the Army Chief requisitioning assistance from his Corps Commanders in Rawalpindi (Lt General Mahmood Ahmed) and Karachi (Lt General Usmani), to dishonour these orders and help effect yet another coup against an elected Political Executive.'

It merits mention that as GOC of the Rawalpindi-based 10 Corps, General Mahmood Ahmed had played a vital role in the coup which General Musharraf had launched leading to Nawaz Sharif's ouster. General Ahmed had sent tanks from the Rawalpindi-based 111 Brigade to surround the houses of the Prime Minister and the TV station where General Ziauddin had placed himself. Some weeks later, however, General Ziauddin also fell out of his mentor's favour as Musharraf reportedly did not make him the COAS after him. 'Gen Ahmed is alleged to have given contrary advice to Mullah Omar during one of his mediation visits to Kabul just after 9/11, to stand up to the Americans. Unconfirmed rumours link him to the terrorist Omar Sheikh, one of the hostages released from the IC 814 plane hijacking who was later implicated in the Daniel Pearl murder. Other rumours allege General Ahmed was aware of Omar Sheikh's role in sending money to the 9/11 plotters in Europe. After the Americans complained to General Musharraf, General Ahmed was sacked as ISI chief and kept in house confinement in Lahore, before being rehabilitated in a Fauji Foundation assignment.'

Since the Musharraf–Sharif episode, all subsequent ISI chiefs have been appointees of the COAS.

General Ashfaq Parvez Kayani was one of the senior officers

of the Pakistan Army in recent times, who has been both the ISI director general and the COAS. The son of a humble Naib Subedar (JCO), General Kayani briefly commanded the Rawalpindi X Corps before General Musharraf (as COAS and President) appointed him as the director general. In the latter appointment, he was involved in parleys with Benazir Bhutto, while she was in exile in UAE. Even the US was keen for Benazir to return to her native land and democracy to once again be given a chance. The Americans were, reportedly, well-inclined towards General Kayani. 'He remained loyal to General Musharraf but underplayed this loyalty during the burgeoning civil society dissent and Lawyers Movement (2007-2008) for restoration of Chief Justice Iftikhar Chaudhary when General Musharraf had to be eased out as President.' He did manage, however, to have General Musharraf, his old mentor, flown out of Pakistan safely. An acute chain-smoker and not much of a speaker, General Kayani witnessed grave embarrassment during his tenure when the US Special Forces raided Al-Qaeda supremo Osama bin Laden's hideout and killed him. General Kayani symbolized the typical senior Pakistani officers who are consistently anti-India and supporters of most anti-India and anti-Afghan terrorist outfits proliferating in Pakistan.

Another aspect for which General Kayani is remembered is his dual policy of keeping the Americans happy whilst keeping lines of communication open with some terror tanzeems in Pakistan and Afghanistan. Ably assisted in this duplicity by ISI Director General, Lieutenant General Ahmed Shuja Pasha, General Kayani did manage to keep Islamic militants in Swat and the FATA regions, besides even the anti-national Tehrik-i-Taliban Pakistan (TTP), in good humour to prevent them from organizing anti-Pakistan terror acts.

ISI: TERROR OPERATIONS AGAINST INDIA

Among the countless diabolical intelligence operations mounted by the sinister ISI since its inception, a majority of them have been targeted against India, in particular. In fact, one of the sub-sections of its Joint Intelligence Bureau is specifically tasked for operations against India.

A few specific acts against India in J&K, Punjab and the Northeast regions have been covered separately in the later chapters. However, many of the ISI's terrorist actions also in the Indian hinterland have been spectacular to say the least. In mid-1977, after General Zia-ul-Haq wrested power in Pakistan, he directed the ISI to work all out to achieve success as conceived in his Operation TOPAC strategy, namely 'bleeding India by a thousand cuts'. General Haq also worked assiduously for his K2 (Kashmir and Khalistan) stratagem and the ISI was his handmaiden to make it happen. Some of the ISI's major terror acts inside India have been the Bombay train blasts on 12 March 1993 in which, on a single day, 350 innocent civilians were killed and over 1,200 injured. This gruesome terror attack was the handiwork of Bombay-based don and smuggler, Dawood Ibrahim on instructions of the ISI. He was assisted by his chief lieutenant Tiger Memon, Abu Salem (currently in Indian custody) and some other Bombay- and Karachi-based smuggling kingpins. The ISI was also involved in the 2006 Mumbai train blasts while its most dastardly terror attack in recent history has been the Mumbai 26/11 terror strike in which over 181 civilians including a dozen foreigners were killed at the iconic Taj Hotel and a few other places. The subsequent arrest of Pakistani terrorist Ajmal Kasab by the Indian police and the joint investigations and interrogation by the FBI and Indian security agencies of David Coleman Headley all revealed, unmistakably, the Pakistani Army, ISI and LeT hand in engineering the Mumbai blasts.

An interesting event pertaining to the earlier terrorist act also deserves mention here. Immediately following the Bombay blasts in March 1993, the masterminds of this ghastly terror attack, speedily disappeared as plotted by the ISI. In a conversation with the author, India's Consul General in Karachi at that time, Rajiv Dogra, recalls the Pakistani subterfuge. A few days after these blasts, Dogra was invited for dinner by a well-known Karachi-based businessman to his house. Traditionally, the Indian Consul General in Karachi was made much off in the city's protocol-driven and cosmopolitan society. On that evening, as Rajiv Dogra walked into the Pakistani businessman's sprawling house, he noticed in the porch a group of invitees standing around a particular individual. As Dogra walked towards the porch, the individual concerned spotted the approaching Indian Consul General and hastily withdrew inside the house—he was perhaps cautioned by those around him. However, this seemingly casual slip was not missed by the sharp Rajiv Dogra. Well-entrenched with the Karachi hoi polloi, Dogra found out that the man who made an exit on his arrival was none other than the chief coordinator of the Bombay blasts—Tiger Memon! His arrival from Bombay via Dubai to Karachi was also confirmed by one of Pakistan International Airlines employees to the Indian consulate's staff.

It was also revealed to the author that during Rajiv Dogra's tenure in Karachi (1992–94), both during the times of PM Nawaz Sharif and then PM Benazir Bhutto, the ISI did their level best to have the Indian Consulate in Karachi shut. A major reason was that the latter's residence was located in the posh Clifton area of Karachi opposite the sprawling Bhutto bungalow and the ISI wanted the Clifton area to be cleared of Indians where they wanted to house the notorious Dawood Ibrahim. After Rajiv Dogra left, the Consulate General's office was instructed to be shut by the Pakistani government on flimsy diplomatic grounds. Subsequently, Dawood and his henchmen were shifted to this prized location. Incidentally, Indian intelligence was more than aware that Dawood, in cohorts with the ISI, planned all his nefarious activities against the Indian state from his Clifton den. Amazingly, the Pakistani government, despite irrefutable proof about Dawood's presence in Karachi, has consistently, even at the highest levels, merrily refused to acknowledge his presence either in Karachi or anywhere else in Pakistan—in the same manner as it had denied the presence of al-Qaeda supremo Osama bin Laden in Pakistan till he was taken out by US Special Forces.

Dawood continues, till today, to run his anti-India operations from Karachi and many other places in Pakistan (known to frequently change his places of residence) via his notorious 'D' Company. Dawood, by any standards, has eminently served his ISI masters not only in countless anti-India terror acts, but also smuggling into India hundreds of crores of counterfeit Indian currency via Nepal and Bangladesh and across the international border between the two nations through J&K, Punjab and Rajasthan. Dawood continues to be one of Pakistan's well-guarded and prized strategic assets and it is wishful thinking by Indian agencies that Pakistan will ever hand him over to them. Pakistan may, on its own, bump him off if it feels that he has outlived his utility to that country—this is also a possibility.

In the last forty years, the ISI has acquired a larger-than-life image among all institutions in Pakistan. With over 25,000 permanent employees and reportedly 30,000 on its rolls as informants and other related roles, the ISI is a well-organized and well-oiled outfit. Within the services, particularly the Pakistan Army, officers in the younger ranks as captains, majors and colonels, try to get a tenure or two in the ISI for the prestige, perks and privileges that serving in the ISI gets them. That the ISI's role has gone far beyond its original charter of the provision of external and military related intelligence for the three services is a reality which no one in Pakistan will ever contest even if they criticize the ISI's unconstitutional powers and its machinations-creating abilities. It truly symbolizes the Pakistani Deep State in all its sinister forays inside Pakistan and outside in the entire region. Terrorist surrogates that Pakistan created against the nation's so-called enemies also have a propensity to strike back at their creators. But regrettably, not only individuals or organizations, but even nations forget that monsters once born tend to become self-serving and defeat the very purpose for which they were originally conceived.

5

Genocide in East Pakistan

> There is a consensus on the imperative need of bringing to book senior army commanders who have brought disgrace and defeat to Pakistan by their subversion of the Constitution, usurpation of political power by criminal conspiracy, their professional incompetence, culpable negligence and willful neglect in the performance of their duties and physical and moral cowardice in abandoning the fight when they had the capabilities and resources to resist the enemy.
>
> —Justice Hamoodur Rahman Commission Report on the East Pakistan defeat, kept under wraps by successive Pakistan governments

The over-involvement of Pakistan's Deep State in the nation's affairs, beyond the usually accepted jurisdictions, is a classic example of how those chartered to defend one's country end up breaking it. The severing of its eastern wing in December 1971 is a telling manifestation of the army's atrocities, widespread corruption, unbridled use of snatched power and the moral laxity of many of its generals in the treatment of the ethnically different yet religiously similar province of East Pakistan. Till date, the main reason ascribed by Pakistan to East Pakistan's breakaway has been, allegedly, a well-thought out conspiracy by India. It is indeed true that when the opportunity arose, India encouraged and supported the Mukti Bahini (a group of Bengali freedom fighters). Subsequently, when matters escalated out of control with a million Bengali refugees streaming across the international border from East Pakistan to India, the latter, under the decisive leadership of Prime Minister Indira Gandhi, mounted a highly successful military action into East Pakistan which resulted in the birth of a sovereign nation—Bangladesh. It is worth analysing the manner in which a new nation was carved out for the first time after World War II, altering the map of South Asia.

SIMMERING DISCONTENT

On 25 March 1969, faced with months of widespread public protests and strikes and with the all-powerful army also discontented with the state of the nation, Pakistan's titular head, President (Field Marshal) Ayub Khan ultimately succumbed to his Army Chief General Yahya Khan's suggestion, and handed over the country to him. Ayub Khan abrogated the Constitution in place and imposed martial law. Thus, once again, Pakistan's quest for the rule of democracy received a severe jolt. Yahya Khan had become the Chief Martial Law Administrator on 25 March 1969 and then assumed the presidency on 31 March.

General Yahya Khan, the country's new dictator and widely known for his weaknesses for the 'good things of life', in his first speech to his nation exclaimed that, '...[his] sole aim in imposing martial law is to protect life, liberty and the property of the people and put the administration back on the rails I wish to make [it] absolutely clear that I have no ambition other than the creation of conditions conducive to the establishment of a constitutional government.' These were familiar words, similar to several other military dictators at the commencement of their rule. Within a month, Yahya Khan proclaimed to his fellow Baloch Regiment officers in Abbotabad that 'we must be prepared to rule this unfortunate country for the next 14 years or so. I simply can't throw the country to the wolves.'

Yahya had indeed inherited political instability and a weak economy, and its eastern wing was gradually getting restive. The primary reasons were the nation's overall meagre investment in developmental projects, poor economic growth in East Pakistan as also the overall representation of Bengalis in the nation's armed forces and its powerful bureaucracy. There were merely 5 per cent Bengali officers commissioned in the army and 30 per cent serving in the bureaucracy. In addition, Pakistani Army officers generally displayed an arrogant attitude towards their Bengali colleagues and did not hesitate to convey that they desired Bengali culture to be purified of its Hindu influence. The West Pakistani civil and military elites believed that the Bengali Muslims, though in majority in East Pakistan, were lesser Muslims owing to their ethnicity and affinity to the Hindu Bengalis. Dismissing them as a non-martial race, the West Pakistanis often referred to the East Pakistanis as 'black bastards'. If the 'one-man, one-vote' system had been followed by Pakistani governments since their independence, then the majority Bengali population would have played a more dominant role in the nation's politics.

Shuja Nawaz sums up the overall situation prevailing in Pakistan during Yahya's early tenure: 'East Pakistan was increasingly coalescing under the banner of the AL under Sheikh Mujibur Rahman, who had once been a junior office holder but now had supplanted Maulana Bhashani as the leading political figure of the province. The PML, a construct of the Ayub government, was now in tatters, an orphan looking for a new master. In the West, the Pakistan's People's Party (PPP) of Zulfikar Ali Bhutto, an upstart political party, had caught the imagination of the youth and the opportunistic politicians of the traditional parties (including the Muslim League).' He further clarifies that, '...presiding over this simmering discontent, the army under Yahya was not equipped to handle the subtleties of political discourse. Trained to fight external enemies, principally India, the military had a hard time comprehending the complexities of civilian unrest within Pakistan. Its response was often too swift and too harsh, defining opposition to the government as "treason". It saw the hidden hand of India in all the troubles in East Pakistan and relied on its military force to quell disturbances, thus fuelling further discord.' Thus, the Pakistan Army's high-handedness, cruelty and arrogance in dealing with its own people had set the ball rolling for the eventual breakaway of its eastern wing.

BATTLE LINES DRAWN BETWEEN THE TWO WINGS

General Yahya, meanwhile, had restored the one-man, one-vote to the electorate all across Pakistan, which was a small but laudable step in the country's search for democracy. However, this step, based on the population strength in the western and eastern wings, gave East Pakistan 169 seats compared with 144 seats for West Pakistan in the National Assembly. In West Pakistan, Zulfikar Ali Bhutto's PPP was gaining in popularity whereas Sheikh Mujibur Rahman was becoming a cult figure with his appeal to Bengali nationalism catching the imagination of Bengali youth and other sections of the society. The battle lines for the ensuing chasm between the two leading political outfits were being inexorably drawn on Pakistan's map.

The results of the general elections of December 1970 produced traumatic results for the Pakistani establishment, totally at variance with the estimates provided by its intelligence organizations. Mujibur Rahman's Awami League garnered 160 of the 162 seats in the eastern wing while the PPP swept to an unexpected majority, winning 81 seats out of 138 seats in the western wing. General Yahya Khan was now faced with the trickiest situation in his life, not knowing how to resolve this impasse in which a recalcitrant Bhutto was not prepared to sit in the Opposition with Mujibur Rahman as the PM. Yahya Khan made frequent appeals and visits to both the contending competitors but to no avail. Bhutto had suggested that the nation appoint two PMs—one each for the respective wings. This was hardly a solution to keep an intra-warring Pakistan united. Thus Yahya, despite many efforts, postponed the gathering of the National Assembly citing constitutional and security reasons. The grounds were then speedily prepared by the army to teach the Bengalis a lesson they would never forget. Yahya uttered to his close circle of advisers that 'we may have to give him (Mujib and his party men) a whiff of the grapeshot, should they refuse to behave and go berserk.'

With the establishment continuing to brand even Bengali Muslims as 'Hindus at heart', the inevitable was thus around the corner.

Sensing the serious situation developing in East Pakistan, the Pakistani government, in December 1970, conceived Operation Blitz, in which the commander of its Eastern Command, Lieutenant General Sahibzada Yaqub Khan, would take over, if the need arose, all powers of the East Pakistani governor and ensure law and order. Initially, General Yaqub Khan also felt that strong punitive action against the dissenting voices in East Pakistan was the answer to quell the rising discontent rapidly. However, the sensible army commander soon realized the folly of his earlier directives to adopt a martial law approach in dealing with the Bengalis. Meanwhile, on 6 March 1971, having failed in his attempts to broker a deal between the Awami League and Pakistani government, the governor of East Pakistan, Vice Admiral Syed Muhammad Ahsan, resigned. Four days later, even General Yaqub Khan followed suit, stating unequivocally that, '…the only solution to present crisis is a purely political one…there is no military solution which can make sense in present situation. I am consequently unable to accept the responsibility for implementing a mission, namely military solution, which would mean civil war and large scale killings of unarmed civilians and would achieve no sane aim.' Some in the army back in Pakistan felt that Yaqub Khan had 'lost his nerve' and by accounts of that period, General Yahya Khan nearly had him court-martialled. Yaqub Khan was, however, immediately replaced by Lieutenant General Tikka Khan, who had earlier earned the sobriquet of 'Butcher of Balochistan' for his brutality against dissident Baloch tribesmen in 1958.

Sensing the doom approaching the country with hardened stances in both the western and eastern wings, and, the army's total animosity towards the Bengalis, General Yahya and Bhutto made frequent trips to Dacca to assuage Mujib. On 23 March 1971, which was Pakistan Day, General Yahya, accompanied by Bhutto, paid another visit to East Pakistan but they found that in many places the Bangladesh flag had been hoisted, making it a Resistance Day. Thus, Yahya Khan decided to leave Dacca ordering General Tikka

Khan to 'sort them out'. A month earlier, Yahya Khan, during a conference, had also stated: '...Kill three million of them and the rest will eat out of your hands.' Thus giving state sanction to the genocide which was to follow shortly.

THE GENOCIDE IN 1971

On the night of 25 March 1971, the army launched Operation Searchlight to quell the Bengali mutiny against the Pakistani state. The operations commenced with full ferocity and unspeakable cruelty against students, professors of Dacca University and other intellectuals named in lists that had already been prepared. Bhutto, who was holed up in the Dacca InterContinental hotel, saw the rising flames and left the next morning for Karachi, terribly saddened. On reaching Karachi and hopeful that the army's actions would prove successful, he made his famous, though wholly inaccurate, statement at the Karachi airport, 'By the Grace of God, Pakistan has been saved.'

Massacre, arson, destruction and rape became commonplace and, within a few days, it turned into a full-scale genocide perpetrated by the army on its own citizens. Within weeks, it was estimated that three million East Pakistani citizens had been exterminated—one of the worst and most inhuman tragedies inflicted on one's own countrymen by any government in human history. The Pakistan Army's bestiality crossed all bounds as they used rape 'as an instrument of coercion'. Susan Brownmiller, in her book, *Against Our Will: Men, Women, and Rape*, observes that, 'Between two to four million women were raped over a period of nine months... Girls of eight and grandmothers of seventy-five had been sexually exploited, assaulted... they abducted tens of hundreds and held them by force in their military barracks for nightly use.' Even General Amir Abdullah Khan Niazi, the Commanding General in East Pakistan, appallingly, exclaimed that 'you cannot expect a man to live, fight and die in East Pakistan and go to Jhelum for sex, would you?'

Over a million refugees fled to neighbouring India, which put up refugee camps and tried its best to provide succour to the extent possible. Many international organizations, including the UN and Red Cross, pitched in to provide some humanitarian relief to the hapless East Pakistani refugees. The influx of refugees in such colossal numbers would soon become a major problem for the Government of India. In addition, one of Mujib's confidants, Tajuddin Ahmad, had fled to Calcutta and declared himself the prime minister of the Bangladesh government-in-exile.

Meanwhile, with the security situation deteriorating rapidly by the day, Yahya Khan sent in Lieutenant General Niazi as the army commander to Dacca. On 10 April 1971, Niazi (who superseded many officers to the rank of lieutenant general) took over the army operations from Lieutenant General Tikka Khan, who later became governor of Punjab and Martial Law Administrator. Years later, General Niazi, in his memoir, *The Betrayal of East Pakistan*, stated that, 'General Tikka Khan instead of carrying out the task given to him, i.e. to disarm the Bengali units and persons and to take into custody the Bengali leaders, resorted to a scorched earth policy. His orders to his troops were: "I want the land and not the people."' Even the Adviser to East Pakistan, Major General Rao Farman Ali, known to be of brutal temperament, had written in his diary, 'Green land of East Pakistan will be painted red.'

Troops from the Bengali units like the East Pakistan Rifles and East Bengal Regiment had deserted and were all marshalled under the command of Colonel M.A.G. 'Tiger' Osmani, who now had become a force to reckon with in East Pakistan leading the rebels. He soon controlled most of the countryside and carried out frequent raids on Pakistan Army convoys and soft targets.

INDIA'S MILITARY AND DIPLOMATIC MANOEUVRES

The summer of 1971 witnessed continuing unprecedented violence perpetrated by the Pakistani Army on hapless Bengalis including innocent men, women and children. The psychological division of East Pakistan was complete by the time the Indian armed forces launched their operations in the first week of December 1971 to liberate Bangladesh.

Initially, as is well known, Prime Minister Indira Gandhi wanted the Indian armed forces to launch its operations in East Pakistan in March–April 1971. But being a pragmatic leader, she heeded to the advice of her Army chief, General (later Field Marshal) Sam Manekshaw, to postpone the Indian Army's advance into East Pakistan later in the year. The militarily sound reasons were, firstly, to avoid the summer rains which render movement difficult for army units advancing in the countryside, and, importantly, for the snows to come in the winters which would discourage China opening another front against India in the high Himalayas. Mrs Gandhi also utilized the additional time thus available to sensitize the world about Pakistan's genocidal activities against its own people and the burden India was facing with the influx of millions of refugees.

As Indira Gandhi quietly gave the armed forces the go-ahead to prepare for the impending invasion into East Pakistan, she also got into full preparations for her diplomatic offensive. In August 1971, observing a clear-cut, anti-India stance of the US administration, spearheaded by US President Richard Nixon and his wily Secretary of State, Henry Kissinger, the Indian Prime Minister found it prudent for India to sign a Treaty of Peace, Friendship and Cooperation with the Soviet Union. This assured India of military and diplomatic support, namely the exercising of a veto by the Soviet Union in the UN Security Council (UNSC), if required.

In October 1971, Mrs Gandhi undertook an extensive tour of many global capitals to explain India's position and Pakistani atrocities heaped upon its own people and the inevitability of possible Indian military intervention. Despite the US embargo on exporting arms and equipment to Pakistan since 1965, President Nixon had discreetly ordered the continuation of arms supply to Pakistan in clear violation of US laws. During Mrs Gandhi's visit to the White House, the US President, reportedly, displayed a cold attitude, bordering on rank discourtesy towards her. This is something India and she never forgave—but then Nixon hardly exhibited the persona US presidents are normally made of.

During this period, China, being wooed desperately by the US, also proclaimed its support for Pakistan and blamed India for the overall situation in East Pakistan. As is well-documented, Pakistan had played a major role in arranging meetings of Henry Kissinger and other US officials with the Chinese establishment during this period. The US was more than keen to isolate their bête noire—the Soviets—in the region and was thus hell-bent to strike bargains with the Chinese. The Pakistanis were convenient mediators to assist the US and Chinese to get together.

With the overall situation in the subcontinent getting out of hand and Pakistan being warned by the US about an impending Indian attack in East Pakistan, the foolhardy Pakistan establishment got provoked into initiating a reckless military attack on India itself. On 3 December 1971, Pakistan launched a pre-emptive air strike against some forward Indian air bases in Punjab, Rajasthan and J&K. This strike, similar to the Israeli strike against the Egyptian Air Force in 1967, however, turned out to be a damp squib—failing miserably and giving the Indians a chance to retaliate with all their might. India opened up both the fronts—namely the western and eastern sectors—with full force. Sensing major military defeats on both fronts for Pakistan, the US did their utmost to pressurize India to terminate hostilities, even threatening India with using their Pacific Command's Seventh Fleet. However, Nixon was not aware of the determination and courage of Mrs Gandhi who dismissed his threats with contempt.

BIRTH OF A SOVEREIGN NATION

The 1971 War was brief and comprehensively decisive. The Indian forces launched multi-pronged offensives into East Pakistan supported by the Indian Air Force and parachute drops. The Indian Navy also played a significant role blockading Karachi with the Indian Air Force successfully blasting the Karachi port and its oil terminals. In merely thirteen days, the Pakistan Army accepted defeat by the Indian Army's Eastern Command on 16 December 1971. Having achieved the nation's strategic objectives, Mrs Gandhi ordered a unilateral ceasefire which was immediately accepted by Pakistan President Yahya Khan. On the western front, the Indian Army made significant gains both in the mountainous and the plains sectors. The war ended with General

Niazi and 93,000 Pakistan Army personnel laying down their arms and surrendering to Lieutenant General J.S. Aurora, India's Eastern Army commander, at a historic ceremony in Dacca.

This war terminated with the birth of Bangladesh as a sovereign nation. It was indeed India's finest hour attributable to the Indian armed forces' matchless professionalism and valour and embellished with Indira Gandhi's determined political leadership.

In Pakistan, General Yahya Khan resigned in favour of Zulfikar Ali Bhutto. Sheikh Mujibur Rahman was released by the Pakistanis and he took over the reins of his newly born nation immediately after the ceasefire.

In March 1972, Pakistan PM Bhutto and his Indian counterpart, Mrs Gandhi, met at Simla to resolve matters pertaining between the two nations as an aftermath of the 1971 War. After protracted negotiations, which nearly ended in failure, both the leaders signed the Simla Agreement, which conformed to the Indian demand of resolving all disputes between the two nations bilaterally and accepting the inviolability of India's borders. Christine Fair, with a slightly different viewpoint, analyses the Agreement, stating, 'Pakistan, for its part, had four objectives, which it largely secured. It sought to have its 93,000 prisoners of war released, to stop Bangladesh from holding war crimes trials of captured Pakistani soldiers, to regain some 5,000 square miles of territory that India had seized in the west, and finally to ensure that its position in Kashmir remained fundamentally unchanged…the salient features of the resulting settlement included the restoration of bilateral diplomatic relations, a mutual commitment to avoiding the use of force to resolve the Kashmir dispute, and a change in the name of the 1948 Ceasefire Line to the Line of Control (LoC).' She further surmises, '…after the war, India emerged as the undisputed power in South Asia… Pakistan's inability to bring ethnic Bengalis into the national project had dealt another serious blow to the two-nation theory, which was and remains the ideological basis of Pakistan and its army.'

The birth of Bangladesh, unparalleled in the history of the period post World War II, has understandably not yet been digested by its parent nation, Pakistan. This defeat in 1971 can be comprehensively attributable to the failings of its own Deep State. In view of similar ethnic divisions currently afflicting Pakistan, history may just repeat itself if its institutions do not pay heed to its myriad fault lines and replicate the same mistakes committed in East Pakistan in the summer of 1971. The tinderbox of ethnic divisions has a propensity of being catastrophic if not handled with fair play and caution.

6

Strategic Deterrence through Nuclear Sabre-rattling

> If India builds the bomb, we will eat grass and leaves for a thousand years, even go hungry, but we will get one of our own.
>
> —Pakistan's Prime Minister Zulfikar Ali Bhutto, 1965

> Pakistan's growing nuclear arsenal and its evolving tactical nuclear weapons doctrine pose increasing risk of an incident or accident.
>
> —Vincent R. Stewart, Director, Defence Intelligence Agency, USA, 2016

Pakistan is one of the nine nuclear states in the world and the only Islamic nation to possess nuclear weapons. Amazingly, most countries in the world, especially the US and Israel, have vehemently opposed the nuclear weapons programme of another Muslim nation—Iran—which the latter denies, but most nations have inexplicably glossed over the nuclear ambitions and the consequent sabre-rattling by an irresponsible Pakistan. The dangers which a nuclear-armed Pakistan poses to the region is a harsh reality of the times.

On 28 and 30 May 1998, with a series of six nuclear explosions in the deserts of Chagai in restive Balochistan, Pakistan declared itself a nuclear power, putting to an end its long practised policy of nuclear ambiguity. Pakistani Prime Minister Nawaz Sharif, then in his second tenure, gleefully exclaimed, '...today, we have settled the score with India.' That Pakistan's entire nuclear programme is India-specific was once again clarified to the whole world. Two weeks earlier, when India had carried out five nuclear explosions as part of its tests in the Pokhran deserts in Rajasthan, the Indian PM, Atal Bihari Vajpayee, had not even mentioned Pakistan in his post-tests speech. Pakistan going nuclear, apart from matching India, is attributable to its obsessive desire to be equal to India in virtually everything and thus be treated by the world as India's peer, counter any nuclear threat from India and, most importantly, deter India from using its overwhelming conventional superiority in the battlefield against Pakistan. It is a well-accepted cardinal rule in Pakistan's strategic thought, among most defence analysts and its establishment, that its nuclear arsenal is the final guarantor of its security against a larger and stronger India by neutralizing the conventional military imbalance between the two nations.

Brigadier Feroz Hassan Khan, who has served in the Pakistan Army's Nuclear Strategic Plans Division (SPD), has adequately expressed in his aptly titled book, *Eating Grass: The Making of the Pakistani Bomb*, that in Pakistan, '...nuclear developments were interwoven with the broad narrative of Pakistani nationalism'. And, that Pakistani nukes 'have evolved into the most significant symbol of national determination and a central element of Pakistan's identity'. He further amplifies that their nukes reflect 'Pakistan's enduring rivalry and strategic competition with India'.

EVOLUTION AND EXPANSION OF NUCLEAR CAPABILITY

Though in today's Pakistan, its military is the final arbiter of the development and deployment of its nuclear weapons, surprisingly, the army hierarchy was rather slow after its independence to press for nuclear establishments to come up in the country. In its initial years, the army including General Ayub Khan, did not feel the need to go nuclear. Ayub Khan believed, rather naively, that apart from the unaffordability of nuclear weapons, they would buy a nuclear bomb 'off the shelf' from one of its allies in case India developed a bomb. In addition, he expressed that Western powers, especially the US, would not take kindly to Pakistan going nuclear. However, after reports of India setting up its atomic energy establishments, Pakistan did send a few young scientists to the West to acquire some rudimentary knowledge of atomic energy.

Pakistan's civilian nuclear programme has its roots in the 'Atoms for Peace' initiative in the mid-1950s started by US President Dwight D. Eisenhower. The Pakistan Atomic Energy Commission (PAEC) was founded in 1956, but its establishment and the work it carried out in its early years was rather sluggish, displaying an 'apathetic attitude'. However, this programme got energized with the appointment of Zulfikar Ali Bhutto as the Minister for Fuel, Power and National Resources. Bhutto established the Pakistan Institute of Nuclear Science and Technology (PINSTECH) in 1962. In 1963, as the Minister for Foreign Affairs, Bhutto began canvassing for Pakistan to develop a nuclear weapon to counter India.

The outcome of the Indo–Pak War in 1965 further strengthened Bhutto's resolve to develop nuclear weapons. Operation Gibraltar in J&K in July–August 1965, of which he was the mastermind, and in which Pakistan infiltrated nearly 5,000 terrorists and military personnel into Kashmir, was a colossal failure. The infiltrators were soundly beaten back or captured by Indian troops in Kashmir. The hope for local uprising against the Indian state never materialized and the locals themselves assisted the Indian Army in rounding up the Pakistani marauders. Importantly, Bhutto also learnt the significant lesson that Pakistan would never ever be able to defeat the Indian Army in a conventional war owing to India's military superiority which Pakistan could never dream of matching. Bhutto's quest to obtain an effective deterrent against India was further reinforced after the 1965 operations, in which India secured a slight military edge over Pakistan and the latter's hope of annexing Kashmir came a cropper.

The resounding defeat of Pakistan at the hands of the Indian military in December 1971 and the break-up of a 'moth-eaten' Pakistan, led to the fall of its military dictator and President, General Yahya Khan. Bhutto's party, PPP, won a majority of seats and he was sworn in as the Prime Minister. Bhutto had his priorities for his country clearly chalked out and shortly after assuming office, revitalized Pakistan's nascent and otherwise listless nuclear weapons programme. At a secret meeting in Multan, Bhutto ordered a team of selected scientists under Munir Ahmad Khan to produce a nuclear bomb for Pakistan in five years from then.

Munir Ahmad Khan, a plutonium expert, led the PAEC to produce weapons-grade plutonium as India had also adopted it in its nuclear programme. It was also a cost-effective option as Pakistan would need only a reprocessing plant to recover the plutonium produced by its civilian reactor. The only problem was that Pakistan's reactor, the Karachi Nuclear Power Plant (KANUPP) was not only inefficient, but was also being monitored diligently by the International Atomic Energy Agency (IAEA) and Western agencies. Mindful of Pakistan being a proliferation risk, these agencies had begun to restrict Pakistan's access to reprocessing technology.

With problems accruing with regards to plutonium reprocessing, Pakistan switched to a less technically efficient but more discreet highly enriched uranium (HEU) route. This shift was prompted by two factors. The first one was India's Peaceful Nuclear Explosion (PNE) in Rajasthan in May 1974 dubbed 'Smiling Buddha'. India's Prime Minister Indira Gandhi had waited for years exhorting the nation's nuclear establishment to acquire the technology for instituting a PNE. The second factor was the arrival on Pakistan's nuclear stage of a crafty and ambitious nuclear scientist, AQ Khan, who was working in the URENCO enrichment consortium in Netherlands. In his work there, he had access to confidential German reports on centrifuge technology. In September 1974, AQ Khan offered to PM Bhutto his assistance in producing a nuclear bomb for Pakistan. The country, lacking the foundation and expertise for a successful nuclear weapons programme, relied on AQ Khan's clandestine network for basic components that were illegally procured from URENCO's key suppliers in western Europe. Meanwhile, Khan's under-the-table activities had alerted the Dutch intelligence. But before they could act, he fled to Pakistan taking away with him relevant designs of centrifuge technology and other necessary details of producing a low-tech nuclear weapon. The rest was, as they say, a nuclear nightmare in the making. Stephen Cohen has dubbed Pakistan's then nascent nuclear programme as 'a triumph of espionage and assistance from a friendly foreign power'.

In the initial years of Pakistan's nuclear build-up, the role of Sultan Bashiruddin Mahmood has not been given due importance. This scientist reportedly obtained complete engineering drawings of a nuclear plant and centrifuges from the Italian Casaccia Nuclear Research Centre outside Rome. He then copied these by hand in his hotel room. After retirement, Mahmood is reported to have met Al-Qaeda supremo Osama bin Laden and Afghan Taliban chief, Mullah Omar. These clandestine meetings with terror chieftains are a poor reflection of Pakistan's security as regards its nuclear programme.

Though Bhutto shared the army's assessment about a 'hegemonic India's' designs against Pakistan, he cleverly kept his army some distance away from the country's predominantly civilian-led nuclear weapons programme for primarily two reasons. Firstly, the development of nuclear weapons would act as a strategic deterrent against India and, secondly, it would prove to be an effective foil against Pakistan's powerful military, which was eating into the nation's meagre resources by over-exaggerating the threat from India. Thus, Bhutto could both 'reduce the army's role and face India on an equal footing'. However, during this time, the Carter administration was getting uncomfortable with Pakistan's clandestine efforts at establishing facilities for uranium enrichment. The year 1977 witnessed a major political change in Pakistan with General Zia capturing power in a military coup and imprisoning Bhutto.

In her book, Christine Fair clarifies Bhutto's summation as regards Pakistan's nuclear forays during that period. She amplifies that, '...in 1979 during the imprisonment that ended with his execution, Bhutto wrote *If I am Assassinated*, an autobiography-cum-manifesto defending his actions and policies. He explains that he, and not the military, achieved Pakistan's weapons capability. Bhutto even argues that the United States (for the sole purpose of preventing Pakistan from acquiring a reprocessing capability) facilitated the coup that overthrew him by backing his political rivals and encouraging the army. Bhutto further insinuates that his opponents, in and out of uniform, sold him, and Pakistan's nuclear future, to the Americans.'

With General Zia's ascendancy to power, the nuclear programme came under strict control of the army. However, in 1979, the US, under the Symington Amendment, suspended military and financial aid to Pakistan after the Americans were convinced about the former's continuing covert construction of a uranium enrichment facility. But the deteriorating situation in neighbouring Afghanistan after the Soviet invasion and occupation of that country was to change the overall geopolitical landscape of the region to the benefit of Pakistan in its nuclear ambitions.

As US, Saudi Arabia and Pakistan got together to launch a 'jihad' in Afghanistan against the Soviets, Pakistan's strategic utility to the US again came to the fore. President Jimmy Carter's national security adviser, Zbigniew Brzezinski, known for his pro-Pak and anti-Soviet stance, famously stated that the US 'security policy cannot be dictated by our non-proliferation policy'. The change in the US presidency with Ronald Reagan entering the White House in January 1981 brought to Pakistan a massive $3.2 billion in economic and military assistance for the next five years. The Symington sanctions were all waived off for Pakistan's assistance in utilizing the mujahideen to combat Soviet troops in Afghanistan. Christine Fair comments that a tacit agreement was thus established between the Zia and Reagan governments: 'The Reagan administration could live with Pakistan's nuclear programme as long as Islamabad did not explode a bomb.' It is thus more than apparent that the US has played a major role in the development of Pakistan's nuclear weapons and if ever they come to regret it, they have only themselves to blame.

The US Congress adopted the Pressler Amendment to continue aid to Pakistan after 1985. But the Congress remained suspicious of Pakistan's record despite assurances of their own presidents. The Pressler Amendment required the US president to annually certify that Pakistan did not possess a nuclear device. Presidents Reagan and Bush continued to certify the same till 1989 when the Soviets withdrew from Afghanistan. Meanwhile, there were intelligence and media reports that Pakistan was covertly procuring technology for nuclear processing from around the world. More importantly, China had supplied Pakistan detailed blueprints for a nuclear bomb. The Pakistanis are reported to have also gifted 50 kg of HEU to China in return for Chinese nuclear favours.

The Soviet withdrawal from Afghanistan followed by the Geneva Accord put an end to the anti-Soviet jihad there. This change in events radically reduced Pakistan's utility to its mentor, the US, who by 1990, was more than convinced of Pakistan's nuclear weapons programme being supported by the Chinese. In October 1990, President Bush refused to furnish the Pressler certification and, accordingly, the US administration cut off all aid to Pakistan. The end of the Cold War also brought down Pakistan's strategic importance to the US. In 1991, then Prime Minister Nawaz Sharif revealed during an interview that though he supported the freeze of uranium enrichment, he was unable to cap the nuclear programme without his army's consent. Sharif had merely reiterated the defining feature of all civil administrations in his country. Even during Benazir Bhutto's tenure as PM, the Army Chief, General Mirza Aslam Beg, had spoken of the army's insistence to control the nation's nuclear programme completely as a quid pro quo to let Benazir Bhutto assume her office.

Throughout the 1990s, Pakistan continued to work feverishly to hone its nuclear weapons programme and development and production of delivery vehicles for nuclear missiles. When Pakistan carried out nuclear tests in 1998 in response to the tests conducted by India, many nations around the world responded with condemnation and imposed sanctions on the nation. But Pakistan felt that it had achieved its long sought mission—strategic deterrence vis-à-vis its permanent rival, India.

The year 1999 was significant for the Indian subcontinent. To improve Indo–Pak relations, Indian Prime Minister Vajpayee undertook his famous bus yatra from Amritsar to Lahore. The signing of the Lahore Accord between the two nations, which incorporated the spirit of the Simla Accord of 1972 signed between Indian PM Indira Gandhi and Pakistan PM Zulfikar Ali Bhutto, generated much enthusiasm. However, the bonhomie between the two leaders soon disappeared with Pakistan army's incursions along the Kargil heights in the Ladakh sector of J&K in the summer of 1999. Both nations were nuclear powers by then, the concept of deterrence, attributable to possession of nuclear weapons, took a beating. Massive and determined Indian counter-attacks by the army with assistance of the air force, without crossing the LoC, threw back the Pakistani intruders, inflicting a large number of casualties on the their troops.

US President Bill Clinton, too, played his part to ensure that the conflict between two nuclear-armed neighbours did not get out of hand and escalate into a nuclear exchange or an all-out war. Nawaz Sharif was hurriedly summoned to the White House by Clinton and admonished for the Pakistani transgressions across the LoC. Nawaz Sharif was presented with proof of preparations being made by his army to arm the nukes. He was bluntly told by the US president to withdraw towards the Pakistani side of the LoC. Prime Minister Sharif and his country were both humiliated by the misdirected Kargil adventure of the army, about which Sharif feigned ignorance. Brigadier Feroz Hassan Khan, now a senior lecturer at the US Naval Postgraduate School in California, USA, has succinctly summed up his nation's predicament during the Kargil conflict, stating that it had 'eventually produced further deterioration in the country's civil–military relations and paved the way for the coup in October 1999. Kargil underscored incoherence in Pakistani governance and strategic decision-making. This was a very shaky beginning for Pakistan as a nuclear power.'

SIGNIFICANT LESSONS

The Kargil conflict also brought about a couple of significant lessons for the Pakistan military to imbibe. Firstly, the Indian military's successful actions highlighted that there exists space in short-duration military conflicts with limited objectives, short of a full-fledged conventional war and a nuclear conflict breaking out. Nuclear states tend to draw 'red-lines'—the crossing of which threatens the commencement of a nuclear exchange. With India having nuclear weapons, Pakistan was not deterred from its audacious intrusion in Kargil and neither was India deterred to throw out the intruders and reconquer the heights. Nuclear weapons with irresponsible nations will definitely lower the nuclear threshold, but international pressures also play their part in preventing the dangerous climb up the escalatory ladder of conflicts. But military prudence also demands that provocative behavioural patterns of such nations are kept under surveillance and check.

Secondly, without formal public pronouncements, Pakistan has, since it turned nuclear, felt that it can use non-state actors from its terror factories far more freely inside India as it will deter the latter to go for an all-out war with Pakistan. India's Operation Parakram in 2001–02, after the Pakistani terrorist attack on the Indian Parliament in December 2001, culminating in the Indian military's massive mobilization (also termed coercive diplomacy), did not escalate to an all-out war. However, the Pakistani security establishment continues to feel that their nuclear arsenal kept Indian retaliation in check.

Thirdly, Pakistan too is aware that the Indian military may utilize its conventional weapons superiority for punitive strikes with limited objectives without crossing the generally known Pakistani nuclear threshold. Accordingly, in this state of nuclear ambiguity, Indian military planners will have to devise out-of-the-box punitive measures to put an end to Pakistan's nuclear bluff and frequent sabre-rattling.

NUCLEAR CAPABILITY

Pakistan has a total of fifteen nuclear sites, of which only three—Karachi, Chashma and PINSTECH—are under IAEA safeguards. Others are under the control of the army and remain unsafeguarded. Additional plutonium enrichment plants are coming up at PINSTECH. Reportedly, Pakistan produces HEU at a rate of 100 kg per year. Its HEU-based warheads require between 15 and 20 kg of HEU each. Pakistan is also producing plutonium for plutonium-based warheads to which they are changing over from HEU. It is reported to have the fastest growing nuclear arsenal in the world with estimates of 120 to 140 warheads in its possession. The development of Pakistan's nuclear delivery systems has been assisted mainly by China and North Korea, while some systems are indigenously produced.

Pakistan's delivery vehicles include modified F-16A/B aircraft and a few Mirage V and Chinese-built A-5 Fantans, under the control of the Pakistan Air Force (PAF) and a variety of surface-to-surface missile systems under the control of the army. The F-16s are likely based at the Sargodha Air Base, located 160 km northwest of Lahore. In August 2007 and May 2008, Pakistan tested the air-launched cruise missile (ALCM) Ra'ad (Hatf VIII), which is claimed to be nuclear-capable possessing a range of 350 km.

Pakistan has three ballistic missiles that are supposedly nuclear capable—the solid fuel Hatf III (Ghaznavi) which has a range of 300–400 km; solid fuel Hatf IV (Shaheen) with a range of 450 km and the liquid fuel Hatf V (Ghauri) with an approximate range of 1,300–1,500 km. In addition, Pakistan is developing the Hatf VI (Shaheen II) which will have a range of 2,000 km. It also claims to have developed the much heralded TNWs, like the 60 km range Nasr and the short-range Abdali, to counter India's Cold Start doctrine. Pakistan Army's official press release calls these TNWs part of a 'quick response system which addresses the need to deter evolving threats'. Sea-based systems are also under development, including the potential purchase of six Qing-class diesel submarines, which would enhance Pakistan's second-strike capability. The lowering of Pakistan's nuclear threshold is of greater concern than the prospect of nuclear terrorism due to theft of fissile material. This aspect is worrisome not only for India and the West, but even for Pakistan. But it claims that its nuclear arsenal is well protected by the army's 20,000-strong SPD, which takes its orders from Pakistan's Nuclear Command Authority.

NUCLEAR DOCTRINE: IRRATIONAL AMBIGUITY

For Pakistan, its nuclear arsenal is an instrument that allows it to wage offensive proxy war and, concurrently, provides it defence against retaliatory punitive action from India. As mentioned earlier and universally accepted, Pakistan's nuclear weapons are a strategic equalizer of power asymmetry, that is, they are supposed to balance India's conventional military superiority. Additionally, the Pakistanis have used their nuclear capability to extract maximum aid from the

US, China, Europe and some nations in West Asia. At the outset, it must be understood that the growth of Pakistan's nuclear programme, conduct of proxy war through terrorism based on an undue faith in its own nukes, its obsessive revisionist agenda for Kashmir and India's proverbial strategic patience, will ensure that strategic stability and mutual deterrence, which is customarily possible between two nuclear-weaponized states, is not likely between India and Pakistan. Importantly, China's support for Pakistan's nuclear programme with assistance in weapons, missiles, reactors and fissile material will continue to drive instability in the Indo–Pak dyad.

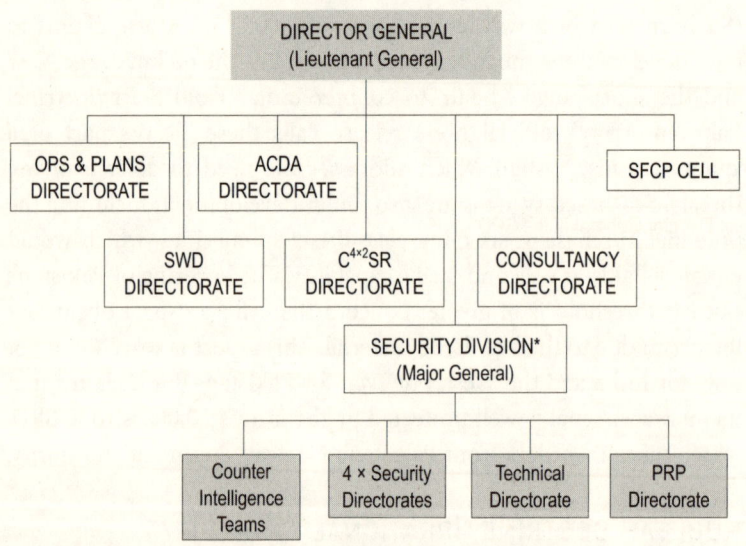

Ops & Plans: Operations and Plans; ACDA: Arms Control & Disarmament Affairs; SFCP: Strategic Forces Command Post; SWD: Strategic Weapons Development; $C^{4\times 2}SR$: Command, Control, Communications, Computers, Surveillance & Reconnaissance; PRP: Personal & Recruitment Policy

*Newly raised after the A.Q. Khan 'fiasco'

Nuclear Command Authority

Prime Minister (Chairman)

Secretariat of the NCA (enjoys maximum powers)
- Strategic Plans Division (SPD)

Employment Control Committee

- Deputy Chair: Foreign Minister
- Minister of Defence
- Minister of Interior
- Minister of Finance
- Chairman Joint Chiefs of Staff Committee
- Chief of Army Staff/Vice Chief of Army Staff
- Chief of Naval Staff
- Chief of the Air Staff
- Secretary: Director General of the SPD
- Others: as required

Development Control Committee

- Deputy Chair: Chairman of the Joint Chiefs of Staff Committee
- Chief of Army Staff/Vice Chief of Army Staff
- Chief of Naval Staff
- Chief of the Air Staff
- Heads of concerned strategic organizations
- Secretary: Director General of the SPD

Services Strategic Forces (Operational Control – NCA)
- ARMY
- NAVY
- PAF

(Technical, Training & Administrative Control)

Pakistan does not have a declared nuclear doctrine and neither has there been any clear articulation of its guiding tenets. As early as 2001, the first and renowned director general of Pakistan's SPD, Lieutenant General Khalid Kidwai, in a well-publicized statement of Pakistan's nuclear intent underscored its employment of nuclear weapons. His nation's thresholds were military, economic, political and survival. At various seminars, he has listed circumstances in which Pakistan would respond to a conventional attack with nuclear weapons: 'India attacks Pakistan and conquers a large part of its territory. India destroys a large part of Pakistan's land or air forces. India blockades Pakistan in an effort to strangle it economically, India pushes Pakistan into a state of political destabilization or creates large-scale internal subversion in the country.' While these verges were some indication of Pakistan's restraint levels, the statement was quickly revoked. Officially, there remains no policy declaration on the grounds that any stated doctrine would create space for conventional conflict. The contradiction here is particularly stark coming in the wake of Kargil conflict, the assault on the Indian Parliament and the continuing use of jihadists as part of military strategy. In another statement, some years earlier, former Army Chief, General Aslam Beg stated, 'An attack by any nation on our nuclear arsenal will automatically trigger a nuclear strike on India.' Weird as this may sound, it is clear that Pakistan retains a certain irrational ambiguity in its policy to use nuclear weapons.

The Pakistan Army has embedded the use of nuclear weapons in their overall military strategy and doctrine as they opine that in their strategy of 'flexible response', escalation from conventional to the nuclear is always possible. However, in their stated stance they have rightly surmised that nuclear weapons are political weapons to be employed as a last resort and that their possession may avoid conflicts. Pertaining to Pakistan itself, it is appreciated that 'on the matrix of a larger power–smaller power equation, such a capability provides to the smaller an unreserved strategic equivalence.' Thus, through ambiguities and a threat of first use, Pakistan has ensured the absence of a formal declaratory policy. Accordingly, the Indian security establishment will have to factor in Pakistan's deliberate nuclear subterfuge in its preparations.

In summation, Pakistan's nuclear strategy embraces the undermentioned facets:

- Pakistan has not abjured the First Use of Nuclear Weapons doctrine and their usage forms an integral part of its military strategy.

- It has taken recourse to deliberately projecting ambiguity in its overall nuclear strategy.
- The military is both the custodian and controller of nuclear assets and professes to have in place a robust command and control system. With fundamentalism on the rise and having penetrated into the services and with terrorists also on the prowl for stealing fissile materials, the dangers of nuclear materials pilferage/safety of nuclear assets remains a major problem.
- China's assistance to Pakistan's nuclear weapons programme is a critical asset for Pakistan with newer technologies, doctrines, command and control facilities and additional lethal infusions of missiles.
- Though Pakistan's nuclear weapons programme and strategy is 'India-specific', it does not recognize India's NFU-declared nuclear intent rejecting it on the grounds that India may not stick to its declared policy during hostilities.
- Pakistan's development and deployment of TNWs is primarily to prevent India from launching its battle groups as part of its Proactive Doctrine. With TNWs, Pakistan has lowered its nuclear threshold, which now results in the creation of additional strategic instability in the subcontinent.
- Pakistan is now shoring up its second-strike capability with the development of the sea-launched submarine cruise missile Babur III, which is likely to have a range of 450 km. It is reportedly moving its major submarine base from Karachi to Ormara as it feels Karachi's closeness to the Indian border makes it more vulnerable.

NUCLEAR PROLIFERATION

Pakistan's nuclear programme, since its inception, has been riddled by controversies, illegal activities and proliferation. Its 'father of nuclear bomb', A.Q. Khan, had initially focused on importing nuclear technology and materials into Pakistan, but shortly thereafter, Khan's network became the launch pad for illegal nuclear exports to many nations. During 1980–2002, Khan reportedly exported technologies and nuclear materials to North Korea, Iran and Libya. However, what has not been clearly established is whether his actions were at the behest of his government or on his own to rake in astronomical amounts for himself. Brigadier Feroz Hassan Khan gives a clean chit to his government stating that AQ Khan 'exploited bureaucratic fissures and that in the absence of a single nuclear command authority he was able to conduct his illegal nuclear commerce without state approval'.

Many Pakistan watchers are firmly of the view that there was 'indisputable evidence that the Pakistani state actively supported and authorized sensitive nuclear transactions'. Matthew Kroenig, of Georgetown University, USA, concludes that A.Q. Khan's nuclear exports were 'state-sponsored by any reasonable definition of the term'.

General Mirza Aslam Beg had a bizarre explanation justifying Pakistan's nuclear proliferation to constrain American power, stating that the 'increased global diffusion of nuclear weapons could lead to a multi-polar world that would better suit Pakistan's interests.'

It is an indisputable fact by now that the Pakistan military was privy to and part of A.Q. Khan's initiative in offering enrichment technology to North Korea. After General Musharraf ousted Nawaz Sharif and captured power in Pakistan in early 2000, he set up the SPD at the Joint Staff headquarters at Chaklala. After CIA chief George Tenet briefed Musharraf regarding Pakistan's lax nuclear security procedures and Khan's illicit nuclear commerce, Musharraf did endeavour to bring the country's nuclear infrastructure firmly under the military's control. He also ordered investigations and many scientists and senior military officers working with Khan were interrogated and a few were imprisoned. This show of strictness was primarily designed to impress the Americans of Musharraf's efforts to cleanse the Kahuta Research Laboratories (KRL) of corrupt elements.

Among the many suspicious incidents which occurred during that time was the murder, in June 1998, of one of A.Q. Khan's house guests, Kim Sa Nae, wife of a North Korean arms dealer. She was invited to watch the Pakistan nuclear tests and it was suspected that she was passing information to US agents. The Pakistanis hushed up the case, though the ISI, to date, has never been able to get its involvement off their chest. During many missile tests in Pakistan, Western journalists have reported frequently on the presence of North Korean and Libyan officials, as also on Khan himself ferreting out letters, audio and video tapes to his daughter in the UK.

During the Nuclear Security Summit (NSS) in Seoul in March 2012 and at many other international conferences subsequently, Pakistan has tried to project that its nuclear security regimen was based on four pillars. Firstly, it has a well-defined, robust command and control system, comprising the NCA, the SPD and the SFC, which exercises control over all aspects of policy, procurement, operations and nuclear security. Much has been made of SPD's Personnel Reliability Programme (PRP), which was introduced with the assistance of the FBI, after many scientists and officers in the KRL were found to be complicit in Khan's clandestine export of nuclear technology. Secondly, it was highlighted that the Pakistan Nuclear Regulatory Authority (PNRA) has established a rigorous regulatory regime covering all matters of nuclear safety, including the physical protection of nuclear materials and facilities. Thirdly, it has been claimed that a comprehensive export control regime is now in place, comparable to standards set by the Nuclear Suppliers Group (NSG) and the Missile Technology Control Regime (MTCR). Lastly, Pakistan seeks international cooperation and is ready to meet international obligations.

Brigadier Feroz Hassan Khan comprehensively sums up Pakistan's nuclear ambitions and raison d'être of being nuclear-crazy by saying that, 'Nuclear weapons are now so deeply embedded in Pakistani security thinking that any attempt to dissuade it from this path—towards disarmament or towards a weapons-free world—would be met with stiff resistance from the entire spectrum within the state. Also there is a strong consensus that Pakistan's nuclear weapons are under threat from hostile countries, which include the United States, Israel and India.'

Considering that Pakistan faces internal stability and self-created terror threats from within, escalating law and order and security problems within its restive provinces of Balochistan and to some extent in Sindh, KPK, FATA and areas along the Durand Line, its obsession with nukes may turn out to be self-defeating in the long run. If it wishes to continue brandishing its nuclear card, it may wish to heed to Michael Krepon's advice that 'escalation control and the nuclear option is a subject matter proven to be remarkably resistant to sensible analysis.' For the world and India, one of the most enduring challenges of the times is for Pakistan's nukes to be neutralized, before they are ever used by the state, their sponsored non-state actors or any rogue elements from the many terror tanzeems dotting Pakistan's unstable landscape.

7

Armed Forces and Their Corporate Interests

> Milbus is military capital that perpetuates the military's political predatory style…military's economic predatoriness increases in totalitarian systems. The military's economic predatoriness, especially inside its national boundaries, is both a cause and effect of a feudal authoritarian, and non-democratic, political system.
>
> —Ayesha Siddiqa in *Military Inc.: Inside Pakistan's Military Economy*

In nations where militaries are excessively and unconstitutionally powerful, they manipulate, if not totally control, the economic agendas of their respective nations, apart from influencing internal politics and foreign policies. In addition to obtaining the lion's share of their national budgets for modernization and maintenance of weapons and equipment, pay and allowances of military personnel and other expenditures required for ensuring the security of the nation, some militaries, over the years, have also developed burgeoning commercial interests for their exclusive and personal utilization. This concept, dubbed as 'Milbus', has been researched extensively by a former Pakistani bureaucrat of the Defence and Accounts Service and now well-known author, Ayesha Siddiqa. Her service in the Pakistani military establishment thus makes her more than an insider with adequate knowledge of the financial shenanigans of the country's armed forces. That she has had the courage to pen down her views for her nation with refreshing frankness, much against the wishes of the military establishment, is a well-known fact acknowledged by many within Pakistan.

In her pioneering book, *Military Inc.: Inside Pakistan's Military Economy*, Siddiqa candidly opines that, 'Milbus refers to military capital that is used for the personal benefit of the military fraternity, especially the officer cadre, but is neither recorded nor part of the defence budget. In this respect, it is a completely independent genre of capital. Its most significant component is entrepreneurial activities that do not fall under the normal accountability procedures of the state, and are mainly for the gratification of military personnel and their cronies. It is either controlled by the military, or under its implicit or explicit patronage. It is also important to emphasise that in most cases the rewards are limited to the officer cadre rather than being evenly distributed among the rank and file. The top echelons of the armed forces who are the main beneficiaries of Milbus justify the economic dividends as welfare provided to the military for their services rendered to the state. Since this military capital is hidden from the public, it is also referred to as the military's internal economy. A study of Milbus is important because it causes the officer cadre to be interested in enhancing their influence in the state's decision-making and politics.'

Ayesha Siddiqa, delving further on the ever-escalating financial muscle of such corporate armies around the globe explains that the 'mechanisms and manifestations' of Milbus vary in different nations. 'In countries such as the United States, the United Kingdom, France, Israel and South Africa, it operates in partnership with the civilian corporate sector and the government. In other cases such as Iran, Cuba and China, Milbus is manifested through partnership with the dominant ruling party or individual leader, while in Turkey, Indonesia, Pakistan, Myanmar and Thailand, the military is the sole driver of Milbus…the direct involvement of the armed forces in making a profit, which is made available to military personnel and their cronies, increases the military's institutional interest in controlling the policy-making process and distribution of resources.'

INSIDE PAKISTAN'S BIGGEST BUSINESS CONGLOMERATE

In July 2016, the Pakistani Senate was informed that the armed forces run over fifty commercial entities worth over $20 billion. Ranging from petrol pumps to huge industrial plants, banks, bakeries, schools and universities, hosiery factories, milk dairies, stud farms and cement plants, the military has a finger in each pie and stands today as the biggest conglomerate of all business in Pakistan. However, the jewels in their crown are the eight housing societies in eight major towns where prime lands in well-manicured cantonments and plush civil localities in the possession of these societies are allotted to military personnel at highly subsidized rates. Even military awards are linked with the grant of farm lands and housing plots to military personnel.

Shuja Nawaz in his book, *Crossed Swords*, expounds the land-grabbing propensities of Pakistani generals. He goes on to say that in the 'late 1980s, as dictator fatigue set in during the Zia period, many army officers refrained from going out into the public in their uniforms as there was much resentment against the military for their over-indulgence in economic activities.' Later in 2007, 'the country saw the jarring banners carried by lawyers who were protesting the removal of a chief justice by the military ruler: "*Ae watan ke sajeele Genrailo; saaray ruqbey tumhare liye hain* (O' handsome generals of the homeland, all the plots are just for you)."'

The 'Culture of Entitlement' in the military started during General Ayub's time when he commenced the tradition of awarding land to army officers (the size of allotment depending upon the rank of the officer) in the border regions of Punjab and in the newly irrigated colonies of Sindh. General Zia also created a novel way of involving serving officers in commercial ventures by placing military lands and cantonments and the provisioning of logistics to the regional corps commanders. Thus, many senior army officers availed opportunities to acquire multiple plots in various cantonments for themselves at highly subsidized rates. These prime properties soon sparked nepotism in allotment and corruption among both the military and civil bureaucracies. After being allotted plots in prime areas, it became common practice for army officers to sell their preferential allotments at exorbitant prices to well-heeled civilians.

The military soon got involved in establishing several foundations ostensibly to help retired service personnel. These institutions virtually penetrated into all sectors of the economy and gradually propelled the military into a major business stakeholder in Pakistan's economy.

The military operates its economic endeavours at three levels with the Ministry of Defence (MOD) being at the top of the economic military network. The MOD controls four major areas—the service headquarters, the Department of Military Land and Cantonments (MLC), the Fauji Foundation (also known as Fauji Group) and the Rangers (a paramilitary force). The Department of Military Land and Cantonments acquires land for allocation to the service headquarters, which distributes it among individual members. The three services have independent welfare foundations, which are directly controlled by the senior officers of the respective services.

The military is also involved in public sector organizations like the National Logistics Cell (NLC), the Frontier Works Organisation (FWO) and the Special Communications Organisation (SCO), which are all controlled by the army. The Water and Power Development Authority (WAPDA) was placed under military control in 1998 with over 35,000 personnel now involved in its operations.

The MOD does not directly manage the economic activities of the organizations under its control, but it is an instrument to mobilize resources, accord legitimacy to the varying commercial and other economic activities of its organizations and even field formations and units which run many subsidiary commercial ventures independently.

In addition, there are four subsidiary organizations that are involved in the economic activities of the military. These include the Fauji Foundation, Army Welfare Trust, Shaheen Foundation (for retired Pakistan Air Force personnel) and the Bahria Foundation (for retired Navy personnel). These foundations, though controlled by their respective service headquarters, are run by retired military personnel. The profits accruing from the commercial ventures of these organizations are distributed to all shareholders who are retired military personnel. These are engaged in ventures like fertilizer and cement manufacture, cereal production, insurance and banking enterprises, education and information technology institutes besides airport services, travel agencies, shipping, harbour services and deep sea fisheries.

The influence of the MOD plays a vital role in securing public sector business contracts and financial and industrial inputs at highly subsidized rates. In recent years, profit making by retired military personnel has acquired even newer dimensions with them providing privatized security services to foreign contractors in security-sensitive regions like the FATA and KPK. This follows the pattern as established by foreign security contractors in adjoining Afghanistan.

The Culture of Entitlement is getting stronger by the day. Several senior service officers have also been parked as ambassadors, governors and nominated on other high-ranking bureaucratic posts in Pakistan. Successive army chiefs have continued with the practice of strengthening the special perks and privileges of their serving and retired personnel with respective civilian governments reluctantly acquiescing to all the fair and unfair demands of the armed forces.

It is an indisputable fact that Milbus contributes towards professionalism taking its toll when the military participates in non-military commercial activities. The case of the People's Liberation Army (PLA) in China is a classic example where some senior Chinese generals fell prey to the temptations of corruption and lucre. True to their style, the Chinese government stepped in and severely punished some of the offenders and thus discouraged the Chinese military from commercial activities.

Milbus in Pakistan is the never-fading and ever-growing clout of its military in its nation's policies far beyond strategic and security matters. A major reason for this state of affairs is the independent, unaccountable financial muscle of the military. Since the Ayub era, no civilian government has ever bothered to tame in the military except, to some extent, Zulfikar Ali Bhutto for a short period. Most civilian governments have looked the other way at the financial handlings of the military's commercial enterprises, primarily to buy peace with the powerful generals. Most members of Pakistan's civil society and even its parliamentarians have wilfully ignored the military's economic empire-building except for some senators like Sherry Rehman and Farhatullah Babar. Among the many constants in Pakistan, Milbus too, in the foreseeable future, is likely to more than thrive as it is coterminous with the power wielded by the military in its national affairs. Currently, there are no indicators whatsoever that the Pakistan military will ever relinquish the primacy and unfettered powers it enjoys in its nation.

8

Stirring the Pot in J&K

…most people have concluded long ago that Pakistan's Kashmir policy has been hurting Pakistan and Kashmir than India.

—Michael Krepon, co-founder of US-based think tank, Stimson Center

The immensely beautiful valley of Kashmir with its unquestionable strategic overtones has overwhelmed and impacted relations negatively between the two neighbours since 1947. Pakistan refuses to recognize the perfectly legal, though tumultuous, accession of the restive state to the Union of India. Notwithstanding the Instrument of Accession duly signed by Maharaja Hari Singh, the ruler of the former princely state, to join India, Pakistan views this event and interprets the later UN resolutions on J&K in its own light. In pursuant of its two-nation theory, Pakistan argues that despite having a Hindu ruler, J&K being a Muslim-majority state should have acceded to it. For India, J&K symbolizes its secularism with religion not being the overriding factor for any state wishing to integrate itself in the inclusive 'Idea of India'.

That the status of J&K remains 'disputed' in international political parlance and is a nuclear flashpoint is also a universal reality. That Pakistan initiated wars and smaller conflicts to wrest Kashmir in 1947–48, 1965, 1971 (slightly different, operationally speaking)

and the 1999 Kargil conflict, besides whipping up insurgency-like conditions in the Kashmir Valley, points to Pakistan's ill-advised but continuing obsession for it. In fact, the so-called intractable problem of J&K has been reduced to a zero-sum game by Pakistan as far as its relations with India are concerned. For Pakistanis, J&K remains a 'core issue' and the unfinished business of Partition, whereas to Indians, the accession of J&K to India is a final and dead issue notwithstanding the on-off-on unrest which comes to the Valley, primarily attributable to Pakistani manoeuvres. In the light of these facts, it is imperative to understand the efforts of the Deep State in 'stirring the pot' in J&K in recent times and the present ground situation.

ISI's DIABOLICAL MISSION

In pursuit of its agenda regarding Kashmir, Pakistan launched a two-pronged mission, despite having unsuccessfully triggered wars to wrest the state from India and having signed the 1972 Simla Agreement to resolve all problems, including J&K, peacefully. The first mission remained the perennial internationalization of the 'dispute' at any given opportunity and at international forums. Significantly, under General Zia, it conceptualized 'Operation Topac' to 'bleed India by a thousand cuts'. Naturally, this diabolical mission was to be executed by the ISI, which had been bloodied by its vast experience in handling terrorism laced with religious fanaticism in Afghanistan. That there existed some resentment in J&K against the Indian state among some of the radical Islamist separatists was a fertile ground for the ISI to cultivate and exploit in pursuit of their mission. The mountainous terrain of the unfenced LoC dividing the two parts of J&K, administered separately by both nations, lent itself for easy infiltration by ISI's terrorists carrying arms, ammunition, explosives and other subversive material required to create mayhem in J&K.

In mid-1998, religious extremists commenced hurling bombs at bars, cinema houses, beauty parlours, video shops and the like, which they considered un-Islamic. Women were also asked to wear burqas and unveiled women were attacked with acid or ink. The reactions to counter the extremists were highly exaggerated by the well-conceived propaganda machinery of the ISI and its paid agents in the Valley. They concocted imaginary accounts of atrocities and rape by Indian security forces. Spearheading the Kashmiri unrest from across the border, the ISI soon marshalled all anti-India forces around a common platform—the All Parties Hurriyat Conference (APHC)—a fraternity of over two dozen disparate groups. Some of these groups demanded independence for J&K, including the parts held by Pakistan, while a few ultra-hardliners were keen on its annexation to Pakistan. And soon, the APHC leadership split. Meanwhile, the impressive turnout of local Kashmiris in the 1987 state elections in J&K, categorically proved to all that the influence of the APHC did not spread beyond the Valley and the populace, though getting provoked off and on, still believed in the Indian state—a fact which the ISI could not ever stomach. The ISI then substantially stepped up its support of the pro-Pakistan faction in the APHC.

German writer Hein G. Kiessling, who has inside knowledge of the ISI, comments in his book, *Faith, Unity, Discipline: The ISI of Pakistan*, that, '...the mujahideen religious warriors are seen as terrorists on one side and freedom fighters on the other side. President Zia-ul-Haq had laid the foundation for what was to happen in Kashmir in the 1990s. From 1988, the ISI began to organize training camps for young militants from the Valley. At the beginning, their partner was the Jammu Kashmir Liberation Front (JKLF), who was responsible for recruiting the fighters, while the ISI delivered training and equipment. Funding came from the Gulf region and the drug trade, and donations were collected in the mosques of Pakistan, US and Western Europe. All this ensured the recruitment and training of new, young volunteers and the deployment of battle-hardened mujahideen from Afghanistan. The recruits came mainly from Punjab and NWFP, but young Muslims were also enlisted from abroad. The training camps for volunteers from Jammu and Kashmir were located in Azad Kashmir, close to the LoC; the camps for the Pakistanis and the foreigners were in Punjab and NWFP.' Kiessling further amplifies that '...once the JKLF, under their leaders Amanullah Khan and Yasin Malik, drifted ideologically towards independence for Kashmir, the party was dropped by the ISI in the early 1990s.'

BIRTH OF RADICAL TERRORIST ORGANIZATIONS

By 1989, the ISI had raised a fanatic pro-Pakistan outfit, Hizbul Mujahideen (HM)—'Party of the Holy Fighters'. Under the ISI's consistent support and guidance, it soon became the most potent and radical terrorist organization for operations inside Kashmir.

Another extremist group, the Harkat-ul-Mujahideen (HuM)—'Movement of the Holy Warriors',—was bolstered after the fall of Kabul in 1992 with fighters from Egypt, Tunisia, Algeria, Bosnia, Tajikistan, Chechnya, Myanmar and the Philippines. They then started to broaden their operations in Kashmir. The HuM also carried out bomb attacks against the US consulate in Karachi and some French assets in Pakistan. The US protested to Pakistan about this organization's links with the al-Qaeda, forcing General Musharraf to ultimately ban it in 2002, while it was operating under its new name, Jamiat ul-Ansar (JuA).

The 1990s witnessed the birth of other powerful militant organizations with two of ISI's favourites being the Lashkar-e-Taiba (LeT)—'Army of the Pure'—and Jaish-e-Mohammad (JeM)—'The Army of Prophet Mohammad'—for their ferociousness and terror specialization skills. The LeT, under Hafiz Muhammad Saeed, also assumed responsibility of the audacious attack on the Indian Parliament in December 2001, while the JeM, under Maulana Masood Azhar, had developed close relations with the al-Qaeda.

As a result of the mass mobilization and deployment of Indian troops along the Indo–Pak border after the attack on the Indian Parliament, the US stepped in strongly to prevent war between the two nuclear-armed neighbours. Counselling restraint to India, it prevailed upon Pakistan's military ruler General Musharraf to wind up the terrorist infrastructure established on Pakistani soil and POK. Musharraf did blacklist some of these militant organizations and made some peaceful noises but, as per well-established practice, these militant outfits continued operating under new nomenclature. For example, the LeT morphed into its new avatar as the Jamaat-ud-Dawa (JuD).

Among the many terror tanzeems operating in J&K till date, LeT has emerged as the most lethal. It has audaciously ambushed security forces, directly attacked their camps and offered determined resistance to Indian security forces. If there is one militant outfit which has terrorized local Kashmiris, it has been the LeT. Composed of foreign cadres and predominantly Pakistanis, it has been indulging in rapes, loot and killing of suspected informers and even innocent civilians in the Valley. Though essentially a hated outfit, some locals have given in to their barbaric ways out of absolute fear. However, for some years, the LeT cadres have been operating in conjunction with the HM and two other Islamic fundamentalist organizations—Al-Badr and Harkat-ul-Jihad-al-Islami (HUJI).

CONGLOMERATE OF RADICAL SEPARATIST LEADERS

To stoke the fires in the Valley, the ISI has, for years, built a faithful conglomerate of radical separatist leaders, like the old war horse Syed Ali Shah Geelani, Yasin Malik, Shabir Shah, Masarat Alam and the woman leader, Asiya Andrabi. It has also carved out a constituency among the so-called moderate separatists like Mirwaiz Umar Farooq (whose father was assassinated by pro-Pakistan elements of the HM), Abdul Ghani Lone and Abdul Ghani Bhat among a few others. Amazingly, Mirwaiz has never found the courage to name his father's assassins and even had the temerity to warn Muslims of the Ahmadiyya sect to stay away from Kashmir. These leaders who have never participated in state elections do carry a vicious clout on the Kashmiri populace, especially among the Sunni Muslims in the Valley. It is a well-known fact that this separatist conglomerate is more than adequately funded by donations from abroad and Pakistan through illegal monetary channels. All these separatist leaders visit the Pakistan High Commission in Delhi whenever a senior leader/functionary from Pakistan visits India or to attend the Pakistan Day celebrations. Even the ISI would be amazed at the fact that successive Indian governments have been naive enough to allow separatist Kashmiri leaders to meet Pakistani leaders whenever they wish to—a facility not reciprocated by the Pakistanis in Islamabad to Indian diplomats to meet separatist leaders of that country.

FLAMES OF INSURGENCY

Over the last few years, the number of terrorist incidents and fatalities among security personnel and civilians has shown a distinct downward trend. However, from 2015 onwards, the ISI has made concerted efforts to change its tactics in whipping up insurgency in the state and redoubled its efforts to energize the waning insurgency in the Valley. It has partially succeeded in doing so and is following it up with vigour in 2017. A new, but disturbing, challenge for Indian security forces since the last eighteen months or so has been that a large number of Kashmiris have been infected with militant propaganda leading to a discernible rise in the number of over ground workers (OGWs) for militant outfits.

Locals in large numbers have been turning out to attend funerals of militants killed by security forces. Another ominous development for the Indian state has been the resurgence of waving Pakistani flags and, alarmingly, ISIS flags at times, after Friday prayers at a few Sunni mosques in the Valley, particularly in Srinagar. On instructions from the ISI from across the border, waving of these flags and pelting of stones at the police and other security forces has been normal tactics of the separatists for some time now. However, the influence of these separatists is restricted to only five out of the total of twenty-two districts in the state. Inside the Valley, Pakistan has been making all out efforts to radicalize the generally secular-minded Kashmiris. As a result, many Salafi madrasas, funded by Saudi and Pakistani money, have started cropping up. Lately, India's National Investigation Agency has been vigorously investigating illegal money transactions into the accounts of separatist leaders in Kashmir and has arrested a few offenders.

The situation in POK and the Gilgit–Baltistan region (erstwhile Northern Areas) is also becoming increasingly worrisome for the

Pakistani state. Atrocities on the Shia population are commonplace in these regions, and many Shias returning from pilgrimage in Iran have been routinely slaughtered by Sunni terrorists. Local Shias have been protesting against the discrimination being heaped upon them by Pakistanis from the plains settling in their province in large numbers. In Indian Kashmir, owing to the Indian government's staunch adherence to Article 370 of its Constitution, no Indian from outside of J&K can settle in the state. However, the Deep State in Pakistan has ensured that the local demographics of the state have changed in POK and Gilgit–Baltistan. With further improvements in the Karakoram Highway and the development of the China–Pakistan Economic Corridor (CPEC), locals of these regions are hardly enthused with the growing Chinese presence, which appears to be near-permanent in these areas. Additionally, media reports indicate that Pakistan has also leased out these regions for fifty years to China. In the overall futuristic context, Pakistan must remain wary of the growing and creeping footprint of the wily Chinese in the Gilgit–Baltistan and POK regions.

The ISI with elements of its terror conglomerate, which are referred to by many as non-state actors—though they are as much state actors as the Pakistani establishment—continue to fan the flames of insurgency in parts of J&K, wherever they can. India is yet to firm up a cohesive and consistent strategy to deal with this mischief in J&K. While dealing with seditious activities firmly, the use of minimum force and a healing touch also has to be ensured by Indian security forces. Recently, in response to a major terrorist strike in Uri in September 2016, Indian special forces had undertaken a swift and strong surgical strike at seven limited objectives against some terrorist camps and infrastructure inside POK. However, terrorist activities of the Pakistanis inside J&K have not abated till date and in the period 2015–17, Pakistanis have made all efforts to up the ante in Kashmir by involving larger numbers of local youth to rise against the Indian state. The numbers of stone-pelters has gone up considerably causing much discomfiture to Indian security forces, who, for obvious reasons, have to exercise maximum restraint whilst dealing with the young protesters.

Political scientist, Stephen Cohen had, a few years ago, maintained that a 'state of stalemate is seen to be more attractive to each side than finding solutions. From the perspective of the Pakistan military, which has an absolute veto over any policy initiative regarding Kashmir, the ability to tie the Indian forces down in Kashmir is an important consequence of the dispute; for India, Kashmir has so many links to the country's secular political order—especially the place of Muslims—that any settlement which appeared to compromise this order is unacceptable.'

The Deep State will have to realize the follies and implications of their machinations inside J&K before matters get out of hand. Currently, the return of peace and normalcy to J&K appears problematic and this state remains a flashpoint between two nuclear neighbours. The Deep State, by all counts, is likely to determinedly follow its avowed policy of the dismemberment of India, and Kashmir for them is just the route and not the end. That Pakistan perhaps misjudges India's determination to stabilize J&K at any cost for itself, may prove disastrous for Pakistan if it continues with its myopic shenanigans in the state. It has to come to terms with the fact that Kashmir is not only the symbol of India's secularism and the inclusive idea of India, but its very guarantee. Till then and in the foreseeable future, Kashmir is likely to remain a zero-sum game for both the nations.

9

Fomenting Communal Troubles and Secessionism in India's Punjab

The border state of Punjab, rightly referred to, many times over, as the 'sword arm of India', has been on Pakistan's radar right since India's independence. Punjab is India's granary, and provides lakhs of uncommonly valiant men for the country's armed forces and bulk of sportspersons to various national teams. The Sikhs who constitute slightly over 50 per cent of Punjab's population have always symbolized the ethos and the spirit of a resurgent India. Thus Pakistan, chafing under the vivisection of its eastern part, conceived deliberate and determined plans to create major problems in Punjab to seek its revenge. Further, the Pakistani establishment had clearly understood its inability to defeat India in conventional wars. Its declared intent of 'bleeding India by a thousand cuts' was launched by General Zia at the commencement of his tenure as Pakistan's military ruler. Thus, Punjab and J&K were the states where Zia's highly violent, secessionist and communal-ridden agendas were launched to damage India from within.

The ISI had been crafting its strategy for fanning secessionism in Punjab since decades, and deviously tapping some politically disgruntled elements among the Sikh community and criminal elements to forge them into a potent force. The redoubtable K.P.S. Gill, who, as Punjab's Director General of Police (DGP), successfully led the campaign against Pakistan-supported Khalistani terrorists, had summed up the developments in Punjab stating that 'the movement for creation of Khalistan was one of the most virulent terrorist campaigns in the world. Launched in the early 1980s by a group of bigots who discovered their justification in a perversion of the Sikh religious identity and supported by a gaggle of political opportunists both within the country and abroad, this movement had consumed 21,469 lives before it was comprehensively defeated in 1993. Thousands of others were injured and maimed; hundreds of thousands were permanently scarred by their experience of dislocation, the gratuitous loss of loved ones, and an unremitting terror they had endured for more than a decade.'* (The valiant K.P.S. Gill passed away just recently.) The ISI, unmistakably, can take most of the credit for conceiving, organizing, funding and training the Khalistani terrorists who had created mayhem in Punjab.

DISAFFECTION IN THE SIKH COMMUNITY

At the dawn of Independence, some Sikhs (other than those with the Congress) were enamoured with the idea of having an autonomous Sikh state within the borders of the new India. The majority of Sikhs stood by Nehru's assurance a year earlier to India's independence when he declared at the All India Congress Committee in July 1946, that 'the brave Sikhs of Punjab are entitled to special consideration'.

During the Partition, the unprecedented violence and mass killings of Muslims, migrating to Pakistan, and Hindus and Sikhs, moving to the new India, had left most in the prosperous and large land-owning Sikh community bitter as they had to leave their centuries-old homes and hearths and other material possessions back in Pakistan. Though the industrious Sikhs soon became prosperous once again in the new India, some disquiet and aspirations among a few politically charged Sikh leaders for greater political space remained lurking. Some within the Sikh clergy also tried to create differences between the Sikhs and Hindus in Punjab.

Most problems, intractable later on, emerge from nowhere and without much provocation. Some local unscrupulous politicians in

---

*https://www.scribd.com/document/139297497/K-P-S-Gill

Punjab did contribute to producing disaffection among the Sikh community. The ever-watchful ISI, right from Zulfikar Ali Bhutto's tenure and then under General Zia's directions, were waiting in the wings to only step up their machinations in Punjab. Not only was the thirst for avenging the break up of Pakistan in 1971 the main motivator, but Pakistani leaders were also determined to give further credibility to the 'two-nation theory' of their founder.

SINISTER OPERATIONS

The ISI established a cell in its organization to coordinate its sinister operations to foment trouble and fan separatism in Punjab. By the early 1980s, the ISI found a willing adherent to its anti-India programmes in a young, fiery radical leader called Jarnail Singh Bhindranwale, who had built up a sizeable following among a section of militant Sikh youth. The ISI set up training camps for these youths in Lahore and Karachi, while the Pakistan Army, through their field intelligence units, organized the training and supply of arms and ammunition near the international border for Khalistani terrorists. The key insurgent groups patronized by the ISI were the Khalistan Commando Force, Babbar Khalsa, Khalistan Liberation Force and the Bhindranwale Tiger Force.

The Punjab cell at the ISI's headquarters adopted a three-stage plan:

1. The first phase sought to precipitate the alienation of the Sikh population from mainstream India.
2. The second phase emphasized the need to subvert the state's machinery and mobilize mass agitation against the government.
3. The third phase was to mark the onset of a genuine reign of terror in Punjab in which the population became victims of violence and counter-violence by the militants and state, respectively.

The ISI, to garner local and religious support for its devious agendas, also tried to establish links with some Sikh religious organizations like the Panthic Committee and even with some radical elements in the Shiromani Gurdwara Parbandhak Committee (SGPC). The latter is the custodian of all Sikh shrines and carries tremendous financial clout besides substantial religious influence over the Sikh community in India and abroad.

Pakistan has a very small Sikh population, but many historical Sikh gurdwaras managed by three Panthic Committees are located there. The ISI, in a bid to further its agendas, managed to get these warring religious organizations to cooperate with each other to spread disaffection among the Sikh pilgrims who would come to visit the gurdwaras from India and other countries. The ISI unleashed a well-conceived psychological warfare campaign against India, built upon the imagined 'plight' and 'sufferings' being supposedly heaped up on the Sikh community. In particular, the propaganda campaigns were directed towards promoting unrest among the Sikh youth in Punjab and eliciting sympathy among the Sikh diaspora for the creation of an independent Sikh state called 'Khalistan' (the land of the pure) in Punjab. That the ISI went the whole hog to make this movement a success has been documented and revealed by many foreign intelligence organizations, friendly nations and India's own Sikh community, which had to suffer for over a decade for no fault of theirs.

OPERATION BLUE STAR AND ITS FALLOUT

Hein G. Kiessling, who stayed in Pakistan from 1989 to 2002, and has excellent contacts with many leading members of the Deep State, has written extensively on the ISI in his book. In his narration of the 'Insurgency in Punjab', Kiessling opines that, 'Many critics in India see Operation Blue Star as an erroneous decision even today, because they feel that moderate elements of the Sikh community were humiliated by what happened, a grievance that lingers till this day. However, for Indian Prime Minister Indira Gandhi the time to act had come. Counter-intelligence reports had stated that Balbir Singh Sandhu, Subheg Singh and Amrik Singh, all three prominent heads of the Khalistan movement, had made at least six trips to

Pakistan between 1981 and 1983.' Meanwhile, the Indian IB had also submitted reports to her stating that weapon training was taking place in gurdwaras in the states bordering Punjab, namely J&K and Himachal Pradesh. In addition, the Soviet KGB, which had close working links with the Indian external intelligence service, R&AW, had also relayed a tip-off that the CIA and ISI were working together on an operation plan for Punjab, code-named 'Gibraltar'.

Kiessling further amplifies that the 'then R&AW chief R.N. Kao had interrogated a Pakistani Army officer in the top secret Counter-Intelligence Centre situated in the Red Fort in New Delhi, and reported afterwards that Pakistan had dispatched over 1000 highly trained men from its Special Service Group (SSG) into Indian Punjab to aid the mad monk Bhindranwale in his fight against the Indian government.' Indian intelligence reports also indicated that the ISI had activated the Indo–Pak smuggler syndicate, which operated in the south, primarily in the Kutch region of Gujarat, and in northern J&K. The Indian security forces had also discovered sophisticated electronic cameras with photographs of military installations and other strategic installations with some of the smugglers who had been apprehended.

With the security situation deteriorating in Punjab and terrorist incidents on the rise against moderate, innocent Sikh elements and Hindus, some resolute action was being contemplated. The Golden Temple, the holiest and most revered shrine for Sikhs the world over, located in Amritsar, had been virtually taken over by Bhindranwale and his bunch of terrorists. Though the terrorist actions masterminded by Bhindranwale against fellow Sikhs from the holy precincts of the Golden Temple did not meet the approval of many Sikhs in Punjab, the fear factor had taken over all across the state.

With the law-and-order situation in Punjab worsening by the day, Prime Minister Indira Gandhi took the decision to cleanse the Golden Temple of Bhindranwale and his band of terrorists holed up there. She did so regretfully and much against her personal wishes, but, in the larger interests of the country as the situation then warranted. That some of Bhindranwale's followers conducted all sorts of immoral activities inside the shrine is generally forgotten by the ultra-Sikh radicals.

Operation Blue Star was launched by the Indian Army on 6 June 1984. In the words of the then General Officer Commanding-in-Chief (GOC-in-C) Western Command, the senior-most officer responsible for the operation, Lieutenant General K. Sundarji, Indian troops went inside the Golden Temple with their shoes taken off as a mark of respect with 'a prayer on their lips and humility in their hearts'. The assault on the terrorists who had fortified the holy shrine from inside was led by a valiant Sikh, Major General K.S. Brar, who even today remains on the hit list of some Khalistani terror organizations. Brar was nearly murdered a couple of years back by Khalistani terrorists when the over 80-year-old General was holidaying in London.

The Golden Temple operations had taken nearly 72 hours to complete. Mrs Gandhi visited the holy shrine along with the then Army Chief, General A.K. Vaidya (who was assassinated later in Pune by Sikh terrorists) and others. As she went inside the sanctum sanctorum to offer her respects, she was reportedly very upset at the damage which had occurred to the shrine and remarked to the Army Chief, 'Is this the minimum damage you had assured me about?' She was only later informed about the ISI-supplied modern weaponry and the huge arsenal built up by the terrorists inside the shrine who had fought the Indian Army attack ferociously.

The ISI, despite putting their complete weight and resources behind the Khalistani terrorists to initiate an armed uprising in Punjab, failed owing to lack of popular support with the terrorists. But the ISI did have the last laugh when Mrs Gandhi was assassinated by her own personal Sikh bodyguards at her residence on 31 October 1984, a few months after Operation Blue Star. Pursuing her secular credentials, she had ignored the IB's warnings that after Operation Blue Star, there was some resentment among her Sikh police bodyguards and she must change them. But then Mrs Gandhi dismissed the suggestion and was not the one to ever doubt her faith in all the peoples of India, which remained unflinching till her last breath and for which she made the supreme sacrifice.

By mid-1986, the Golden Temple had been restored, but again, had come under the control of a radical group—the Damdami Taksal.

Despite the army action in Operation Blue Star and its mopping-up operations in Operation Woodrose later to arrest/eliminate armed terrorists roaming around Punjab, fatalities against innocent civilians and some moderate political leaders continued to rise. The ISI was regularly pumping in arms and ammunition besides instructions to terrorists inside Punjab, whose back had still not been fully broken by the Indian security forces. Statistically speaking, there were 5,070 fatalities during 1978–89, while in just two years (1990–91), there were 5,058 civilian deaths. These high fatalities are attributed to the ISI that inducted the much sought-after AK-47 in the Sikh terrorists' arsenal. As Kiessling quotes Punjab super cop, K.P.S. Gill that 'though crude bombs extracted a steady toll of innocent lives, it was only after 1990 that sophisticated explosives became an essential component of the terrorist gear supplied by Pakistan. The scale of killing, consequently, was directly connected with the gun power available to the terrorists.'

Kiessling further narrates that one intriguing revelation about the training of Khalistan insurgents in Pakistan came from a member of the Babbar Khalsa who was arrested and interrogated by Indian authorities in the early 1990s. He described the ISI inviting him to join a flight training school in Bombay (now Mumbai). At an advanced stage of his training, during a solo flight he was to crash his plane into an offshore oil rig. He rejected the plan; however, as the Sikh faith forbids suicide assassinations.' The ISI did try to motivate some Sikh insurgents to attempt suicide missions, but these were all refused by the Sikh youth on religious grounds.

One of the major and painful terrorist actions initiated by the Babbar Khalsa during this period was the blowing up of Air India Flight 182 in 1985. The flight, which took off from Canada, was blown up mid-air by a bomb smuggled into the luggage of one of the passengers, resulting in the death of 329 innocent people. This inhuman terrorist act shook the conscience of millions the world over, including several Sikh leaders in India, at the intensity of Punjab-related terror. Many Sikh clerics criticized the handiwork of Khalistani terrorists and swore then to work for amity within Punjab. One of such leaders was Sant Harchand Singh Longowal, who was assassinated by Khalistani terrorists while delivering a sermon inside a gurdwara in Punjab.

Meanwhile, the ISI simultaneously endeavoured to influence and rope in the Sikh diaspora for the Khalistani cause, especially in nations like Canada and the UK which had large number of migrant Sikh communities. They found a willing figure in a former Akali minister of Punjab, Dr Jagjit Singh Chauhan, the self-proclaimed 'President of Khalistan'. Chauhan was hyperactive and, flushed with ISI funding, made frequent trips from his London base to many nations to marshal support from the expatriate Sikh community in Western countries for his cause.

OPERATION BLACK THUNDER

After Rajiv Gandhi assumed India's prime ministership, he, along with the then Punjab Chief Minister Surjit Singh Barnala, an Akali leader, endeavoured to defuse the situation in Punjab through stringent security measures and some political sops. They were largely successful as K.P.S. Gill, the Punjab Police DGP, coordinated the security countermeasures determinedly to take on ISI-supported terrorists. Gill oversaw Operation Black Thunder which he describes in his own words as, '...the most significant...was the loss of the Golden Temple and the Gurudwaras as shield and sanction. Rape, extortion and murder had been the business of the terrorists from the very beginning of the movement; but in its initial phases, and right up to the Black Thunder period, the top leadership was apparently distanced from these activities, concentrated as they were in the Golden Temple. Their vice and depravity in the hallowed place remained unknown to the large mass of Sikhs and while lesser terrorists were often seen to "stray from the path", the highest motives could still be ascribed to the militant leadership...divested of the sanctuary of the Golden Temple and the Gurudwaras, the leadership was forced to live life as fugitives in the Punjab countryside, on the one hand, their own deeds exposed them even further, since they were now believed to be condoned, even encouraged, by these leaders.'

The Khalistani terrorists, despite full support of the ISI, were on the run by 1992–93 and it was just a matter of time that the ISI-sponsored terror operations in Punjab were squarely defeated. The major reason remains that the illogical and irreligious Khalistani movement had no popular support.

However, evil ambitions never fade and despite the many knocks on its head the Pakistani establishment continues to make all efforts to keep the Khalistani issue somewhere on its agendas to destabilize the Indian state. Will it ever change is not a million-dollar guess—all current tabulations point to the contrary for the ISI can never depart from its sinister ways. This remains a challenge which India will have to factor in its overall political strategy and security preparedness. Punjab's politicians of all hues, in concerted effort, will have to combat Pakistani mischief to revive separatism and terrorism in the state. India also has to reach out to the huge Sikh diaspora across the world which remains a favourite hunting ground for the ISI.

10

Northeast:
India's Backdoor Beckons the ISI

The ISI has made widespread efforts to engage soft targets all over India. If Kashmir has been the front through which Jehad has got a foothold, the northeast with its unending influx of illegal immigrants is the backdoor, invitingly beckoning the ISI.

—Lieutenant General S.K. Sinha,
former Vice Chief, Indian Army

In its framework for India's destabilization, the ISI has, since decades, relentlessly looked for opportunities all over the Indian landscape to foment trouble. Not only in the neighbouring states of J&K or Punjab, but prior to 1971, the ISI also used the large and porous international border between erstwhile East Pakistan and Indian states to actively assist local insurgencies with supply of arms, ammunition, explosives, drugs and counterfeit money. Even after the emergence of Bangladesh, the ISI continued with its nefarious activities by utilizing its old contacts and a well-established network in the safe havens of the region bordering China, Myanmar and even inside Bangladesh.

India's Northeast comprises the states of Arunachal Pradesh, Assam, Manipur, Meghalaya, Mizoram, Nagaland and Tripura (referred to as the seven sisters) and Sikkim. This region accounts for about 8 per cent of India's geographical area, but roughly only 4 per cent of its population. The region borders China, Bhutan, Bangladesh and Myanmar and is connected to mainland India by a stretch of territory approximately 130 km long and just 25–30 km wide at Siliguri in the north of West Bengal. This small strip of land, called the Siliguri Corridor, bordering Bhutan, Bangladesh and Nepal, is also referred to as the 'Chicken's Neck' owing to the strategic challenge it imposes on India.

The Northeast is known for its ethnic, cultural, linguistic, religious and physiographical diversity. In addition, violent internecine rivalries have also been a part of its landscape since centuries. Tribes in the hills and plains and the non-tribal population spilling all over this region have differed with each other on various counts leading to conflicts among them and, at times, against the Indian state on perceived discrimination—a fertile ground for being exploited by powers inimical to the Indian state. China, Pakistan and earlier even Myanmar have endeavoured to exploit the grievances of the people of this region for their own selfish interests.

The British in the twentieth century, busy with two world wars, establishing its political authority over the rich plains of India and overly worried about the Russian expansionism from India's northwest frontiers, hardly devoted any time or resources to adequately link India's Northeast with the rest of the mainland. Immediately after Independence, while the government of India set about integrating the rather far-off Northeast region, a few local political organizations had taken root to establish their own areas of influence and political control. Some of these outfits took recourse to violence and initiated insurgency against the Indian state, also seeking assistance from countries in their neighbourhood.

INDIA'S NORTHEAST ON THE ISI RADAR

One of the first underground organizations to whip up the insurgent movement in the Northeast was the self-styled Federal Government of Nagaland. Apart from areas in their state, their violent authority even spread to the Naga-dominated regions of neighbouring Manipur by 1956. Some of the other insurgent outfits which took birth and indulged frequently in violence and terrorist activities were the National Socialist Council of Nagaland (NSCN), the United Liberation Front of Assam (ULFA) and the People's Liberation Army of Manipur (PLA) and the National Liberation Front of Tripura (NLFT). The ISI soon established nefarious links with these organizations. These outfits maintained their headquarters and training-cum-logistics bases in neighbouring Burma. Even after the emergence of independent Bangladesh, right from the early 1970s, the ULFA, NSCN and PLA had established a few camps both in Bangladesh and Burma. The Pakistani embassy in Dacca was active, through the ISI, in coordinating insurgent activities against India. Though the 1971 War did put a temporary halt at material assistance and funding emanating from the ISI for the diverse insurgent groups, this assistance got revitalized by close cooperation between the ISI and Bangladesh's Directorate General of Forces Intelligence (DGFI) under the umbrella of the political party in power—Khaleda Zia's Bangladesh Nationalist Party (BNP). This traditionally anti-India party has customarily enjoyed the support of pro-Islamist forces in the country. The ISI has always taken advantage of this reality to support anti-India forces in Bangladesh and in the region. Even the outspoken former director general of ISI, Lieutenant General Asad Durrani, has highlighted the manner in which the ISI has worked closely with Bangladesh-based radical outfit, HuJI. He even publicly stated that the ISI gave ₹50 crore to the BNP leader and former PM Khaleda Zia for her election campaigns. The ISI has always maintained close contacts with the Jamaat-e-Islami (JeI), the radical political ally of BNP.

Kiessling recounts in his book that, 'In January 1991, with the help of the ISI, several high-ranking ULFA leaders travelled to Pakistan to sign a training agreement for ULFA cadres. In the same year, two 6 member ULFA groups arrived in Islamabad for training; a third 10 member group followed in 1993. The ISI's auxiliary support for operations of this kind covered more than just the training courses in Pakistan. Well in advance, new identities and fake passports had to be procured, travel routes determined and the financing of the whole operation had to be secured. In this way, the Pakistan Embassy in Dhaka became an important ISI station, the hub of its operations in northeast India.' In addition, Indian intelligence also discovered that support, both financial and supply of arms and ammunition, was also extended to other anti-India underground groups.

'Indian security forces at one point arrested and interrogated a member of the NLFT, who revealed that between 1997 and 1998 some of their top brass had gone for training with the ISI in Pakistan. The detainee mentioned the names of the NLFT leaders, thereby uncovering the whole structure of task distribution and kinship within the top echelons of the group.

'It is also a fact that parallel to the Muslim resistance in Kashmir, other Islamist organizations in northeast India were also increasingly active in the 1990s. In Thailand, after the collapse of the Khmer Rouge regime in Cambodia from the 1980s onwards, light weapons and light machine guns awaited prospective buyers, so new supply opportunities opened up…the ISI provided weapons to a group of 240 NSCN members. Small boats brought the cargo to Cox's Bazaar, a port in Bangladesh, which became the hub for weapons supplies in the region. In week-long treks the NSCN and ULFA fighters themselves fetched weapons from Bangladesh and brought them back to their bases. In the initial years of the new arms supply channel, the ISI was obliged to procure and finance the weapons. According to a prominent Naga fighter imprisoned by the Indians, in the 1990s, he received three instalments totaling $1.7 million from the ISI for weapon purchases. Later on, the rebels often funded the purchase themselves. Bank robberies, tax extortions, blackmail and the drug trade supplied the means; terror began to be self-financing. Such weapons supply routes were running throughout the 1990s and into the new millennium, with Bangladesh as the main trans-shipment point.'

However, the ISI was not alone in supporting Indian insurgents. Over the years, they have received fair support from their Chinese friends, who have maintained contacts with both the ULFA and the NSCN using traditional routes and even through Bhutan. In 2000, 'high ranking officials of the organization (NSCN) negotiated with the

Chinese authorities in Kuming province for new weapons assistance. In December of that year, the NSCN-IM received a delivery valued at $750,000 via Cox's Bazaar; and that same month a delivery by road reached the Burmese border town of Tamu, conveniently situated opposite Moreh in Manipur...this was proven by India which successfully traced back a transaction of $1 million to a Chinese state company.'

NEFARIOUS STRATAGEMS CONTINUE

Among the states which constitute the Northeast, three of them—Arunachal Pradesh (which borders China), Meghalaya and Mizoram—remain peaceful. But the ISI has been active in the other four states owing to diverse tribe populations and inter-tribal rivalry also accentuated by foreign machinations. For some years, it has also targeted unemployed youth among the Muslim population. Additionally, the number of mosques and madrasas has multiplied in the largest and most populated state of the Northeast, Assam, and the vast areas bordering Bangladesh and West Bengal. An official report to the Assam Assembly submitted by Chief Minister P.K. Mahanta in April 2000 regarding ISI operations in Assam stated that the ISI is 'promoting indiscriminate violence in the state by providing active support to local militant outfits...creating new militant outfits along ethnic and communal lines by instigating ethnic and religious groups...promoting fundamentalism and militancy among local Muslim youths by misleading them in the name of Jihad...promoting communal tension between Hindu and Muslim citizens by way of false and inflammatory propaganda...sabotaging oil pipelines and other installations, communication lines, railways and roads.' ISI agents and officers have also been intercepted and arrested by Indian security forces a few times, but that has never discouraged the ISI from continuing with its sinister agendas in India's Northeast.

With a substantial improvement over the past few years in the overall situation in the Northeast, democracy taking firmer roots and the states undergoing rapid development and economic growth, the

ISI is at its wits' end on ways and measures to rekindle insurgency in this region. They are thus now targeting unemployed Muslim youth to rekindle their machinations in this region. Fortunately for India, the friendly regime of Sheikh Hasina (daughter of Bangladesh's first PM, Sheikh Mujibur Rahman) is keeping a check on the ISI's anti-India activities and the many radicalized elements existing in Bangladesh. However, the fact remains that some elements of Bangladesh's DGFI still retain their old affiliations with the ISI. India's Northeast may be relatively peaceful, but the nefarious collusive stratagems of the ISI and the Chinese are not likely to subside in the near future.

11

Eternal Quest for Strategic Depth in Afghanistan

…a pure Islamic state in Afghanistan not only promised to neutralize Pashtun irredentism but also helped to train and indoctrinate jihadis for the struggle against India in Kashmir.

—Dr Marvin Weinbaum, Director for Pakistan Studies, The Middle East Institute, Washington, D.C.

Islamabad viewed its Afghan policy through the prism of denying India any advantage in Kabul.

—Ahmed Rashid, journalist and author

Once a 'graveyard of empires' and the region where the 'Great Game' raged, Afghanistan unfortunately continues in the same groove despite the passage of centuries. Impoverished, fratricidal violence-ravaged and suffering from grave political instability, the land of the Hindu Kush has defied varying solutions, often bred from conflicting geopolitical interests of its neighbours, and remains a pawn for newer Great Games.

Whether in the past or in contemporary times, Afghanistan's strategic significance for the entire region cannot be ever overstated. It lies at the fulcrum of South Asia, West Asia and the CARs.

Within itself, its extreme diversity has fractured it along multiple fault lines—geographical, ethnic, tribal, sectarian and linguistic. Its quest to become a single unified state has been found wanting, since centuries, and till date.

THE DURAND LINE AND BEYOND

With rugged terrain and the few passes in the formidable Hindu Kush mountains, Afghanistan has historically accorded some security to the frontiers of the Indian subcontinent from its northwest. In the eighteenth and nineteenth centuries, the British Indian Empire, constantly wary about the creeping ambitions of Tsarist Russia, made all efforts to keep Afghanistan as a buffer state. Both the Russian and British empires competed for dominance in the regions of Central Asia and the areas which are now Afghanistan, Iran, Balochistan and the NWFP. These sparsely populated areas were the focus of British concerns to prevent any Russian advances into this expanse. The frontier areas of the empire were emphasized upon as the British had realized that Persia was considered unreliable to stave off any Russian onslaughts in this region. During these times, Afghan warlords also perfected the art of extracting benefits from the two contending empires—a habit which lingered on for years. To strengthen Afghanistan as a buffer and bulwark against the Russian Empire, the British signed an agreement on 12 November 1893, with the Amir of Afghanistan. Known as the Durand Agreement, it defined the southern and eastern limits of the Amir's dominion, beyond which he supposedly renounced any territorial claims. However, post India's independence in 1947, Afghanistan did not approve of this Agreement, dismissing it as having been signed under duress. In addition, many among those who advocate Pashtun ethnic unity and claim the Afghan nation extending even beyond Afghanistan, extend the boundary for 'Pashtunistan' till the Indus River also incorporating some areas of KPK and Balochistan. Pakistan is naturally keen for Afghanistan to formally recognize and accept the Durand Line as the international border. However, much free movement, including of terrorists, across this boundary continues on a daily basis, though a few checkpoints do exist on the so-called international border between the two nations.

Relations between Afghanistan and Pakistan remained uneasy during the early years after independence. Pakistan's leadership was also rattled by Afghanistan pitching for an independent Pakhtun state comprising Pakistan's Pakhtun areas (Pashtun, Pakhtun or Pathan carry the same connotation). General Ayub Khan, who always displayed a propensity to blame India for all of Pakistan's ills, maintained that Afghanistan's attitude towards Pakistan was owing to 'constant Indian propaganda that Pakistan could not survive as a separate state. The Afghan rulers believed this to be true and decided to stake a claim to our territory before Pakistan disintegrated… In this way the idea of an artificial State of Pakhtoonistan inside our borders was made an issue by the Afghan rulers…in this claim the Afghans were backed by India whose interests lay in ensuring that in the event of a war with us over Kashmir, the Afghans should open up a second front against Pakistan on the North West Frontier. They also reasoned that if they had this understanding with Afghanistan we would not be able to use the Pathan tribesmen against them. The Indians thought that they would be able to hem us in and embarrass us by a pincer movement.' Ayub's view on any such India–Afghan convergence is shared by most Pakistani security analysts and their military, though it is also a matter of record that India has never publicly supported the Afghan position on the Durand Line.

Apart from not recognizing the Durand Line as the international border between the two nations, Afghanistan was the only nation which opposed Pakistan's entry into the UN. Diplomatic relations were severed in 1955 and 1962 following border skirmishes between the two nations, as Afghanistan protested against what it termed as illegal occupation by Pakistan of some areas in then NWFP and Balochistan. Pakistan, of course, had only inherited what the British government had left for them, except for its forcible annexation of Kalat and some other areas in Balochistan. As is well known, the Khan of Kalat had desired an independent state for the Baloch people.

Notwithstanding Pakistan's consistent misgivings about Afghanistan's relations with India, Kabul supported Pakistan in its 1965

War with India. However, Afghanistan maintained strict neutrality during the 1971 War. When Zulfikar Ali Bhutto assumed control of Pakistan as its first civilian martial law administrator, he felt that the geopolitical environment after the secession of Pakistan's eastern province was more challenging, thereby increasing the dependence on Iran and even Afghanistan to bolster the country's security interests. Bhutto thus made a trip to Kabul to ostensibly thank Afghanistan's monarch, King Mohammed Zahir Shah, for the latter's neutral stance during the war. He also tried, in vain, to get Afghanistan on the Pakistan side vis-à-vis India. Later in 1973, Zahir Shah was overthrown by a leftist-leaning (probably with Soviet connivance), Mohammad Daoud Khan, in a bloodless coup. Daoud was the King's first cousin and Afghanistan's prime minister since 1953 and was known for his reformist agendas, emancipation of women and Pashtun nationalism. A pronouncedly anti-Pakistan Daoud strongly supported the independent 'Pakhtunistan' movement, besides providing arms and sanctuaries to Baloch rebels. In addition, Daoud brought to the notice of the UN the alleged atrocities and human rights violations by the Pakistani military on the Pashtuns and the Baloch people in Pakistan. He also sought the support of the Soviets and Indians. Thus, from the mid-1970s, PM Bhutto encouraged radical Pashtun leaders like Burhanuddin Rabbani and Gulbuddin Hekmatyar in order to wean them away from the Pashtun fraternity that threatened to become a united force in Kabul's affairs. Pakistan supported Islamic fundamentalists under the Ikhwanis to keep Kabul in check and infuse radical Islamism in Afghanistan. In the border regions, both nations ensured peace, off and on, by buying off restive Pashtun tribal chieftains. In 1978, the Afghan communists had Daoud assassinated and replaced with a pronouncedly pro-Soviet regime. The Soviet invasion and occupation of the country rekindled an ideological armed conflict not witnessed in the land of the Hindu Kush for centuries.

GENESIS OF THE AFGHAN TALIBAN

The Soviet occupation was a game changer for Pakistan's myriad ambitions in the region. By reconstructing its role as the conduit for American arms and equipment for Afghans combating the Soviets in their land, Pakistan was able to divert the attention—both globally and regionally—from its objectives in Afghanistan. The clever Pakistanis seized this golden opportunity come its way and obliged the US by resisting the Soviet forces in Afghanistan. With massive US military and financial backing augmented by support from other Western nations and Arab governments, Pakistan successfully expanded the scope and tenor of their arc of influence inside Afghanistan, which they had originally endeavoured for the last many decades, though without much success.

However, the events in neighbouring Afghanistan during these years also caused tremendous unease in Pakistan. PM Zulfikar Ali Bhutto had commenced training and arming of radical Afghans under the umbrella of the Afghan Ikhwanis to take on the Pashtun and Baloch rebels. After Bhutto's removal and with military rule established by General Zia, the latter redoubled his activities against these rebels. Zia also articulated his Afghan policy with resoluteness and the necessary ferocity. With his avowed hatred towards India, he put into place an anti-India, anti-Soviet strategy in Afghanistan. He successfully gave a jihadi orientation to the struggle of the Afghan people against the Soviets, far beyond the natural movement for indigenous freedom. In this clever stratagem, the Americans also saw their chance to embarrass their Cold War rival, and willingly opened their doors to give Pakistan the requisite military and financial support. The ISI masterminded the entire anti-Soviet operations and with the concurrence of the US, managed to cobble up a strong 'mujahideen' force consisting of Muslim fighters from many Islamic nations the world over. For these jihadis, it was merely serving the Islamic Ummah and not for territorial gains in any country. General Zia, in keeping with his fundamentalist leanings, had more ambitious agendas for his nation and the region. He deftly managed the anti-Soviet jihad, not only raking in massive American military and financial support, but also encouraged the Pakistani Pashtuns to join hands with their Afghani counterparts to synergize their activities against the Soviets. The seeds of the birth of the Afghan Taliban germinated during this time.

Ahmed Rashid has further amplified the developments in the region during that period stating that, 'Zia also promoted the idea of Afghanistan offering "strategic depth" to Pakistan—a military doctrine conceived as a counter to an Indian attack with the Pakistan Army having little geographical depth to wage a counter attack from. Elements of the Pakistani Army could retreat or regroup in Afghanistan where Pakistani aircraft and even some of its nuclear arsenal and rockets could be kept out of harm's way. The latter was seriously considered by military officers after the Taliban captured Kabul.' Rashid clarifies the theory of 'strategic depth' stating that this concept 'was so thoroughly rubbished in the 1980s by critics— including retired generals—that it disappeared, until it was resurrected in 2009 by Army Chief General Ashfaq Kayani, who described it not as a military doctrine but as political justification to show Pakistan's need for a friendly government in Kabul. However with India and Pakistan now nuclear powers such conventional warfare talk of territory, geography and safe havens had become even more meaningless.'

DAWN OF THE DARK ERA

The resounding defeat of the Soviet Army in Afghanistan and the withdrawal of the pro-Moscow regime from Kabul in 1988-89 did not usher in an era of peace and stability for the Afghan people. On the other hand, the intervening period between 1989 and 1996 (when a resurgent Taliban captured power in Afghanistan) is one of the nation's darkest periods in recent history. This fratricidal fighting took place initially between the former mujahideen groups and later against the Taliban by some of these groups who did not coalesce with the Taliban owing to the latter's fundamentalist ideologies and, importantly, sensing Pakistan's machinations towards their land.

The disengagement of both the Soviet Union and the US during this period allowed Pakistan to step up its interference in Afghanistan. Iran and Uzbekistan were also meddling in Kabul's affairs but far less than Pakistan. Prominent anti-Soviet resistance leaders and Afghan Islamists like Ahmad Shah Massoud and Gulbuddin Hekmatyar were given refuge and generously supported inside Pakistan. However, Masood, realizing Pakistan's intended mischief for his native land, gradually distanced himself from his hosts. On the other hand Hekmatyar soon became a hot favourite with the ISI owing to his penchant for adopting radical and violent methods even against his own countrymen at the behest of the Pakistani establishment. For his loyalty and dedication to the ISI (including rocketing Kabul), Hekmatyar received a lion's share from international assistance funds. He had even called for an Afghanistan–Pakistan confederation when Soviet withdrawal was imminent.

The ISI's relationship with the radical Hekmatyar and Haqqani networks and Masood was at the heart of the Pakistani stratagem for Kabul's control and a major cause of the imposed civil war in Afghanistan. If it had not been for Masood's skilful parleys with the communist government in Kabul, the fate of Afghanistan during that era would have been different. Hekmatyar and the ISI nearly succeeded in establishing a pro-Pakistan pliant regime in Kabul.

Once Pakistan realized Hekmatyar's inability to capture power in Kabul, it took recourse to a newer strategy. Professor William Maley observes in his book, *The Afghanistan Wars*, that the then Pakistan interior minister in Benazir Bhutto's cabinet, Major General Naseerullah Babar, also considered the 'Godfather of the Taliban', became the new hero for the ISI, replacing Hekmatyar. The latter was surprised when the ISI informed him that the Taliban had reached the gates of Kabul in September 1996. In her own flip-flop strategizing of her relations with Afghanistan and India, Benazir Bhutto fanned both the Afghan jihad and supported the extremist elements in J&K.

It merits mention that even after the Soviet withdrawal, Pakistan continued to be unduly apprehensive about the so-called threat from a militarily far weaker neighbour, Afghanistan. The army felt that though Afghanistan could not militarily threaten their nation, but in collusion with or instigated by the then Soviet Union, India or even Iran, it could cause major internal security and stability problems for Pakistan, besides border-related challenges from Pakhtun and Baloch dissidents. Such apprehensions continue to persist in the minds of the Pakistani military to date.

As mentioned above, the 1980s and '90s witnessed substantial Pakistan support for the Sunni-Islamist Pashtun elements in Afghanistan, which was primarily instrumental in the creation of the Afghan Taliban. The latter controlled Afghanistan from 1996 to 2001. It was a period marked by medieval cruelty and countless executions of innocents who did not subscribe to their version and orientation of Islam. Regrettably, the Taliban also destroyed Afghanistan's historical non-Islamic monuments, including the famed heritage Bamiyan Buddha statues.

COBRAS IN THE BACKYARD

The emergence of the Pakistani Taliban from the ranks of the vast terror conglomerate nurtured by Pakistan for years is an interesting phenomenon. The mercenaries that Pakistan trained for terrorist acts in Afghanistan and Kashmir turned their backs on them. This was fittingly summarized by former US Secretary of State Hillary Clinton during a visit to Islamabad, where she famously admonished her Pakistani hosts that, 'If you rear cobras in your backyard, be prepared for them biting you one day.'

The Tehrik-i-Taliban Pakistan (TTP) is one such terror group. The TTP and Afghan Taliban, though both predominantly Pashtun, vary immensely in their history, leadership and ultimate goals as they pursue their diabolical agendas. Though the TTP claims allegiance with the Afghan Taliban in the latter's insurgency in Afghanistan, the two groups have no direct or operational affiliation with each other. For the Pakistan Army, the TTP symbolizes the 'bad Taliban', while the Afghan Taliban are the 'good Taliban'. Pakistan forgets that no differentiation among terrorists of any hue can ever be justified for any reason. The TTP was responsible for the dastardly terror attack at the Army School, Peshawar, where nearly 140 innocent children and school staff were massacred in December 2014. In addition, the terror group has been frequently involved in terror attacks on numerous Sufi shrines all over Pakistan.

STRATEGIC OBJECTIVES

Pakistan's unflinching strategic objectives in Afghanistan may be summarized as follows:

- Establishing a pro-Pakistan government in Afghanistan to prevent the emergence of a New Delhi–Kabul axis.
- Ensuring strategic depth against India (in the event of an all-out war) by redeploying critical military assets in Afghan territory.
- To nurture and foster a radical Sunni Islamist policy in conformity with Pakistan's own religious proclivities.
- To establish training camps and safe havens for Pakistan-trained extremists and terrorists for operations inside Afghanistan and particularly in India.
- Having an economic corridor towards the CARs to meet Pakistan's growing demand for oil, gas and other products, whilst acting as a bridge between the CARs and warm water ports on the Arabian Sea.
- To nullify any efforts by rebel Pashtuns for carving out an independent 'Pashtunistan' and ensuring the sanctity of the Durand Line.
- Leverage both economic and security support from regional (read China, Russia, Iran) and extra-regional powers (the US and European Union) and keep India totally out of exercising any influence in Afghanistan.

Bearing in mind the above considerations, the Pakistan military has persistently endeavoured to stymie the development of an Indo–Afghan axis. Summarizing Pakistan's ambitions in the region, Frederic Grare opines that, 'According to Pakistan whatever India does in Afghanistan is a ploy against Pakistan, be it economic investment, infrastructure, or any related matter… As a result, Pakistan has ensured that Indian interests would be blocked whenever and wherever possible.'*

---

*Savita Pande. 'Pakistan's Afghanistan Relations: A Strategic Shift. *CLAWS*, Summer 2015.

IN THE AFTERMATH OF 9/11

The overall situation in Afghanistan underwent a traumatic change with the 9/11 attacks. US President George W. Bush launched the Global War on Terror (GWOT), which embraced a range of objectives—military, political, legal and importantly, ideological. These were to be achieved by speedily initiating massive military intervention in Afghanistan and in the latter's border regions with Pakistan which have been, and still continue to be, sanctuaries for terrorists of many hues. The primary objective of Operation Enduring Freedom was to eliminate all terrorists and their infrastructure that posed a threat to US interests anywhere in the world, and take on the global terrorist conglomerate of the al-Qaeda. It was to target al-Qaeda and the Taliban and remove the latter from power, which it had captured in Kabul and the rest of the country since 1996. These objectives were endorsed internationally in 2001 when the United Nations Security Council adopted Resolution 1373 that obliged states to criminalize all terror activities in their regions and synergize all activities to combat global terror.

Prior to the launch of the US invasion of Afghanistan, Lieutenant General Mahmood Ahmed, the ISI chief, was removed from his post and sent on retirement by a reluctant Pakistani President General Musharraf. General Ahmed was unceremoniously sacked owing to his role in wiring $100,000 to Mohammed Atta, the World Trade Centre (WTC) hijacker-attacker. Despite the enormous loss of lives and tremendous destruction caused in the US homeland, and the swift launch of Operation Enduring Freedom, the Americans did not act decisively against many in the Pakistani establishment who were directly or indirectly involved in the carnage.

The US went into Afghanistan without a clear-cut strategic aim. Ultimately, the destruction of al-Qaeda and other terror outfits operating in that nation took centre stage and the holistic aim of establishing peace and stability in that impoverished and violence-ravaged land took a back seat. Under Pakistan's influence, the US failed to integrate all the diverse tribal groups inhabiting Afghanistan and played into the hands of Pakistan and its devious tactics. In the initial years, as Pakistan controlled the major supply route from its Karachi port to Afghanistan for the foreign troops stationed there, it managed to extract from the US more than adequate financial and military support for itself. In addition, General Musharraf was successful in selling his distinction of the 'good Taliban' and the 'bad Taliban' to the naive US establishment, who were led to believe that the Afghan government and the US could engage in some talks with the 'good Taliban' to usher peace in Afghanistan. The Pakistanis were clear that if elements of the Afghan Taliban could be made to agree to some form of power-sharing in Kabul, the Pakistanis would be able to hold a lever of power inside Afghanistan in the future. The same state of flux and duplicity by Pakistan continues till date.

Notwithstanding Pakistan's double-dealings with its mentor during the conduct of Operation Enduring Freedom, their protégés—the Taliban—were swiftly defeated by the troops of the Northern Alliance, predominantly non-Pashtun groups with overwhelming support from US Special Forces and its air power. However, the success of these military operations directed against the fundamentalist and terror fraternity in Afghanistan did not bring the much-desired tranquility to the violence-wrecked land. Nascent Afghan nationalism embracing all its diverse ethnic groups fell once again into the pitfalls of Islamist radicalism represented by terror groups of various hues masterminded by the wily ISI. The Americans continued to look the other way at this persisting Pakistani mischief. To ensure the safety of their convoys from Karachi port to Afghanistan, the US, at times, directly and mostly through the ISI, continued to pay-off terrorist groups inside Pakistan and the Taliban within Afghanistan.

Meanwhile, the murder of former Afghan President Burhanuddin Rabbani, who, during his tenure, maintained cordial relations with Pakistan without acquiescing to all of ISI's orders, generated a lot of anger against the Pakistani establishment in Kabul. President Hamid Karzai, who took over the reins in Kabul in December 2001, endevoured determinedly to give a fresh orientation to Afghanistan's foreign policy towards its neighbours. Accordingly, he signed a strategic agreement with India to provide his country with increased economic aid, supply of non-lethal military equipment and additional training facilities for Afghan military personnel. During the simultaneous presidential tenures of Musharraf in Islamabad and Karzai in Kabul, relations between the two neighbours remained frosty and were marked by frequent violence in Kabul and other towns of Afghanistan, engineered by the ISI with its protégés like the Afghan Taliban, Hekmatyar and Haqqani outfits and the remnants of the al-Qaeda. The major terrorist targets for the ISI in Afghanistan were obviously Indian infrastructure projects and importantly, Indian consulate offices in Kandahar, Jalalabad, Herat and Mazar-e-Sharif. Thus, the Pakistani security establishment kept up its efforts to keep Kabul destabilized and Indian presence, even in civil infrastructural and welfare projects, under constant terrorist threat.

ENDGAME

In view of the diverse pulls, pushes and assorted machinations of many nations simultaneously at play, the outcome of the endgame in Afghanistan, remains currently fuzzy.

Ashraf Ghani, who took over as the Afghan President at the end of Hamid Karzai's tenure in September 2014, endeavoured to normalize and improve relations with Pakistan. Ghani made the unprecedented gesture of visiting the Pakistan Army's GHQ at Rawalpindi during his first official visit to the nation. However, the Afghan president soon realized that the Deep State's agenda for his nation was hardly altruistic and the Af–Pak relationship soon came back to its originally restive and mutually suspicious orientation.

The endgame in Afghanistan is currently underscored by a few significant factors whose likely contours in the future are going to shape Kabul's destiny. First is the stability of President Ghani's fragile National Unity Government (NUG), and the manner in which he and his Chief Executive, Abdullah Abdullah, can cooperatively function without compromising the larger interests of their nation. Both of them will have to steer clear of the conspiracies of nations like Pakistan. Second is the ability of the NUG to strike an equitable deal with the Taliban which is clearly on the resurgence in a majority of the Afghan areas. The ISI, duly pressured by the US, Saudi and even China, has been masquerading since the last three to four years as the negotiator between the Taliban and the NUG, but has consistently followed its own agenda with the Taliban. Thirdly, it will be equally important for the Trump administration to revisit its Afghanistan strategy, as the US participation in the longest war in its history has distinctly fatigued it both militarily and financially. However, the US scaling down its already depleted forces (not more than 12,500 foreign troops in Afghanistan now) will further exacerbate the security situation for the ill-equipped and beleaguered Afghan National Army (ANA) to successfully confront a resurgent Taliban with a more-than generous Pakistani support.

Further, the emergence in the last two years of the formidable West Asian Islamic terror organization, the Islamic State of Iraq and the Levant (ISIL), generally referred to as the Islamic State (IS), is a cause of great concern not only for Afghanistan, but also for all countries in South Asia, notably India. The way it shapes up in the immediate future will also be an important contributing factor for Afghanistan's stability. Barring the remnants of the al-Qaeda, it is felt that elements of the Afghan Taliban—fragmented that they are currently—are not favourably disposed towards the IS. Its spread in the eastern portion of the country was, however, halted after a collective offensive by the Afghan and Coalition Forces. The IS has had no compunctions in engineering a few suicide blasts in Kabul, killing innocent civilians and Afghan security guards. However, the Taliban, sensibly for a change, see the IS as competitors and are not overly enamoured of the IS radical jihadi agendas vis-à-vis their own nationalist moorings.

The Taliban, however, now under the command of Mawlawi Haibatullah Akhundzada (after the death of their supremo Mullah Omar and the killing of Omar's successor, Mullah Mansour in Balochistan by a US drone in May 2016), have also kept up their violence levels in Afghanistan and hardly shown any serious inclinations for peace talks with the NUG. The year 2016 was a difficult one for Afghanistan which included Taliban's sway in more than half of the country, especially in the eastern part, including the Taliban's temporary capture of the strategic provincial capital of Kunduz for a second time. The ANA had to suffer many casualties in fierce battles to retake Kunduz and many other targets which fell to the Taliban. The provinces of Faryab, Jawzjan and Baghla in the north and Helmand and Urzogan have been sites of many bloody battles between the ANA and the Taliban.

Poppy cultivation in Afghanistan has witnessed an unprecedented rise. Its export to neighbouring countries is synonymous with the fuelling of insurgency in Afghanistan and helps its various regional warlords fund their warring tribesmen and smuggle arms from neighbouring nations.

Another problem currently afflicting the country is massive unemployment. The adverse security environment has resulted in the large-scale exodus of professionally qualified, secular-minded educated Afghans to Europe and India. This migration does not bode well for the country in the long run.

President Ghani, having failed to get Islamabad's Deep State on board to work for a united Afghanistan and its stability despite genuine and serious outreach to Pakistan in the last year-and-a-half, has now crafted an independent foreign policy for his nation. At the last 'Heart of Asia Conference' in Amritsar, India, in December 2016, Ghani openly lashed out at the Pakistan establishment and blamed them for backing the main insurgent groups that have wrecked his nation's peace and stability. He refused a $500 million Pakistani aid offer for Kabul. Ghani stated that if Pakistan stopped meddling in his country, the Kabul government would be able to contain terrorism within a month.

In concert with India, Afghanistan has been reasonably successful in isolating Pakistan, both regionally, and to some extent, internationally on the issue of terrorism and its role as a terror-exporter in the region. The battle lines between President Ghani and Pakistan's Deep State are now clearly drawn on challenges afflicting Afghanistan. The Afghans, currently and near-unanimously, blame Pakistan squarely for all their ills. However, Ghani also knows that his options are not unlimited. With the presence of a mere 12,000–13,000 US/NATO troops in his country and a beleaguered ANA to handle the precarious security situation, Ghani had signed the Bilateral Security Agreement (BSA) with the US. The manner in which US President Donald Trump reacts to the security scenario in Afghanistan will determine its future geostrategic contours in South Asia.

Afghanistan will have to carve out a cogent foreign policy to balance the conflicting geopolitical ambitions of the regional players. It will have to reach out to the likes of India, China, Russia, Iran and the CARs, while clarifying to Pakistan that as it will brook no interference from it, Afghanistan will reciprocate in equal measure to bring in much needed peace in the region.

Russia too has shown greater interest in Afghanistan in recent times by organizing conferences with China and Pakistan, and surprisingly leaving out the Kabul government from it. Reportedly, Pakistan and China have offered the use of the Gwadar deep sea port for Russian trade. In an amazing change of stance, Russia has dubbed the Taliban as a 'political and social movement'. The Russian volte-face clearly shows that the pursuit of own interests does go to make strange bedfellows.

Media reports also point to neighbouring Iran raising a 15,000 plus strong local militia, the Liwa Fatemiyoun, comprising Afghanistan's Shia Hazaras to protect Iran's interests in Afghanistan. Iran's own Sunni population, concentrated in the area bordering Iran, Afghanistan and Pakistan, has also evinced more than a keen interest in Afghan affairs and is becoming as influential as the pro-Pakistan Quetta Shura. Each of these various groups meddling into Afghan affairs, regrettably, has its own selfish and local motives to achieve.

China, which has a deep interest in tapping Afghanistan's mineral wealth, is likely to play a major role in the years ahead. It will desire that some of the Islamic terror groups based in Afghanistan do not train and export any native Islamic Uighur militants to its restive Xinjiang region. However, with China now developing its ambitious $56 billion CPEC in Pakistan-held Gilgit–Baltistan and the POK regions, it will hardly be in a position to tame or caution its protégé, Pakistan, to avoid interfering in the internal affairs of Afghanistan. Thus, China's agenda in the land of the Hindu Kush may prove to be of some economic advantage to Afghanistan initially, but in the long run, with China's increasing footprint in the country, could Pakistan be far behind with its ever devious agendas?

Notwithstanding the international community's sympathy and support for the hapless Afghan people, in the ultimate analysis, Afghanistan will have to assert itself from within to resolve its problems to stay as a unified state. The friction between the two halves in the NUG will have to be bridged between President Ghani and his deputy, Abdullah Abdullah. Both these leaders will have to cooperate and get down to serious governance and curbing corruption, which has been a long persisting cancer in the Afghan administration. Importantly, the Taliban has to be managed, independent of Pakistan's mentoring of it and other Afghanistan-based radicalized groups. Currently, the Taliban is in no mood to engage in any fruitful talks with the NUG. Thus, the Afghan government will have to further weaken the Taliban and its other violent cohorts militarily to pressurize it to display an accommodative approach to any power-sharing arrangements in Kabul.

As Afghanistan and, importantly, India endeavour to get regional stakeholders on board to stabilize the former, the role of the US administration would be critical for Kabul's future—the US must not exit Afghanistan without having ensured a reasonable level of peace, economic growth and political stability there. The UN may consider keeping a moderate level of peacekeeping force in Afghanistan. In addition, the international community will have to support the Afghan government financially, at least for the next ten years or so.

India, which is highly respected in Afghanistan, must augment its soft-power forays by increased assistance to the people in civil developmental projects, infrastructure, education, power supplies, medical facilities, etc. India must also step up training of the Afghan National Security Forces (ANSF) and, without hesitation, provide military equipment including for at least four artillery regiments, two T-72 tank regiments, two mechanized infantry battalion equipment (BMP-2), radio sets, five to six attack helicopters and mobile field hospitals to empower the ANSF. Friendly governments must make Kabul militarily self-reliant and far more combat-capable than in its current configuration.

Apart from regional stakeholders putting aside their personal ambitions and reigniting a newer version of the Great Game, it is critical that the US and Russia also mend their fences, at least for this region. Close monitoring and strict measures must be undertaken to ensure the elimination of the IS influence spreading in Afghanistan and beyond and any convergence taking place between them and the al-Qaeda. In addition, the UN and its drug-enforcement agencies, adequately supported by the global community, must do its utmost to eliminate/reduce the growth and export of poppy, opium and drugs. By current estimates, in the areas controlled by the Taliban, poppy cultivation has gone up by approximately 43 per cent from 2015.

The world must never forget that Afghanistan is the nation where the world's first GWOT was launched. Accordingly, it is imperative for the global community to work unitedly and zealously to eliminate terror in all its manifestations and accord a modicum of stability and peace to this long-suffering country. The current efforts by Russia, China and Pakistan and, to some extent even Iran, to commence negotiations with the Taliban are likely to prove self-defeating, for the Taliban represent radicalism and violence which Afghanistan can do without.

The world also needs to factor in Pakistan's unending machinations to keep the pot boiling in Afghanistan. Till Pakistan does not end its interference in Afghanistan's internal affairs, peace and stability will continue to elude the Afghan people. It will be prudent for all stakeholders in the region to heed to India's advice for Kabul's stability that any peace process for that nation has to be also 'Afghan-controlled'. Hopefully, President Trump will heed to his local US military commanders based in Afghanistan who wish the US not to exit before they achieve credible military success, and a sound and stable government in Kabul. The US Air Force recently bombed an IS base in Nangarhar employing one of the largest 11 tonne non-nuclear bombs in the world which heralds, perhaps, Donald Trump's determination to go all out against Afghanistan-based terrorists. This act, however, drew strong condemnation from former President Karzai who expressed that he now wanted the US out of Afghanistan. The region, in particular, and the world, at large, has been waiting anxiously for the Trump administration to firm up its policy for Afghanistan in a far more determined manner than both the previous US presidents did. George Bush treated Afghanistan as a stepchild and even Obama failed to usher in peace owing to hesitation on his administration's part to rein in Pakistan and deploy meaningful resources to contain the Taliban. On 21 August this year, Trump announced America's newly calibrated policy* for Afghanistan. He unequivocally castigated Pakistan, stating: 'We have been paying billions and billions of dollars at the same time they are housing the very terrorists that we are fighting.' Trump further warned, '...that will have to change and that will change immediately.' An additional 4,000 US troops were to be inducted into Afghanistan and Trump indicated that the US troops will stay there until peace is restored. Praising India's assistance in the development of Afghanistan, he requested for additional Indian economic help for the country.

In addition, and importantly, the US and Russia have to be on the same page to bring peace and normalcy in Afghanistan aided by regional powers like India, China and Iran contributing their bit for the same goal. Regional powers have to forsake their narrow national interests to prevent Afghanistan's further slide towards total chaos. The proud people of the long-suffering Afghanistan need peace, stability and, importantly, political and economic empowerment—something which has eluded them for decades. That will only be possible if all key stakeholders ensure a modicum of convergence in their respective strategies for this unfortunate land. Any further deterioration in the overall political stability, security situation, economic conditions and further radicalization of hapless Afghanistan will be disastrous not only for the nation but also for the whole region.

---

*'Trump announces new Afghanistan war strategy with few details', *The New York Times*, 21 August 2017.

12

The Deep State and the US: A Turbulent Relationship

In the years ahead, the United States may face no greater challenge than Pakistan. Home to a variety of militant groups that attack both US and Pakistan government targets, a growing nuclear arsenal and a very precarious relationship between military and civilian authorities, conditions in Pakistan threaten its own stability, its neighbours and vital US interests. The US-Pakistani relationship has been a dangerously uneven one.

—Ryan C. Crocker, former US Ambassador to Pakistan and Afghanistan

Since its independence and the decades thereafter, Pakistan has been, by and large, a near-favourite protégé of the US. The latter has been more than generous with its economic and military aid to an oft-erring Pakistan. The US has even turned a Nelson's eye to Pakistan's rise as a nuclear state and its consistent penchant in adopting the export of terrorism as an extension of state policy towards its neighbours and many parts of the world, including the US.

Pakistan, under General Musharraf, was reluctantly sucked into the US GWOT launched after 9/11. Nevertheless, many nations and analysts continue to question whether Pakistan is America's friend or foe in the GWOT? Former Pakistani diplomat, Husain Haqqani, surmises in his book, *Pakistan: Between Mosque and Military*, that, 'After 9/11, the selective cooperation of President Musharraf in sharing intelligence with the United States and apprehending Al-Qaeda members led to the assumption that Pakistan might be ready to give up its long-standing ties with radical Islam. But Pakistan's status as an Islamic ideological state is closely linked with the Pakistani elite's world view and the praetorian ambitions of its military.' Haqqani further amplifies, 'Nevertheless, terrorists continue to operate in, and from Pakistan. The country is now a target and staging ground for terrorism while simultaneously being seen by US policymakers as the key to ending terrorism in South Asia.'

TRACING THE HIGHS AND LOWS

Barely two months after Pakistan's independence, the US became one of the first nations to establish diplomatic relations with the new state. Christine Fair observes that, 'Academic accounts of this period focus on Pakistan's destitution, mounting refugee problems, eviscerated institutions, and critical human capital shortages. Within just two months of becoming a state, Jinnah "invited the United States to become the principal source of external support" for Pakistan and requested for a $2 billion dollar loan over five years. As Jinnah envisioned it, these funds would be used to help Pakistan build up its armed forces and to jump start various agricultural and industrial projects. While Pakistan's leaders really sought assistance to underwrite its security vis-à-vis India, they were aware that America's principal concern was the Soviet Union and thus couched all requests within strong anti-communist rhetoric.' However, PM Liaquat Ali Khan was keen to establish fraternal relations with both the US and the Soviet Union. But many in west Pakistan, especially the ruling pro-American PML, and other religious organizations were not too eager as they felt that the Soviets, being communists, were anti-religious. Even the Soviet Union had rebuffed Pakistan's requests for military aid. The Pakistani PM, during his first, and much requested for, visit to the US received a mixed response to his appeal for US assistance, as the latter were, at this juncture, hoping to rope in India in their sphere of influence. PM Khan, meanwhile, declined to lease an air base to the CIA, as requested by US President Harry Truman. With PM Nehru, a strong votary of non-alignment, not responding enthusiastically to US overtures, it was just a matter of time that the US roped in Pakistan for its Middle East strategies.

In the following years, especially after PM Khan's assassination in 1951, ties between the two nations gradually strengthened with the ambitious US Secretary of State, John Foster Dulles, personally moving the relationship forward. Bilateral relations were consolidated with the signing of a mutual defence treaty in 1954. A US Military Assistance Advisory Group (MAAG) was also set up in Rawalpindi. Thereafter, hundreds of Pakistani military officers were sent to the US regularly for training in various nuances of the military art.

During the Cold War, Pakistan allied itself with the US against the Soviet Union. In 1958, it willingly joined the US-led CENTO and SEATO organizations, which were formed as a bulwark against the spread of communism in the world. By joining these organizations, Pakistan became the recipient of substantial modern military aid from the US, ostensibly to be employed against China or Russia. However, Pakistanis were looking for likely deployment against neighbouring India as one of the major spin-offs of this arrangement. During an official visit to the US in 1954, while he was the Army Chief (and not yet the military dictator), General Ayub Khan famously told a senior US army officer, 'I didn't come here to look at barracks. Our army can be your army if you want us. But let's make a decision.' After he ousted the civil government in Rawalpindi, relations between the two nations got better substantially and even the Pakistani public was construed during that era to be pro-American.

In 1960, Ayub Khan granted permission to the US to establish a spy base in Peshawar, which was modernized and upgraded to fly out U-2 reconnaissance planes to carry out missions over Soviet Union and China. It was during this time that one of the US spy missions over the Soviet Union resulted in the downing of a U-2 plane and its pilot, Gary Powers, was captured by the Russians. Notwithstanding this incident, the US military and the CIA continued to strengthen their relationship with the Pakistani establishment. However, the launch of the ill-fated Operation Gibraltar by Pakistan in 1965 to seize Kashmir led to the US imposing both economic and military sanctions on it, which hurt Pakistan far more than it hurt India. Ayub subsequently had to give way to his Army Chief, the pro-American Yahya Khan, who assumed power and faithfully continued with the pro-US stance of his predecessors.

By this time, Pakistan and China too had developed close ties. The US, under President Richard Nixon with his Secretary of State Henry Kissinger, conceived their strategy to isolate the Soviets and thus desired establishing contacts with China. It was in pursuit of this strategy that Pakistan assisted the US by arranging a secret visit by Kissinger to China in 1972, which resulted in some normalization of relations between the US and China.

The events of 1971 further consolidated the US–Pak relationship. Declassified CIA intelligence documents revealed that 'India intended to dismember Pakistan and destroy its armed forces, a possible loss of US ally in the Cold War that US cannot afford to lose.' It also merits repetition that US President Richard Nixon, who was avowedly against both India and Indira Gandhi, had dispatched the USS Enterprise and Task Force 74 of their Seventh Fleet into the Indian Ocean as a pressure tactic against India. However, this development did not shake the determination of PM Indira Gandhi to budge from her decision to liberate East Pakistan from the cudgels of its oppressive parent nation. The rest was history.

After the Pakistan Army's spectacular defeat in December 1971, the charismatic Prime Minister Bhutto, though a land-owning aristocrat, had socialistic leanings, and early in his rule, did try to get closer to the Soviet Union. His efforts to maintain some balance in Pakistan's relations with both the superpowers were scoffed at by the US. Bhutto once stated about his nation's relations with the US, that 'when differences develop, a small country should not take on a great power head-on, it is wiser for it to duck, detour, side-step and try to enter from the back-door.'

Though Bhutto was also reasonably close to Richard Nixon, the US–Pak relation nosedived with Jimmy Carter's election to the White

House. President Carter did not approve of Bhutto's minor flirtations with the Soviets or Pakistan's nascent nuclear programmes being conceived for the future. Bhutto did not heed to the US advice not to pursue nuclear weapons research in Pakistan on which the US kept a close watch. Not the one to be bullied even by his nation's mentor, Bhutto also vehemently criticized US policies for nations seeking nuclear status. He declared, time and again, his objective to launch Pakistan's own atomic bomb programmes.

In 1974, after India carried out its nuclear tests, Bhutto immediately pleaded unsuccessfully with the US government to impose sanctions on India. But instead, Kissinger personally warned Bhutto in a meeting in 1976: 'If you do not cancel, modify or postpone the Reprocessing Plant Agreement, we will make a horrible example of you.' But the determined Bhutto refused to succumb to threats or blackmail.

Pakistan's atomic bomb project became fully mature in 1978 and the first cold test was conducted in 1983 (Kirana 1). Bhutto even appealed to the Organisation of Islamic States (OIC) to bring the Muslim world together on the nuclear bomb issue. However, the nuclear programme for Pakistan did falter, to some extent, with Bhutto's hanging in 1979.

HONEYMOON PERIOD BEGINS WITH A BANG

US–Pakistan relations were destined for a major change after the Soviet invasion of Afghanistan in December 1979. Immediately, President Carter enunciated the creation of a collective security framework for the region. It envisaged augmentation of combat troops with the US Central Command (CENTCOM) and an undertaking for the defence of Pakistan, incorporating new defence strategies to combat the Soviet occupation in Afghanistan. The Pakistan Army's honeymoon period with the US defence forces thereafter commenced with a bang. General Zia exploited US inclinations to the maximum, extracting generous US military and economic aid ostensibly to fight the Soviets but, more importantly, to bolster his own economy and arsenal.

In 1981, the US granted a $3.2 billion military and economic assistance programme to Pakistan. The latter organized many multidimensional covert training programmes to employ Afghan fighters to combat the occupation of Soviet troops. Zia, very adroitly, handled the Americans during this period and after dismissing President Carter's initial aid offers as 'peanuts' bided his time for the next US president to occupy the White House. During his tenure, the next US president, Ronald Reagan, was clear and forceful to end the Soviet occupation by all means and thus for Pakistan, Reagan's assumption of the US presidency was nothing less than a windfall. The US during this period supplied the Pakistanis with F-16 fighters, naval warships, several force multipliers, nuclear technology, intelligence training and various state-of-the-art communications equipment.

GROWING MISTRUST

US–Pak relations took a beating with the sudden and the still unresolved mysterious death of General Zia. The next two prime ministers—Benazir Bhutto and Nawaz Sharif—found the US taking much tougher stands on Pakistan's nuclear development ambitions. Gradually, the US government also made efforts to vastly improve relations with India, which irked Pakistan no end. In addition, Pakistan's duplicity was apparent to the US when, in its unending quest for strategic depth in Afghanistan, it reinforced its contacts with anti-US forces like the Hekmatyar and Haqqani networks apart from establishing closer ties with the Taliban.

The 1990s witnessed growing mistrust between the US and Pakistan primarily over the latter's covert nuclear weapons development programme. Notwithstanding US objections to the clandestine nuclear forays, both Benazir Bhutto and Nawaz Sharif persisted during their respective tenures with the nuclear programme of their nation. Consequent to the Indian nuclear tests in 1998, Nawaz Sharif ordered his nuclear community to conduct their nuclear tests (Chagai-I and Chagai-II). Irked by this defiance, US President Bill Clinton immediately instituted a number of economic and military sanctions against Pakistan.

The 1999 Kargil War further worsened US–Pak relations as the US did not approve of Pakistani perfidy vis-à-vis India. President Clinton summoned Nawaz Sharif to Washington to ensure non-escalation of conflict between the two nuclear-armed neighbours. In Washington, Clinton admonished Sharif for Pakistan's deceit and instructed him to pull back all his troops on their side of the LoC. Gravely embarrassed, the Pakistanis ordered an immediate ceasefire. Meanwhile, Sharif's stock had fallen in the eyes of his countrymen though he has expressed many times over that he was not aware of his Army Chief General Musharraf's Kargil plans. It was thus a matter of time that he was subsequently ousted from power and history repeated itself with the Army Chief assuming power in Islamabad in late 1999.

OPERATION ENDURING FREEDOM

The terror attacks of 9/11 again altered the relationship between the Pakistani Deep State and the US. Pressurized by President George Bush, Pakistan became a frontline ally of the US in the GWOT for US operations being conducted in Afghanistan and along the Af–Pak border.

In 2003, the US administration formally wrote off $1 billion of Pakistan's debt for their support to the US for Operation Enduring Freedom. General Musharraf acknowledges the US bounty in his book, *In the Line of Fire*: 'We've captured 689 [terrorists] and handed over 369 [terrorists] to the United States. We've earned bounties totaling millions of dollars.' Nevertheless, a large number of Pakistanis were unhappy at Pakistan getting too close to the US and going after some of the terrorist groups. However, in reality, Pakistan remained selective in its counter-terrorist operations. They refused to hand over or target any among the Taliban leadership or members of the al-Qaeda or importantly, Osama bin Laden—all considered strategic assets by them. But Pakistan did provide the US with adequate number of military bases and airports for US forces to strike at terrorist targets, besides logistical sustenance for their troops operating inside Afghanistan.

In the initial years of Operation Enduring Freedom (now rechristened Operation Resolute Support), Pakistan was the recipient of billions of dollars in aid and was designated as a major non-NATO ally in June 2004. This enabled Pakistan to purchase advanced American military technology. With the US opening its doors to Pakistan to purchase off-the-shelf modern weaponry supposedly to combat terrorists, Pakistan, expectedly, obtained many force-multipliers like F-16 fighters, Harpoon anti-tank missiles, night vision devices for their tank fleet and ammunition of various types to bolster their forces, in reality, against the Indian military. The Americans, as in the past, looked the other way.

The Pakistanis had perfected the art of duplicity in dealing with the US during the conduct of anti-terrorist operations in Afghanistan and along both sides of the terrorist-infested Durand Line, where operations continue till today. The supply lines to Afghanistan for logistical sustenance of US, International Security Assistance Force (ISAF) and the other NATO troops run along two overland supply routes from the Karachi port to Afghanistan. The northern supply artery via the famous Khyber Pass enters Afghanistan at Torkham and terminates at Kabul. The southern route from Karachi goes through the restive Balochistan province and enters the border at Chaman and ends at Kandahar in Afghanistan. Thus, the US troops were hopelessly dependent on Pakistan's goodwill to let the supplies reach them. With frequent terrorist attacks and violent disruptions along these two routes, some reportedly sponsored by the ISI to stay relevant, the US belatedly developed the Northern Distribution Network (NDN). The US had to lobby hard with Russia, Kazakhstan, Uzbekistan and Kyrgyzstan for this network for non-lethal supplies for its troops. However, all munitions and weaponry are airlifted from some ports in the Persian Gulf to Bagram/Kabul air bases inside Afghanistan. The costs of the aerial supply route are supposedly ten times that of the cost of movement by road through Pakistan. Transporting supplies over the NDN is twice as much as the cost along the relatively unsafe Pakistani land supply routes.

Pakistan's duplicitous policies towards Afghanistan and its obsession to keep India totally out of that impoverished nation has also led to major strategic divergences with the US in the handling of Afghanistan.

UNRELENTING ANTI-US NARRATIVES

By many Western accounts, the US, after World War II, was hardly affected with the formulation of South Asia's global geopolitical priorities. Nevertheless, Pakistan was drawn into the US arc of influence and patronage in this region immediately after independence. By any standards, the US has been one of the major architects of Pakistan's growth, both economically and militarily, despite ups and downs in their tormented relationship. Incredulously, notwithstanding generous doses of political support, military and economic aid to Pakistan in the last seventy years, barring very limited periods, the Pakistani public has remained consistently anti-American, particularly in the last two decades. However, the Deep State leadership, in full knowledge of the indispensability of the largesse obtained from the US for Pakistan's survival, has been privately effusive about US generosity though publicly muted in their appreciation. Thus, what most Pakistanis term as American duplicity, is, factually speaking, Pakistani duplicity towards their mentor.

Many Pakistani analysts have successfully endeavoured to confuse their public about the nuances of American assistance to them. Being overly anti-India, these votaries have never forgiven the absence of staunch US support to Pakistan in the wars of 1965 and 1971 and the Kargil conflict. These Pakistani interlocutors forget the fact that one's sins cannot be washed away by supporters, for apart from morality, national interests of one's supporters will transcend the not-so altruistic ambitions of those being supported.

A typical but telling commentary has been articulated by Brigadier Tughral Yamin who states that, 'Pakistan's early decision to move into the American camp was basically premised on the national security threat from India...the Americans exploited Pakistan's geo-strategic position by integrating it within their overarching strategy to contain the rising tide of communism...naturally, [the Americans] were aware of Pakistani threat perceptions from India, but as long as it suited their convenience, they were willing to turn a blind eye.' Yamin opines that the Americans 'relentlessly pursued the Pakistani leadership and literally seduced it into submission'. In his assessment, 'Pakistan bears no responsibility for undertaking commitments not to attack India while at the same time seeking military aid to do just that.' In an essay for *Hilal* (the official journal of Pakistan's armed forces), Yamin, alluding to American deceit suggests that 'we should never again allow our young men to become cannon fodder in somebody else's war'.

Way back in 1967, even the seemingly staunch Western ally, Ayub Khan, confounded many analysts with his unexpected comments on the US–Pak relationship. Ayub explains that Pakistan joining the CENTO as well as the SEATO was 'exclusively in terms of the defence of the country. I was anxious to take maximum advantage of this arrangement to build up the defence forces of Pakistan.' He further laments that Pakistan 'lost her (Soviets) sympathy…since we had never been a party to any design against her.' Ayub Khan's double-faced statements would have certainly riled the US who, by any standards, generously assisted Pakistan during his rule.

Christine Fair maintains that, 'Pakistani accounts of US-Pakistani relations devote considerable space to the 1980s, when the United States, Saudi Arabia and Pakistan worked to eject the Russians from Afghanistan. Pakistani military authors writing about this period typically minimize the benefits Pakistan obtained through its alliance with the United States and at the same time exaggerate the costs that this relationship forced Pakistan to bear. These narratives depict Pakistan as a passive pawn of US strategies and often—but not always—omit Saudi Arabia's massive contributions to the jihad against the Soviets.' However, in her telling analysis, Fair highlights a fact which is brushed under the carpet: 'Most importantly, they leave out any mention of Pakistani involvement in Afghanistan prior to the Soviet invasion and ignore Pakistani attempts to get America involved in Afghanistan even before the Soviets crossed the Amu Darya. These narratives also tend to conflate the Taliban with the mujahideen who fought the Soviets. This allows Pakistani interlocutors to lay a whole host of problems at Washington's door including typical claims that the Americans created the Taliban and Al Qaeda; that America abandoned Pakistan to a drug, gun, and jihad culture; and that America created Pakistan's purported madrasa problem.' According to Fair, '...this narrative is most pernicious because it blames the United States for Pakistan's current Islamist insurgency and turns a blind eye to the role played by decades of Pakistani government support for Islamist proxies.'

During his presidential election campaign, Barack Obama opined that the US had made the mistake of 'putting all our eggs in one basket', in the form of General Musharraf. However, after Musharraf was forced out of office, and Asif Ali Zardari took over as a democratically elected President, Obama did open up to Pakistan with increased military and economic aid, primarily to to give a fillip to the country's civil institutions.

In the last few years, with the US forces mounting aerial attacks against the militants holed up along the Durand Line, the US complained many times to the Pakistani establishment of the latter's duplicity of tipping off jihadists so that they could escape before the American drone attacks were launched against them. This 'cat and mouse' game has been a regular feature of the US–Pak relationship in dealing with terrorists as Pakistan has followed a policy of terrorist discrimination, namely supporting the good terrorists—those it has nurtured for operations against the Kabul government and India—and taking on bad terrorists, like the TTP.

After the Pakistan-sponsored terrorist attacks in Mumbai on 26 November 2008, which also claimed the lives of a few American citizens, the US asked Pakistan to cooperate fully with India to bring the perpetrators to book. However, even till date, Pakistan has not taken action against the 26/11 mastermind Hafiz Saeed and LeT, the terror outfit that engineered this dastardly attack.

In a candid interview on 14 September 2009, General Musharraf admitted that American aid to Pakistan had been diverted on various occasions from its original purpose of fighting the Taliban to preparing for war against India. Nevertheless, the US administration, as in the past, faithfully continued to assist its ally. President Obama while stating that 'combating Islamic extremism' was a shared endeavour, the US was committed to help Pakistan realize 'the great potential of its people'. Between 2002 and 2010, Pakistan received more than $20 billion, and under Obama, there was 'significant improvement' in the relationship between the two nations.

Even before President Barack Obama assumed office, veteran American diplomat, Richard Holbrooke (later nominated by Obama and Hillary Clinton as the US Special Representative for Af–Pak), after a visit to Pakistan in 2008 after General Musharraf's ouster from power had laid down the priorities for the US in Pakistan for the immediate future. He desired Washington to send a 'clear and consistent' message to Pakistan, stating: 'democracy, reconciliation, the military out of politics, a new policy for the tribal areas and more democracy'. Former US State Department official turned author, Daniel S. Markey, in his book, *No Exit from Pakistan: America's Tortured Relationship with Islamabad*, expresses that, 'Once in office, Holbrooke set about putting his money where his mouth was. Washington's primary policy tool for helping Pakistan's civilian government was to be a vast infusion of cash…the legislative effort was driven by three US politicians—John Kerry, Richard Lugar and Representative Howard Berman.' This led to the famous KLB (Kerry–Lugar–Berman) Bill, which tripled US assistance to Pakistan for non-military projects, raising it to roughly $1.5 billion a year for the next five years. With Holbrooke spearheading Obama's South Asia team, this compensation was to encourage democracy to find firm feet in military-dominated Pakistan. But it did also lay down some conditions for the Pakistani military which created a furore in the country as many leaders in Pakistan called it an infringement of their sovereign rights. Daniel Markey also comments that, 'Why did KLB use language that was certain to ruffle Pakistani feathers? Pakistani conspiracy theorists, including some national political leaders, saw the "evil hand" of Indian lobbyists at work on Capitol Hill. The truth was more mundane.' Also, soon enough, as always, the US was disappointed as to the never-changing attitudes of the military in Pakistan. Importantly, Holbrooke's untimely death in December 2010 did dampen US policies towards Pakistan, notwithstanding President Obama's personal interest in the successful culmination of the KLB mandate.

However, 2011 was rated by the BBC as a 'disastrous year' in the US–Pak relationship. The year saw a CIA agent based in Lahore, Raymond Allen Davis, shoot down two Pakistani would-be assassins, and despite US appeals to the Pakistanis, the latter prosecuted Davis and lodged him in jail. However, after the US paid handsome sums to the families of the deceased, Davis was quietly flown back home. In September 2011, the well-fortified US embassy and NATO headquarters in Kabul were subjected to a major attack, suspected to be the handiwork of the Haqqani network. At a testimony to the US Congress after this incident, Admiral Mike Mullen, Chairman of Joint Chiefs of Staff Committee, called the Haqqani network a 'veritable arm of Pakistan's Inter Services Intelligence'. During this time, even some Islamist groups in Pakistan issued 'fatwas' proclaiming jihad against the US.

On 26 November 2011, during an aerial attack by US forces on suspected insurgents hiding along the Af–Pak border, twenty-four Pakistani soldiers were killed. This incident led to severe criticism of the US by many public organizations in Pakistan. The government too officially protested to assuage the growing public resentment against what was conceived as American high-handedness.

However, it was the elimination of al-Qaeda supremo Osama Bin Laden by US Special Forces on 2 May 2011 in the Pakistan garrison town of Abbotabad in a daring operation code-named Operation Neptune Spear that proved to be the turning point in US–Pak relations. That for many years the most prominent al-Qaeda leader and the world's most wanted terrorist was closeted along with his large family in a reasonably large mansion near the Pakistan Military Academy at Kakul, without the knowledge of the ISI, would be hard to believe by anyone, let alone the Americans. Though details of Laden's hiding for so long remain shrouded in mystery, the US officially claims that on receipt of hard intelligence about his hideout, they carried out the raid to eliminate him unilaterally without anyone in the Pakistani establishment knowing about the operation. Some analysts reveal that the ISI themselves, under sustained and strong pressure from the US, revealed Laden's location to the latter. The charade of the Pakistanis being unaware of the operation was just a face-saver for them. Nevertheless, Laden's elimination did cause a lot of heartburn and acute embarrassment to the Pakistani establishment. The trust deficit between the two nations, at least publicly, had become rather acute.

It was only after a couple of years after Laden's elimination that relations between the US and Pakistan saw some improvement. US forces intensified their drone strikes in 2014-15 in which many militant leaders, including Mullah Fazlullah of the anti-Pakistan TTP, were killed. Meanwhile, the Pakistan Army had also stepped up their operations against the militants holed up in the North Waziristan region launching the much-heralded Operation Zarb-e-Azb. This operation continues till date, with the Army achieving relative success. The US in 2015-16 responded with a dose of another billion dollars and additional modernized eighteen F-16 C fighters, 500 AMRAAM air-to-air missiles, gravity bombs, Bell helicopters, 500 Sidewinder missiles and Phlanax close support naval guns. American munificence comes regularly to the Pakistanis provided they tow or at least pretend that they are towing the US line in matters of combating terrorism. That all these modern force-multipliers and state-of-the-art munitions meant for prosecution in the GWOT will have been diverted for possible employment against India is well-known to all, including the US.

The trajectory of US-Pak relations since the last seventy years, despite its ups and downs, has followed a predictable path. However, a partnership between two unequal allies cannot be stress-free. The US has always been eager for Pakistan to move determinedly on the path of democracy. But it has always disregarded this aspect whenever the Pakistan military stepped in to assume power, as long as the military, according to the gullible Americans, would do their bidding. It was a tall order even earlier but now with China's overwhelming presence and unstinted support for Pakistan in the region, the Pakistanis know that they can arm-twist the Americans a trifle more. More dangerously, Pakistan's ascendancy in its nuclear weapons capability threatens to endanger even US interests, both in the region and in their homeland. How effectively it monitors the safety and security of Pakistan's rapidly growing nuclear arsenal will be critical for the US.

In addition, though the US may not be able to extricate itself in a hurry from Afghanistan—repeating an Iraq there will be detrimental to the US image as the sole superpower—it cannot take Pakistan's support in Kabul for granted. As a matter of fact, in the years since 9/11, Pakistan's strategic interests in Afghanistan have been at a divergence with those of its mentor—from whom extracting military aid and dollars remains Pakistan's overriding and sole priority. It has thrived all these years propagating a self-serving narrative, embracing both Afghanistan and nuclear blackmail as its main pillars to vouch for its significance to the US. China's ascendancy in the region and its deep relationship with Pakistan makes the latter now acquire more significance. However, the burgeoning Indo–US strategic partnership has had a negative impact on the US–Pak relationship.

Overall, US–Pak relations have been shorn of a larger conceptual strategy or a shared vision which should have been conceived and implemented by the Americans in the first instance. The US, according to some analysts, has only thought short-term in its dealings with Pakistan, which is why there is not much to show in Pakistan's record for the huge investments the US has made in it. But then, is it not the same American experience elsewhere?

America's options for handling Pakistan, both in the external dimension and for Pakistan's internal stability, do not lend themselves to easy answers. The army, which remains the most powerful institution of its nation—a fact which the US has always acknowledged and been reasonably comfortable with—is unquestionably also politically driven. Thus whenever the US has expressed its disapproval of Pakistan's duplicity in the GWOT, the Deep State, employing its well-oiled media machinery, stands up to the US 'bullying' for their public consumption. Surveys have shown that American approval ratings in Pakistan, despite generous doles delivered by the US in all these years, remain an abysmal 15 per cent. Pakistan Army's Inter-Services Public Relations (ISPR) outfit regularly churns out stories for its public about Pakistan's ability to stand up to any US pressures. However, when it comes to China, the ISPR does not display any such steadfastness.

In summation, the US acknowledges the geopolitical significance of Pakistan in this region and thus has tolerated many of its shenanigans since the birth of their tormented relationship. The Pakistani conundrum for the US becomes more acute with the country's nuclear ambitions coupled with the huge terror conglomerate present there, making it an apocalyptic cocktail. Thus the US has to strive to motivate Pakistan to abandon its terror proxies and cease cross-border terrorism both in India and Afghanistan. Pakistan has to be denied the dividends of terror which it has been thriving upon. Not that the Pakistani Army may fully agree, but it must be drummed into them that democracy is a far better option than trying to run and thus ruin their nation.

13

Enduring Sino–Pak Relationship

> The China–Pakistan axis plays a central role in Asia's geopolitics, from India's rise to the prospects for a post American Afghanistan, from the threat of nuclear terrorism to the continent's new map of mines, ports and pipelines. Pakistan lies at the heart of China's geo-strategic ambitions, from its take-off as a global naval power to its grand plans for a new silk road connecting the energy fields of the Middle East and the markets of Europe to the mega cities of East Asia. Yet Pakistan is also the battle ground for China's encounter with Islamic militancy, the country more than any other where China's rise has turned into a target.
>
> —C. Christine Fair

It is indeed a unique fact of recent geopolitical history that no two nations which share neither a common culture nor similar human values have had such distinctive synergy in their strategic convergence and common long-term ambitions as China and Pakistan. Though national interests remain paramount and permanent for nations, and not necessarily friends, yet in the case of China and Pakistan, the rather amusing rhetoric of their relationship being 'higher than the Himalayas, deeper than the oceans, and sweeter than honey' is indeed reflected in reality. That the most contributory cause of this nexus is just one reason—the long-term and common animosity for India—is a fact which all security analysts will agree to. That this relationship dates back to 1949 and has remained more or less consistent in its moorings, notwithstanding the ups and downs of regional geopolitics in South Asia, exemplifies the singular motivation driving the two nations. Thus China, in recent months, has been deferring to Pakistan, even wrongly, in international forums without batting an eyelid. This does not appear to worry China overly, notwithstanding its rising status as a reckonable global player which demands it to play a more mature and a stabilizing role.

It is also a historical reality of the recent times that China has successfully utilized three nations to stymie its potential adversaries. China has used North Korea to frustrate Japan and even the US to some extent. Secondly Iran, to contain US strategic designs in the Middle East, and importantly, Pakistan, to contain India and have the latter boxed in South Asia, unable to emerge to fully compete with the growing Chinese influence in this region.

A UNIQUE SYNERGY DEVELOPS

Pakistan was the third non-communist nation to recognize the People's Republic of China (PRC) in 1949 in an era when, under US influence, not many nations either recognized China diplomatically or supported its admission to the United Nations General Assembly (UNGA). Despite Pakistan joining US-led anti-communist military pacts like the CENTO and SEATO, China was not unduly perturbed as they correctly analysed that Pakistan's motivations to join these pacts, apart from obtaining military aid from the Americans, were directed against India and not them. In addition, the Chinese, masters of realpolitik, publicly placed the blame on the US for 'foisting these alliances on a desperate Pakistan'. Right from the early 1950s, the Chinese plotted to employ Pakistan in diverse ways to keep India preoccupied within the subcontinent and thus unable to challenge China beyond the region. At the 1955 Afro-Asian meet in Bandung (Indonesia), Chinese Prime Minister Zhou Enlai and his Pakistan counterpart, Mohammad Ali Bogra, agreed to intensify mutual cooperation in various fields between the two nations with the

Pakistani PM declaring that they did not fear any aggression from China. Bogra, in his speech at the same summit, tried to differentiate between China and the Soviet Union claiming that the latter was 'an imperialist power' whereas the Chinese had never brought any nation 'under its heel'. On the other hand, China was also keen to use Pakistan's geostrategic location and influence in the Islamic world as a bridge to forge relations with them. Importantly, China was also looking at physical land access to the Arabian Sea and the Indian Ocean.

However, this warm relationship did undergo some coolness when Ayub Khan, considered pro-West, took over the reins of his country. Under American pressure in 1959, Pakistan was also a co-sponsor of the UN resolution criticizing China for the Tibetan uprising and its overly harsh actions against local Tibetans while quelling the rebellion.

The late 1950s and early '60s were witness to some geopolitical turbulence in the region. Sino–Indian tensions along their disputed boundaries were rising, the Chinese relations with the powerful leader of the communists, the Soviet Union, were in disarray and US–India relations were getting better. Even Pakistan had changed its political stance on China's admission to the UN. But soon Ayub Khan realized that in the event of an Indo–Pak war, the US would not side with them, and with the Soviets getting closer to India, the only safe bet was the enemy's enemy—China. After 1961–62, relations were on the upswing with China agreeing to sign a boundary pact with Pakistan on the condition that Pakistan would support China's entry into the UN. In Chinese maps, Hunza (part of the Northern Areas) was shown as part of Tibet, but the Chinese gave in amicably to their junior partner.

In 1963, Pakistan illegally ceded 5,180 square kilometres in the Shaksgam Valley in POK to China. The Chinese scoffed at India's protest that this area was part of the erstwhile J&K which had acceded to India, and was under Pakistan's illegal occupation and thus a disputed territory. A few years later, work on the strategic Karakoram Highway (KKH) connecting western China and the mountainous northern Pakistan, through the Khunjerab Pass, commenced with vigour. By bringing the Chinese footprint into POK, Pakistan has cleverly ensured that the problem of J&K is no longer confined to India–Pakistan, but has now extended to India–Pakistan–China.

As mentioned earlier, Pakistan facilitated then US Secretary of State Henry Kissinger's secret visit to China in 1972 which was the precursor to President Richard Nixon's intended visit to China. Pakistan, during this time, was rewarded by the US for it services with some additional financial doles and military equipment. The coming years saw both China and the US provide military and financial support through the ISI to the Afghan guerrillas fighting the Soviet occupation forces in Afghanistan.

The 1980s witnessed China transferring nuclear weapon designs, centrifuges, ring magnets and fissile material to Pakistan. A.Q. Khan, while sharing nuclear secrets with Libya, reportedly on his own volition, sold these designs which had detailed instructions in the Chinese language. This proved the China link in the assistance to Pakistan's nuclear programme. Libya subsequently shared this information with the IAEA in Vienna.

AREAS OF COOPERATION IN THE TWENTY-FIRST CENTURY

In the last two decades, the enduring Sino–Pak cooperation has diversified to many fields and includes several important milestones. China began construction of the Gwadar deep sea port in the restive Balochistan province. Located at the mouth of the Persian Gulf, a Chinese naval presence will allow it to monitor ship traffic through the Arabian Sea as well as the movement of the United States Naval Forces Central Command (NAVCENT), the naval component of the CENTCOM headquartered in Bahrain. Further, the Chinese Navy, and the Pakistan Navy, which will also be able to use this port in addition to Karachi, would pose a grave threat to the Indian Navy. Some other strategic aspects which need being factored are as under:

a) China's continuing assistance to Pakistan in each and every aspect of the latter's nuclear and missile ambitions have been on the upswing. China has dishonoured all rules of the international nuclear regime in its quest to arm Pakistan. For example, even the transfer of M-11 short-range ballistic missiles is in violation of the MTCR as the M-11 missile could potentially carry a 500 kg warhead to a range of 300 km. The *Bulletin of Atomic Scientists*, in an October 2015 report, 'Pakistani Nuclear Forces 2015', confirms the Chinese assistance to Pakistan's clandestine nuclear programmes since the 1970s. Since the end of the 1990s, Pakistan, with Chinese assistance, has diversified to the plutonium route and has constructed four dedicated plutonium reactors at Khushab. China is also building a 1100 MW nuclear power plant in Karachi for $6.5 billion. Even Saudi Arabia has pitched in with the hope of Pakistanis also helping them upgrade their solid fuel DF-21 IRBMs with Chinese assistance.
b) Importantly, China appears to have helped Pakistan in building the sea leg of its nuclear triad. This is centred on a Chinese air-independent, propulsion-equipped conventional submarine that would be possibly armed with the Babur-III nuclear-tipped cruise missiles.
c) Sino–Pak joint venture multirole fighter JF-17 is already in operational service. Pakistan is to get eight diesel-electric attack submarines from China by 2028. The deal, valued at $5 billion, is the largest arms deal between the two nations. The Indian Navy, currently struggling with numbers in its submarine fleet, is concerned about its operational capability in submarine warfare vis-à-vis the Pakistan Navy in the near future, and collusively with the formidable Chinese Navy supported by the Pakistan Navy.
d) Pakistan and China have signed nineteen agreements related to the ambitious CPEC, which is considered by both nations as a game changer for the region and, importantly, reinforcing permanent cooperation between the two nations. The CPEC will allow China to get over its 'Malacca Dilemma'

as it shortens access to the Persian Gulf—source of 80 per cent of China's energy requirements.

e) Twice in the last one year, China has blocked India's move to get Pakistan-based JeM chief, Maulana Masood Azhar, blacklisted as a terrorist by the UNSC. This act by China shows the extent to which it can go to keep its terror-exporting ally in good humour.

f) China has continued to stonewall India's bid to enter the 48-member NSG. It has reiterated that it will have no objection to India's entry if Pakistan is also allowed into the NSG. Re-hyphenating India with Pakistan is rather amusing keeping in view Pakistan's poor, universally known record of being one of the world's worst nuclear proliferators.

In the foreseeable future, the China–Pakistan axis will acquire permanence with an intensity rarely seen in bilateral relations between any two nations. Pakistan's original, long-term and reasonably generous mentor, the US, appears to be strategically, militarily and even financially fatigued, unless US President Donald Trump injects more energy and resources into reshaping US objectives in Asia. That is yet to be seen, but the fact remains that China, to some extent, will fill in the American void for Pakistan.

China too has a stake in a stable Pakistan for it does not wish any radical Islamic group from the Af–Pak region, with whom the Pakistani Deep State has close links, to assist the ongoing Islamist Uighur insurgency in the Xinjiang region. Importantly, China also looks at Pakistan to provide security for the CPEC from Baloch and Pathan insurgents. Thus, Pakistan's coffers will likely overflow with the Chinese yuan, while US dollars will continue, perhaps in a diminished measure.

Another important player in the new Great Game—Russia—is showing heightened interest after years of laying-off from this region. The Russians would not like anyone from the vast terror conglomerate extending their activities to the CARs and thence onwards to Russia. Additionally, the resurgent Russians under Putin will prefer US influence to gradually fade away from the energy resource and mineral-rich Afghanistan and the CARs. The new US policy for Afghanistan enunciated by President Trump on 21 August this year which strongly reprimanded Pakistan for fostering anti-US terrorists and contributing to the growing instability in Afghanistan, immediately prompted China coming to Pakistan's assistance by rebutting* the US charges.

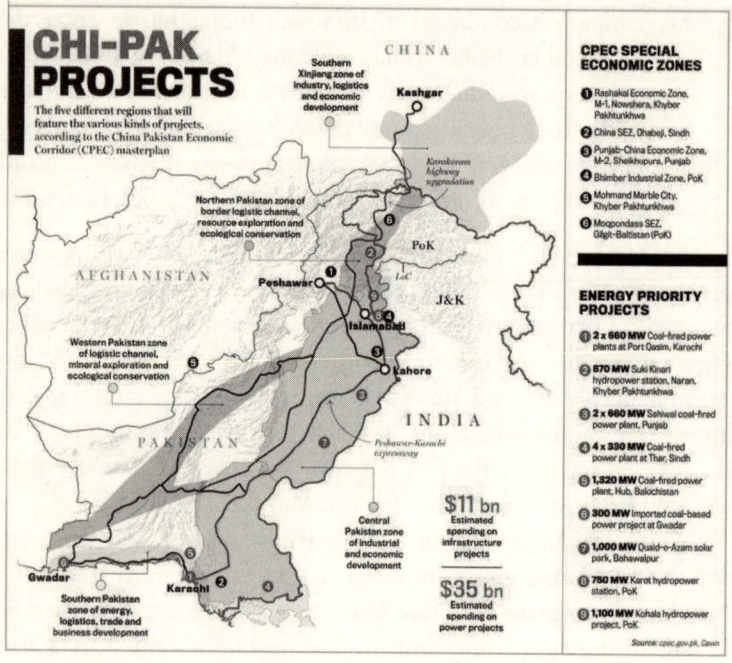

Sketch: Not to scale
Reproduced with permission from India Today. Ananth Krishnan; 'Pakistan China's new colony? Leaked papers reveal Beijing's stake in economy, key project'; July 20, 2017; http://indiatoday.intoday.in/story/china-pakistan-relations-implication-for-india-cpec-obor/1/1006432.html

As both China and Pakistan cement their all-weather friendship, China may wish to heed to former Indian Foreign Secretary Shyam

---

*'China defends all-weather ally Pakistan after Trump's warning on terror safe havens', *Daily Pakistan*, 22 August 2017.

Saran's observation that, as 'Pakistan descends into dysfunctionality and international isolation, it may become as big a millstone around China's neck as North Korea is'. Pakistan has itself to be wary that for some transient financial salvation and make-believe strategic gains, it does not get colonized in the coming years by the world's newly emerging colonial power—China.

Epilogue

India–Pakistan: The Way Forward

You can change your friends, not your neighbours.

—Atal Bihari Vajpayee, former Indian Prime Minister

Pakistani nationalism comprises 95 per cent India hatred. They call it Islam because that is how we learn to differentiate between ourselves and India.

—Khalid Ahmed, leading Pakistani thinker

Seventy years after India's Partition, relations between the two nations born from the womb of the same mother, remain stubbornly on the downward spiral. Pakistan's motivations and mindset stem from its eternal quest for a separate identity. Its anti-India narrative takes shape as Pakistan dubs itself as the 'fortress of Islam', especially in South Asia, while its religious paranoia propels aspirations for it to rise as the global laboratory of Islam. Its obsessive desire to shake off anything even remotely Indian, despite nearly a thousand years of coexistence in the Indian landmass and Indian Muslims contributing handsomely to the composite Indian civilization and culture, precludes rational thinking among its decision-makers. However, this vehemence is not necessarily echoed as intensely by Pakistani commonfolk and many members of the dwindling yet elegant civil society. However, reinforcing the official mindset, Pakistani academic Waheed uz Zaman succinctly observes that, 'If the Arabs, the Turks, the Iranians, God forbid, give up Islam, the Arabs yet remain Arabs, the Turks remain Turks, the Iranians remain Iranians, but what do we remain if we give up Islam?' General Zia, one of the chief architects of both the anti-India narrative and Islamization of Pakistani society further amplified this thinking. 'If Pakistan does not become and remain aggressively Islamic, it will become India again. Amity with India will mean getting swamped by this all enveloping embrace of India.'

The roots of the seemingly unbridgeable, yet totally unwarranted, chasm between the two neighbours lie in Jinnah's two-nation theory and, more so, in the British imperial power partitioning the country in haste and leaving it behind in a mess. Most problems bedevilling the two nations remain firmly rooted in the history of their division and Pakistan moving away from the vision and dreams of their founder, Mohammad Ali Jinnah. Despite his determination and ultimate success in creating a separate nation for the Muslims of the subcontinent, Jinnah never expressed any ill-will for the minorities or Muslims from leanings other than Sunnis. Yet Pakistan has been treading a different path.

The combination of a fractured freedom, attributable to the British and growing radicalization of Pakistan's society by successive civil and military rulers, has aggravated the India–Pakistan divide. But more than these factors, Pakistan's Kashmir obsession and its quest for equivalence, or a permanent hyphenation, with India in virtually everything, drives it towards irrational behaviour regards India.

In its anti-India tirades since many decades, Pakistan has been distorting history inside its nation and poisoning the minds of its children and youth with contrived narratives; not only in madrasas but also in other schools/colleges, history books with totally false narratives, facts and figures conditioning young minds with anti-India propaganda. Somewhere, however, the country's perception propagandists will, sooner than later, meet their Waterloo at the hands of the global Internet where computer-literate Pakistani youth will realize the truth about India and its values. Bollywood films, highly popular the world over including Pakistan, too portray and project Indian values in a befitting manner, perhaps a trifle dramatically. Unquestionably, truth in today's highly information-connected world cannot be suppressed for long.

In his book, *India vs Pakistan: Why Can't We Just Be Friends?*, Husain Haqqani summarizes Pakistan's dilemma and stimulus in dealing with India. He expresses that, 'Sixty nine years after Partition it is hard to believe that Gandhi wanted to treat Pakistan as an estranged brother or that Jinnah wanted to retire in India after serving as Governor-General of Pakistan.' Jinnah had wished for India and Pakistan to have 'an association similar to that between the United States and Canada.'

Haqqani further argues that, 'Indians, beginning with Nehru and Patel, chose to punish Pakistan for breaking away instead of wooing it. In doing so they reinforced the effort by Jinnah's successors to militarize and Islamize Pakistan. The new country, burdened by the inheritance of a larger military than economy, ended up by building its identity to invent a version of history that stretched Hindu–Muslim rivalry over centuries, casting the two communities as irreconcilable enemies. The Kashmir dispute, terrorism and the advent of nuclear weapons in the subcontinent have all aggravated that rivalry. In Pakistan's case, treating India just as a neighbouring state has proved difficult because of India's centrality to Pakistan's identity as a separate nation. Indians often think that it helps if they accentuate similarities between the two countries but it actually scares Pakistanis even more. India's evolution as a secular country with almost as many Muslims as Pakistan also feeds mistrust, which in turn fuels the need to emphasize differences.' Haqqani, to reinforce his viewpoint, quotes a 'liberal Pakistani official' summarized Pakistan's dilemma by asking an American reporter in 1980: 'If we are not Muslims, what are we, second-rate Indians?' It is indeed an unfortunate fact that right to this day, Pakistan's military leadership adamantly refuses to alter or even dilute the country's radical ideological orientation. It harps consistently on Pakistan remaining an ideological state and perpetuates the theory of India's status as an existential threat to it, which is a totally ridiculous assessment in today's world. Even when some Pakistanis refer to India as hegemonistic, they totally falter when asked to give any solid proof. The narrative about India remains not only false but also borders on the laughable.

The first decade of the twenty-first century was, perhaps, more than tumultuous in the history of Indo–Pak relations coming in the aftermath of Vajpayee's historic Lahore bus yatra and the Kargil conflict, both in 1999. The audacious attack on India's Parliament on 13 December 2001 by Pakistan-trained terrorists was the first trigger for relations to deteriorate in the new century. This led to India's massive military mobilization along the international boundary and the LoC, and war between the two nuclear neighbours became a distinct possibility. The US played a major role in defusing the situation to prevent a nuclear conflagration in the region, but not before it extracted General Musharraf's assurances to stop allowing terrorists to use Pakistani territory for terror acts against India.

DISCERNIBLE IMPROVEMENTS IN RELATIONS

General Musharraf must be given some credit for at least publicly altering Pakistan's policies towards terror, to some extent, beginning early 2002. Whether it was owing to the strong diplomatic pressure from the US or India's coercive diplomacy bearing fruit by the massive troop mobilization, Musharraf announced wide-sweeping internal reforms on 12 January 2002. In the words of Dr Syed Husain, Musharraf addressed the nation and 'condemning radical Islamists who had set up a state within a state, he declared his determination to rid Pakistani society of their pernicious influence. He announced a ban on all sectarian activity, and set up speedy trial courts to punish terrorists. Most significantly, he banned six extremist Islamic groups involved in sectarian campaigns in the country, including LeT and JeM, both of which had already been designated as terrorist groups by the US State Department. Signalling a qualitative shift in Pakistan's involvement in militancy in Kashmir, President Musharraf had hoped that, 'No organization will be able to carry out terrorism under the pretext of Kashmir.'

As a result of Musharraf's statements assuring India that he would ensure Pakistani groups did not support armed militancy in Kashmir, some discernible improvements in relations did occur. India lifted most of the diplomatic and economic curbs put on Pakistan after the December 2001 Parliament attack. In a major change in Pakistan's Kashmir policy, Musharraf publicly stated on 17 December 2003, that 'though we are for United Nations Security resolutions… now we have left that aside.' All these steps, especially the 6 January 2004 meeting between Vajpayee and Musharraf, led to the resumption of the stalled composite dialogue between the two nations.

India and Pakistan commenced their stalled Composite Dialogue in February 2004. The steps agreed to between the two nations to improve relations included:

a) The November 2003 ceasefire along the LoC was to be implemented with sincerity as, despite occasional incidents, it was effective in putting an end to over thirteen years of cross-border firings.

b) Conclusion of several nuclear confidence building measures (CBMs), establishment of a permanent hotline between the two foreign secretaries and the pre-notification of missile tests was to be undertaken.

c) Reducing the risks of nuclear accidents and unauthorized use of nuclear weapons as well as preventing incidents at sea.

d) Resumption of bus service between the two capitals in the state of J&K, namely Srinagar (J&K) and Muzaffarabad (POK).

e) Opening of the LoC at five points after the October 2005 earthquake in POK to enable meetings between divided families and provision of humanitarian assistance.

f) Launching of a truck service on the Srinagar–Muzaffarbad route in May 2006.

g) Linking Poonch in J&K with Rawalakot (POK) by a bus service.

h) Reopening of additional rail and road links across the International Boundary between the two nations. These include a bus service linking Amritsar with Nankana

Sahib. A railway link between Munabao in Rajasthan with Khokhrapar in Sindh.
i) Resumption of bilateral trade through Wagah at the International Boundary.
j) Agreement to restart shipping routes.
k) Reactivation of the Joint Economic Commission and Joint Business Councils to promote commercial activity between the two sides.
l) Setting up of the Joint Working Group (JWG) to explore prospects for Iran–Pakistan–India (IPI) gas pipeline.
m) Creation of an India-Pakistan anti-terrorism institutional mechanism to identify and implement counterterrorism initiatives and investigations.

RELATIONS UNDER STRESS

On 26 November 2008, ten well-armed and trained terrorists from Pakistan launched a massive attack on India's commercial capital of Mumbai at various places, including the iconic Taj Mahal Palace Hotel, causing nearly 181 casualties including twenty-five from eight foreign nations. This gruesome terror incident masterminded by the LeT with assistance from rogue elements within the ISI caused total disruption to the ongoing India–Pakistan parleys and the CBMs initiated earlier.

A few months before this ghastly terror incident, Musharraf was also facing the heat in his country. He was under strong criticism within Pakistan for ordering a military assault on the Lal Masjid (Red Mosque) in Islamabad, which had become the centre of violent radicalism in Pakistan by then. This military operation had caused a large number of fatalities including to the civilian hostages inside the mosque. The incident also caused a spate of terrorist attacks and bombings inside Pakistan. Musharraf's decision to dismiss Chief Justice Iftikhar Chaudhry had also sparked off vehement protests by lawyers all over the country. The tragic assassination of former PM Benazir Bhutto with whom Musharraf had supposedly struck a deal to permit her to return to Pakistan, totally muddied the waters creating further political instability in the country. Despite an agreement with Benazir, her tragic assassination also cast suspicion on Musharraf being a party to her violent death. Thereafter, General Musharraf's hold over the country's polity and his credibility took a sound beating.

The year 2008 witnessed a steady deterioration in Indo–Pak relations. Pakistan viewed India's growing footprint in Afghanistan—notwithstanding those being just soft power forays assisting the Kabul government in various developmental and educational projects—as against its interests. On 7 July 2008, the ISI through its cohorts in Afghanistan mounted a massive terror attack on the Indian Embassy compound in Kabul inflicting over fifty fatalities. Thus, even before the Mumbai terrorist attack, relations were already under stress.

As in the past, Pakistan denied the involvement of its state agencies in the Mumbai terror attack despite India handing over credible evidence to Pakistan. Then Prime Minister, Manmohan Singh, called Pakistan 'the epicentre of terrorism' while then Home Minister, P. Chidambaram, warned Pakistan of dire consequences in case such an attack was ever repeated. In a sign of perhaps Pakistan changing tack in its relations with India, the mastermind of the Mumbai terror attack, Hafiz Saeed, was released by the Lahore High Court for lack of sufficient evidence. As always, the Deep State's views in matters dealing with India prevailed. The so-called non-state actors were always crucial to the notorious ISI in its violent machinations against the Indian state.

General Musharraf's departure from Pakistan's political scene also witnessed a downward slide in India–Pakistan relations, though the new president, Asif Ali Zardari, made some feeble efforts to improve the vexed relationship. Pakistan did arrest Zaki-ur-Rehman Lakhvi, a senior LeT leader and five others identified by the Mumbai terror attack operative Ajmal Kasab who was in Indian custody. Indian agencies' investigation of David Coleman Headley clearly revealed the collusive handiwork of the ISI, Pakistani Army officers and the Lashkar-e-Taiba in staging the Mumbai attack. Notwithstanding concrete evidence implicating Pakistan, the latter continues, till date, to deny its involvement—one of the reasons which have perpetuated bitterness in India–Pak relations.

In the coming years, relations kept deteriorating with the Pakistanis also now accusing India of militant activity in Balochistan and along the Af–Pak border. India's growing warmth in its relations with Afghanistan also rattled Pakistan which continued to attack Indian civil assets through its many proxies in that land. The period between 2010 and mid-2014 saw many ups and downs in relations between the two nations with the Composite Dialogue, now referred to as Comprehensive Dialogue, taking place, and then being called off, time and again.

RELATIONS UNDER PM MODI'S LEADERSHIP

All Indian prime ministers at the commencement of their respective tenures have desired to improve relations between the two neighbours. For all of them it has been something of a legacy issue, but no one has managed to succeed.

Prime Minister Narendra Modi swept to power with a powerful mandate in May 2014, and invited his Pakistani counterpart Nawaz Sharif along with all other prime ministers of the SAARC region for his swearing-in ceremony. That Sharif accepted Modi's invite despite his army's apparent objections was indeed creditable. This gesture did lead to a flicker of hope for improvement in Indo–Pak ties for the future. But these hopes were soon laid to rest with heightened tensions along the LoC, and the ISI upping the ante in the Kashmir Valley through its proxies. Whether it was the Deep State at its characteristic best or the elected government being totally powerless was an easy guess.

In his characteristic style, PM Modi, flying back from Kabul after inaugurating the Afghan Parliament constructed by India, made an unscheduled stopover at Lahore to visit Nawaz Sharif at the latter's sprawling farmhouse in Raiwind on 25 December 2015. The visit made international headlines and the bonhomie generated by this brief meeting between the two leaders pointed towards better days. However, as in the past, this hope was very short-lived. Within a week of this initiative, terrorists of the JeM mounted an audacious attack on the Indian air base at Pathankot on 1-2 January 2016.

Though all terrorists were eliminated, relations were once again back to being tense between the two nations. India supplied all the credible technical data-based evidence of this attack to Pakistan including, for the first time, permitting a Pakistani investigation team inside the Pathankot air base. Barring some cosmetic actions taken by Pakistan, JeM and its terrorist chieftain, Zakiur-ur-Rehman Lakhvi, continued to roam free inside the country. As ever before, the ISI would shield its strategic assets belonging to anti-India terror outfits from the clutches of Pakistani judicial system. This time, the ISI craftily employed the JeM and not the LeT to confuse all concerned as regards to the antecedents of those having mounted the terror attack.

In 2016, the Deep State was in full flow against India. In September, Pakistan-based militants carried out a major terrorist strike in Uri against an Indian brigade headquarters, inflicting nineteen fatalities to Indian troops. India retaliated, conducting a swift, bold surgical strike, over a 250 km frontage across the LoC, a few kilometres inside POK. However, Pakistan denied that such a strike had ever been mounted. This denial permitted Pakistan not to be forced into any major retaliation, and perhaps, was the reason for it to deny the launch of such an attack. The overall situation, currently, remains tense with sporadic firing continuing along the LoC and Pakistan doing its utmost to keep the pot boiling inside J&K.

The year 2016 represented one of the worst years in recent history in the rollercoaster relationship between the two nations. Now towards the end of 2017, are there any chances of the India–Pakistan relations achieving a modicum of normalcy and peaceful neighbourliness or are they marching in unison towards fresher problems or mutually assured near-annihilation?

PROGNOSIS FOR THE FUTURE

To my mind, much depends upon the attitude of Pakistan. If it can transform itself from merely being an ideological state to a truly normal and functional state, and thence not just the two nations but the entire region will prosper. How peace and normalcy can be established between the two nations—one of them persistently running away from its roots—is worth more than serious introspection for the survival and good of nearly a billion and a half people who inhabit the subcontinent. Well-meaning people and governments on both sides of the borders must factor in the persistent efforts of the many determined spoilers who have vested interests in sabotaging the rapprochement between the two nuclear-armed nations. Further, it should never be forgotten that some of those forces who are against Indo–Pak bonhomie lie beyond the borders of the subcontinent.

Notwithstanding a long history of conflicts, both India and Pakistan also have a record of many diplomatic negotiations which have resulted in some agreements and accords. Both nations have engaged, sometime or the other, in bilateral negotiations on diverse issues like border demarcations, boundary adjustments, water distribution, terrorism, Kashmir, trade and commerce, protection of minorities, among many others, to resolve differences. Since 1997, all these aspects have been discussed as part of the Composite Dialogue Process (CDP) involving primarily eight issues—peace and security including CBMs, J&K, Siachen, Sir Creek, Tulbul navigation-Wullar Barrage project, terrorism and drug trafficking, economic and commercial cooperation and promotion of friendly exchanges in various fields.

What is normally not well-known is that despite many differences over important issues, India and Pakistan have many agreements in place with a fairly good compliance record by both nations. Some of the significant agreements have been the 1950 Nehru–Liaquat Agreement, the Indus Waters Treaty of 1960, Tashkent Agreement of 1966, Simla Agreement of 1972, the vital 1988 Agreement (by Rajiv Gandhi and Benazir Bhutto) on prohibition of attacks against each other's nuclear facilities and installations and the Lahore Declaration of 1999. Even the unwritten understanding in November 2003 between General Musharraf and Manmohan Singh on the ceasefire to be observed along the international boundary, LoC and the AGPL was successful barring a few stray incidents till 2009. If Pakistan could ensure the same for many years during the Musharraf regime, surely it can do so now. But during that period, Musharraf was both the Army

Chief and the President, and there was thus no conflict of interest on policy issues between the Army and its civilian government.

Most security analysts and thinkers, predominantly Pakistani, generally summarize enduring India–Pakistan differences consequent to four major factors. The first one is attributable to the opposing ideologies, religious and sociocultural practices and beliefs between Hinduism and Islam in the Indian subcontinent. Though to some extent this may be true, but for centuries, barring few clashes, wherever there was strong administration and fair governance, many kingdoms and states in undivided India managed to keep their diverse populations in peace and harmony. As a matter of fact, in the Indian subcontinent, Islam also contributed substantially to the emergence and flowering of a composite Indian culture. I think a vast majority of Indians today and even many members of the Pakistani civil society will hardly give much credence to this outdated notion of differences in faith overriding political pragmatism in the current world. Myths and distortions about India and Hindus in text books in Pakistan need to be totally discarded. Pakistani youth have to be educated that patriotism is not xenophobia and they can do without radicalism and hatred in their own lives for their own good.

The other factor which appears to cause anxiety to Pakistan is the sheer asymmetry, both militarily and economically, between the two nations. It has thus driven Pakistan to develop a mania to achieve and be talked about with equivalence and hyphenation with India. Husain Haqqani opines that 'reason would suggest that Pakistan would benefit from changing its goal from seeking parity with India to ensuring national security and economic development. Pakistan can no longer count on the United States as an equalizer in its quest to be on a par with India. China—already a close ally of Pakistan— cannot tip the balance in Pakistan's favour on its own. All nations have sovereign equality in international law but realpolitik demands acknowledgement of the difference of size between nations… India's population is six times larger than Pakistan but its economy is ten times bigger. Notwithstanding problems of poverty and corruption (which Pakistan also faces), India's $2 trillion economy has managed consistent growth whereas Pakistan's $245 billion economy has grown only in spurts. Over time, the economic gap will widen.'

Haqqani rightly complains that 'the discord between India and Pakistan is also holding back the entire South Asian region, home to around 1.7 billion people living in eight countries—Afghanistan, Bangladesh, Bhutan, India, Maldives, Nepal, Pakistan and Sri Lanka... It is the least integrated region in the world. There are few flights between the region's capitals, and road and rail links are in poor condition or non-existent.'

Thus, Pakistan must eschew its obsession to be India's equal and realize that even if equivalence is not possible for a variety of reasons, it can still live at peace and with dignity with its larger neighbour without compromising its well-being, sovereignty and security. Pakistan must overcome its feeling of vulnerability attributed to make-believe Indian threats.

Some in Pakistan revel in conjuring up Indian designs to break up the country and undo the Partition. Though some of Pakistan's security concerns could be legitimate for itself, Indians anywhere now have no great wish to undo Partition and reunify the subcontinent, thereby adding Pakistan's manifold problems to itself. India considers Pakistan a sovereign and independent nation and no reasonably thinking Indian in the last forty to fifty years has harboured any such outdated concept. It is a matter of fact that till the 1950s, there were some prominent Indian leaders who had misplaced romantic notions of an India getting reunited, but by peaceful means and the pull of history, and never militarily. The legacy, trauma and the finality of Partition should now be consigned to history books and academic discussions.

Another myth which some Pakistani scholars and writers indulge in—only for their domestic constituencies as no other nation in the world acknowledges this absurd allegation—is that India is a regional hegemon that the Pakistani Army has to resist. In later years, this myth became a popular selling gimmick in text books in Pakistan. However, the first author to propound this utterly dismissive concept was no less than General Ayub Khan, who in his autobiography, *Friends Not Masters*, argues that all of the India–Pakistan frictions are attributable to 'India's ambition to absorb Pakistan or turn her into a satellite... From the day of Independence, Pakistan was involved in a bitter and prolonged struggle for her very existence and survival... Indian efforts in the field of foreign policy were all directed towards one aim, the isolation of Pakistan and its disintegration.' I think it is high time for Pakistan to discard such negative and baseless thinking. It must not delude itself that India is even remotely an existential threat for it.

To India and a clear majority the world over, the major problem which has sorely prevented a possible thaw in Indo–Pak relations is Pakistan's dogged adherence to employing terrorism as an extension of state policy and fanning secessionism in some parts of India. It is worth mentioning here that after the Mumbai terrorist attacks, US Secretary of State Condoleezza Rice told Pakistan's National Security Adviser, Major General Mahmud Durrani, that the US knew that Pakistan had all the information to shut terrorist operations forever. She reportedly warned him saying, 'I realize there could be instability if you go after the jihadi groups but you will be consumed if you do not.' Rice further stated that, 'Focusing your energies on an Indian threat that does not exist is a colossal mistake.' According to her, Pakistan could not 'keep these people as an option because keeping contacts with various jihadi groups is not acceptable.' Former CIA Director Michael Hayden, in his book, *Playing to the Edge: American Intelligence in the Age of Terror,* expressed that Pakistan's ISI's links with the many terror tanzeems were deep and abiding. Even Lieutenant General Ahmad Shuja Pasha admitted to the then Pakistan Ambassador to the US, Husain Haqqani, in 2008 that 'the people involved in the Mumbai attack were ours but it was not our operation.' Pakistan has caused enough havoc inside India, especially in J&K, and India will never tolerate Pakistan continuing with this violent disruption. Thus, for relations to improve for mutual benefit, Pakistan must move away from fostering terrorism and thereby rid itself of being dubbed the citadel and incubator of regional and global terrorism.

To a majority of Pakistanis, the major problem preventing improvement in relations between the two nations is the Kashmir imbroglio. Noted Pakistani academic, Dr Syed Rifaat Hussain, explains the Pakistani viewpoint in Kashmir's standing in the continuing Indo–Pak impasse. He expounds that 'being the fundamental cause of the first two wars between India and Pakistan, and a trigger for the May–June 1999 conflict in Kargil, Kashmir is universally recognized as a nuclear flash-point and a serious international security issue'. Amplifying the efforts of Manmohan Singh and General Musharraf to resolve the vexed issue, he informs that between '2004 and 2007, New Delhi and Islamabad used back channel links to develop a shared understanding in the form of a "non-paper" for a final resolution of the dispute.' Dr Hussain's chapter, 'The India Factor' in the book *Pakistan: Beyond the Crisis State*, reveals that 'in these secret talks, Pakistan was represented by President Musharraf's principal secretary, Tariq Aziz, while India was represented, first by JN Dixit, Prime Minister Manmohan Singh's national security adviser and following his death by former Ambassador Satinder Lambah.' From the Indian side, Manmohan Singh had categorically ruled out any 'redrawing of boundaries' to which Musharraf had agreed even publicly. According to Dr Hussain and also corroborated by noted American journalist Steve Coll, the agreed points were:

- No change in the territorial layout of Kashmir currently divided into Pakistani and Indian areas.
- The creation of a 'softer border' across LoC.
- Greater autonomy and self-governance within both Indian and Pakistan controlled parts of the state.
- A cross-LoC consultative mechanism.
- The demilitarization of Kashmir at a pace determined by the decline in cross-border terrorism.
- From accounts circulating in informed diplomatic circles, it appeared that the above-mentioned Manmohan–Musharraf formula had some chances for fructification had General Musharraf not been made to unceremoniously resign after his altercation with Pakistani Chief Justice Iftikhar Chowdhury in 2008.

Dr Hussain adequately sums up the Pakistani viewpoint on factors adversely impacting the current Indo–Pak relationship.

He opines that 'because of the divisive impact of these factors relating to ideology, the violent legacy of partition, images of the enemy, and the unresolved issue of Kashmir, India and Pakistan have been constrained to pursue their security policies within the framework of unilateral security, where intended gains for one side are supposed to result in an equivalent loss for the other. But this unilateralist way of thinking about security has become untenable in the wake of South Asia's passage to overt nuclearization in May 1998.'

BREAKING THE LOGJAM

The Indian subcontinent, beset with thousands of years in poverty, lacking in basic standards of living, education, health, sanitation, food and clean drinking water and myriad other deprivations, could do well to strive for the dividends of peace. That this simple fact of life is not lost on anyone is a truism. Yet Pakistan refuses to accept the basic principles required for good neighbourliness, mutual amity and growth. Pakistan's continuing misfortune is that its Deep State intoxicated with its 'culture of entitlement' which it will never let go, will remain a stumbling block towards amelioration in Indo–Pak relations. That maintaining a confrontational relationship with India feeds the Pakistan Army's capricious appetite for its own self is a universally accepted phenomenon.

Mian Nawaz Sharif, a three-time Pakistani PM who never could complete any of his five-year terms, has just been unceremoniously disqualified by Pakistan's Supreme Court on grounds of corruption attributable to leaks associated with the Panama Papers. Such an overreach by Pakistan's top court based on the findings of its Joint Investigation Team, comprising mainly officers from the ISI and Pakistan military intelligence, does indicate some unholy collaboration between the Pakistan Army and a pliant judiciary. With Nawaz Sharif's ouster, it is clear that the Pakistani Deep State is, once again, likely to rule the roost in the affairs of Pakistan with its civil government in a subservient role.

Notwithstanding the above stated and rather bleak prognosis for the future, millions of people in both the nations dream of peace and thus mutual prosperity—both conditions which have eluded the two nations. The world and countries of this region are more than conscious that both nations could be sucked into a nuclear conflagration attributable to a Pakistani sponsored major terrorist attack—even by so-called non-state actors. This is a grim reality that India and Pakistan cannot ignore. Further, the fact some among these non-state actors may be out of control of even the ISI now makes the overall situation now additionally hazardous.

With relations between both nations currently at virtual rock-bottom, what then is the way forward? Unquestionably, both have to make sincere efforts to break the logjam before traumatic and tragic events overwhelm the well-being and safety of their people. A nuclear Armageddon lurks around the corner if sanity does not pervade the two nations.

In the last three years, despite cordial meetings between Prime Minister Modi and former PM Nawaz Sharif on the sidelines of the Ufa Summit of the Shanghai Cooperation Organisation (SCO) in July 2015, a couple of 'secret' meetings between the respective National Security Advisers (NSA) of the two nations, there has not been any forward movement on the contentious issues confronting the two nations. Pakistan insists on discussing all outstanding issues—a euphemism to include Kashmir, while India's prime contention is to discuss terrorism in all its forms, which implies even state sponsorship of terror. However, whenever talks are scheduled, a terrorist attack is staged, which ensures cancellation of these parleys. To the list of contentious issues, a few more, equally significant problems, which have bedevilled relations between the two neighbours, will have to be included. These are Afghanistan, the Indus Waters Treaty, Pakistani contacts with Hurriyat leaders in India and the recent one of an alleged Indian spy, Kulbhushan Jadhav, supposedly abducted from Iran by the ISI. In addition, the China-sponsored CPEC which traverses through the disputed territory of Gilgit–Baltistan has further aggravated differences between the two nations. China's well-heralded and determined entry into this disputed region, via the CPEC, will further aggravate the already fragile India–Pakistan relations. Pakistan, despite all the financial problems it suffers from currently, must not wish away its political autonomy to the crafty Chinese.

A sore point for India has been the inordinate delay in the finalization of the case in Pakistani courts of the seven accused in the Mumbai terror attacks, even as the chief perpetrators, Zaki-ur-Rehman Lakhvi and Hafiz Saeed, continue spewing their anti-India propaganda. Tariq Khosa, former director general of Pakistan's Federal Investigation Agency has expressed that, 'Pakistan has to deal with the Mumbai mayhem planned and launched from its soil. This requires facing the truth and admitting mistakes. The entire state security apparatus must ensure that the perpetrators and masterminds are brought to justice. The case has lingered for too long.'* In another of his writings, Khosa further laments that Pakistan 'has acquired the art of turning its strategic follies into triumphs. It is this Deep State that has curtailed and trimmed democracy, ensuring the country stays rigged in favour of small but self-aggrandizing elite. And until that changes, democracy in Pakistan will remain imperiled.'**

BRIDGING THE GAP

Among the many sensitive issues vitiating Indo–Pak bonhomie, some can be resolved with alacrity as the chasm is eminently bridgeable. Some of these, perhaps, would have been resolved had there not been frequent disruptions in the planned bilateral meetings.

The dispute of Sir Creek can be resolved with slight mutual accommodation between the two viewpoints. It is merely a minor cartographic interpretation problem with no strategic or tactically significant overtones. Both Indian and Pakistani teams have carried out joint surveys of the disputed land border in this area, located old boundary pillars and exchanged non-papers. Pakistan recommends

---

*'Tariq Khosa admits: 26/11 Mumbai mayhem was planned, launched from Pakistan.' *The Times of India*, 4 August 2015.
**Tariq Khosa. 'Power of the Establishment.' *Dawn*, 22 February 2016.

the Sir Creek eastern boundary to conform to the Green Line of the 1914 map, while India prefers the boundary as shown in the 1924 map of the area. Importantly, India has suggested the acceptance of the median line principle to conclude the maritime boundary claims from a base island at the mouth of Sir Creek. Both nations, in effect, could easily arrive at a solution reconciling each other's cartographic sensibilities.

Normalization of trade ties between the two nations can prove to be an effective CBM besides bringing great economic benefits to both. The annual current trade from Delhi/Mumbai via Dubai to Karachi and Lahore and vice versa, is estimated to be between $2 and $4 billion, as the journey is nearly eleven times longer and thus, four times more expensive. Greater trade integration will give producers in both nations access to much wider markets in both countries and increase in trade follows will naturally be mutually beneficial to each nation's economies. India had accordingly granted Most Favoured Nation (MFN) status to Pakistan, which the latter has not reciprocated. However, in recent times, Pakistan's former envoy to India, Abdul Basit, has expressed Pakistan's willingness to grant Non-Discriminatory Market Access (NDMA) to India once the dialogue resumes. The connectivity between the two nations, however, needs further improvement as currently there is only one land route through Attari and Wagah in Punjab for rail and road transport of goods. Two more land routes, like the Munabao-Khokhrapar in Rajasthan and Hussainiwala-Ferozepur in Punjab, will have to be opened to handle the larger volumes of trade.

Since many years, India has been seeking transit rights to Afghanistan through Pakistan, which Islamabad has so far refused. Once transit rights are approved by Pakistan for Indian goods, a trade corridor for India to the CARs will open up. Indian companies have offered to supply surplus electricity from India to Pakistan at one-third the rates that Pakistanis are currently paying for electricity, but Pakistan has been shy of even this offer.

The issue of gross indulgence in terror activities in India by both Pakistani state and non-state actors over the last thirty years has irked India. Pakistan's record on this issue is well-known internationally.

Meanwhile, instead of putting a clamp on terrorism in all its forms, Pakistan has commenced vigorously on a strategy to paint India in a light similar to Pakistan's own poor image internationally. To take some load off itself, it has commenced conjuring up India's involvement in terrorism inside Balochistan, along the Af–Pak border and India's R&AW establishing links with the TTP. The ISI, through the Taliban, managed to abduct former Indian naval officer, Kulbhushan Jadhav, who was doing business in neighbouring Iran and have planted a case of Jadhav indulging in espionage and fomenting trouble in Balochistan.

Unlike in the case of Ajmal Kasab, Pakistan adamantly refuses any consular access to India to meet Jadhav. Pakistan's complicity in terror activities, despite numerous warnings from the US, will remain a major impediment in the improvement of bilateral relations. Further, India also has to be careful that Pakistan is prevented from relocating its terror assets from Afghanistan to next-door J&K.

The issue of demilitarization of the Siachen Glacier region currently cannot be resolved in the present stressed circumstances. For India, the Saltoro Ridge, which lies immediately to the west of the glacier, is indeed a very strong defensive feature, and vacating that will be, militarily, tactical stupidity. With China in adverse possession of 38,000 square kilometres in the Aksai Chin region, immediately to the west and in the north, occupation of 5,180 square kilometres in the Shaksgam Valley, illegally ceded to it by Pakistan in November 1963 to enable it to construct the Karakoram Highway, the Siachen region has its own very special military significance to India. In the event of India vacating the Saltoro Ridge/Siachen region, the Chinese and Pakistan troops could then converge and easily reach the Ladakh Range, which guards the approach to Leh via the Khardung La and Chang La passes. Turtuk (captured by Indian troops in 1971), Chalunka and Partapur will easily fall to any invader apart from Chushul and much of eastern Ladakh. In addition, Pakistan refuses to agree to the Indian interpretation of the 1972 delineation of the AGPL, which states that the boundary in this region between the two nations runs from NJ 7842* and thence northwards to the glaciers. Importantly, the Siachen Glacier is the source of the Nubra River, which flows into the Shyok River which in turn flows into the Indus. With the Indus Waters Treaty continually under stress, giving up the source of the waters for the Indus River will hardly be strategically prudent for India. Though deployment of troops is, undoubtedly, costly both in terms of weather-related casualties and a financial burden, the occupation of Saltoro Ridge is a vital military imperative considering the collusive machinations of China and Pakistan. I have had the entire Ladakh sector as my operational responsibility and can vouch for the strategic significance of this region to India's vital interests. India cannot be munificent on the Siachen issue and its demilitarization should only be considered with the overall discussions on J&K along with the Gilgit–Baltistan, POK and Shaksgam Valley—all part of the erstwhile princely state of J&K.

Pakistan underplays the point regarding Balawaristan (pre-historic name for the Gilgit–Baltistan region). Pakistan's claims to sovereignty over a predominantly Muslim population was thrown out by their own Supreme Court ruling in 1999 which expressed unequivocally that 'Balawaristan was disputed territory and the government of Pakistan has no claim over it.' Thus it should be amply clear to any Indian government that for the people of Gilgit–Baltistan, any withdrawal of Indian troops from the Siachen Glacier would leave them at the mercy of an expansionist Han army and a obsequious Pakistan that has already ceded the Shaksgam portion of Gilgit–Baltistan to China long ago and is now preparing to hand over suzerainty of the rest of the Pakistan-occupied territory to its all-weather friend.

---

*The northern-most point of the LoC which ends in Ladakh, short of the Siachen sector. After this point starts the 110 km-long Actual Ground Position Line in the Siachen Glacier whose alignment is not agreed upon by the two nations. The demarcation of the LoC was agreed upon by Indira Gandhi and Zulfikar Ali Bhutto through the Simla Agreement. The LoC till NJ 7842 has been agreed by both the nations.

For Pakistan, J&K remains the core issue for any discussions between the two nations. Pakistan's overly obsessive J&K centricity is the major stumbling block in improvement of relations between the two nations. It may wish to understand India's straightforward and unwavering position on the Kashmir issue. J&K has more than special significance to the Indian state. India has the second largest Muslim population in the world, more Muslims than Pakistan itself. In India, unlike in Pakistan, all hues of the Muslim faith flourish—the 'Idea of India' is embellished and strengthened by its secularism and plurality. Thus, Kashmir is not only the symbol of India's secular nationhood, but more crucially, its guarantee. Pakistan, in the last seventy years, has left no stone unturned to wrest Kashmir from India employing all possible overt and covert measures but to no effect except bringing misery to the Kashmiris. As Pakistan frequently quotes the UN Resolutions for a plebiscite to decide on the future of J&K, it conveniently forgets that the UN Resolution in 1949 clearly stipulated that Pakistan will have to withdraw its armed forces from the areas forcibly captured by it before any plebiscite can be conducted. The Indian Parliament in 1994 has also passed a unanimous resolution calling for all territory of the erstwhile state of J&K held by Pakistan, to be reverted to the Indian state.

With total disagreement between the two nations on this issue, a possible answer lies in freezing this territorial dispute (as Pakistan calls it and not India) for the time being. This could be the first CBM, and whenever there are two strong governments in place in New Delhi and Islamabad, and an environment conducive to further parleys, the reasonable solutions for J&K discussed during the Manmohan Singh–Musharraf era could be further delved into. Without redrawing of boundaries and enforcing any political changes which are unacceptable to people and institutions in both nations, increased trade between the parts of the state and other interactions, and making the LoC irrelevant could be considered for a long-term solution when India–Pakistan relations achieve a degree of cordiality and trust. It will be relevant to point out here that after General Musharraf's resignation from his appointment and departure from his country, even Pakistan's Foreign Office had totally denied the existence of any details with them regarding the Kashmir formula that had been worked out between Musharraf and Manmohan Singh. Since then, all Pakistan governments are back to their old chants of the Kashmir problem to be resolved by implementation of the 1949 UN Resolution, regardless of its validity and geopolitical relevance.

Meanwhile, to improve relations between the two nations and end further misery to Kashmiris, Pakistan must desist from stoking the fires of insurgency in Indian Kashmir. In addition, India also has to look at all options of solving the problem in Kashmir afresh. India has to seriously address getting the Kashmiris emotionally integrated with their parent nation.

Importantly, Pakistan, for some short-term financial salvation and imaginary strategic gains over India, must not barter the sovereignty and well-being of Kashmiris in the parts currently under its administration, to the Chinese. Additionally, India will have to keep a careful watch on the growing Chinese footprint in POK and Gilgit–Baltistan as India's northwest will, most likely, witness a newer version of the Great Game owing to China's ambitious strategies for this region.

Overall, if Pakistan continues to benchmark its relations with India only on Kashmir, the future contours of this association appear rather bleak. The Pakistan military has never shown any willingness to mend relations with India. With China's financial largesse to Pakistan via the under construction CPEC and massive infusion of modern weaponry for Pakistan's armed forces, the Deep State is currently on a high.

Stephen Cohen describes the current relations as 'a hurting stalemate' and opines that this situation will continue for 'two, five or ten years, let alone to 2047', with fluctuating 'more or less tensions'. US diplomat Ashley Tellis calls the relationship between the two nations as one of 'ugly stability'.

Husain Haqqani maintains that 'India is expanding by most measures of national power while Pakistan has been able to keep pace with it only in manufacturing nuclear weapons and their delivery systems. Pakistanis are often not told of the widening gap between the two countries in most fields, including education, scientific research and innovation. Pakistan vehemently opposes a permanent seat for India in the United Nations Security Council and membership of the Nuclear Suppliers Group. Pakistan cannot realistically expect either for itself but would like to deny them to India as well.' Haqqani further suggests that ' Instead of breeding competition with India in the national psyche, Pakistan could concentrate on building its democracy, eliminating terrorism, improving its infrastructure and modernizing its economy.'

Ashraf Jehangir Qazi, a respected former High Commissioner to India, insists that, 'For Pakistan to be simultaneously locked in a zero-sum game with two of its most immediate neighbours (India and Afghanistan) is pure folly. Pakistan can never be stable in such a situation.' He further adds that 'Pakistan must address India's core concerns and move towards a principled compromise settlement acceptable to the Kashmiris.' Former Indian Foreign Secretary Nirupama Rao sums up the current Indian approach to Pakistan rather pessimistically, and maybe realistically, expressing that 'the approach to Pakistan will continue to be tough, since the terrorism issue agitates the public sentiment deeply, and there has been little or no give from Pakistan…there is really no public support for dialogue with Pakistan. The field lies fallow.' However, veteran Pakistani general and a regular participant at Track 2 Dialogues, Talat Masood, states that one view espoused by Pakistani analysts is that by pursuing a hard line towards Pakistan, India further strengthens the role of the military there. It is not surprising in this sense that the BJP being in power in India suits the military in Pakistan, enabling it to justify its policies. This, in turn, boosts the arguments of hardliners in India. The resulting dynamic only perpetuates antagonism between the two countries.

Notwithstanding the many contentious issues which afflict the state of relations, maintaining current negativities and hostile approach towards each other will hardly assist India and Pakistan in their economic growth or ensuring the security and well-being of their people. Thus governments, well-meaning personalities and institutions on both sides will have to make sincere and relatively non-partisan endeavours to ensure peace and some normalcy between the two neighbours. This can be achieved by a continuous process of engagement and dialogue. Continuing tensions on the LoC/international boundary are indeed a wasteful activity, even militarily speaking, and Pakistan, I am afraid, stands out as the perpetrator of keeping up the ante along the borders. Hundreds of their infiltrators apart from poor, innocent villagers have been the victims on both sides and to no effect. Pakistan must realize that the instrument of terror or even aiding and abetting insurgency inside India is not going to materially change India's map whatsoever. So why indulge in unproductive, self-defeating activities which will be costly to Pakistan itself?

Pakistan will do well to imbibe the point made by India in response to their PM Nawaz Sharif's tirade at the UNGA in September 2016. The Indian delegate, Eenam Gambhir, eloquently stated: 'The land of Taxila, one of the greatest learning centres of ancient times, is now host to the Ivy League of terrorism. It attracts aspirants and apprentices from all over the world.'* Faced with the spectre of rising terrorism within itself, Pakistan will do well to change tack and join India and Afghanistan in combating the scourge of terror before the combined evil forces of Al Qaeda, ISIS, LeT, JeM, Haqqani network, Taliban, TTP and scores of other terror tanzeems, roaming with impunity in the Af–Pak region, bring death and destruction to it. Pakistan may recall that most of these terrorist organizations, though Islamic, have caused the maximum damage to their fellow Muslims all over the world. Thus religion and sectarianism do not contribute to geopolitical prudence.

Former R&AW chief, Vikram Sood, referring to India's traditional restraint in dealing with continuing Pakistani provocation and mischief, stresses that perpetual restraint as a response to unending provocation is a policy based on unreal hopes. Restraint has not worked, concessions will be even less. If the world expects India to continue its policy of restraint, then the world must escalate

---

*'India's Response To Nawaz Sharif's Speech At UN.' NDTV, 22 September 2016, http://www.ndtv.com/india-news/full-text-of-indias-response-to-nawaz-sharifs-speech-at-un-1464985

its responses. So instead of plying the culprit with money and weapons, maybe deprivation of this and an ability to call his bluff would succeed.'

India, being the larger and the most powerful nation in South Asia, will have to show the way in addressing all contentious issues confronting both nations with equanimity and accommodation. India will also have to rein in some of its right-wing elements in influencing the government's policies towards Pakistan, as the latter has, unfortunately, developed a propensity for erratic behaviour towards India. It is also a matter of fact that, India too has its share of apologists for Pakistan, who wrongly believe that civil governments in Pakistan, whenever they have existed, are not to blame for lack of cordiality in India–Pakistan relations and that only their army is to blame. This is a faulty assessment, by any standards, as both these institutions are equally instrumental in contributing to the adverse trajectory in India–Pakistan relations. Even Pakistan's judiciary cannot be absolved of overlooking its army's extra-constitutional shenanigans.

The most grave question which stares India–Pakistan relations in the face is—will the strategic manipulations of China, the 'culture of entitlement' and the unbridled powers of the omnipotent Deep State, the powerless civilian government in Pakistan and the many terror tanzeems ever let bilateral relations assume normalcy? That is the lament and apprehension of many eminent Pakistanis who I have had the pleasure to meet abroad. I have no hesitation to state that some of them, in reality, hardly respect their own army and desire to confine itself to defending the nation and permit democracy and the rule of law pervade their land. The Pakistan Army, the most formidable constituent of the Deep State, in the larger interests of the nation it is sworn to protect, will have to shed its 'culture of entitlement' and like armies in democracies the world over, 'return to the barracks' and obey the directions emanating from democratically elected civilian governments. In my considered opinion, which is shorn of any anti-Pakistan sentiment, only the Pakistani people can save themselves by crusading for the establishment of genuine democracy in their nation. Equally, the Pakistani people, while they adhere to the tenets of their faith, have to shun radicalism in all its evil hues. The Pakistani people have to become crusaders, even in their most adverse circumstances, to strive for an alternative paradigm in the relations of their nation with India. The collective wisdom and will of the people can never be throttled.

Importantly, Pakistan has to see itself and its future, as envisioned by its founder, Mohammad Ali Jinnah, and not through the prism of its Deep State. As the elder sibling, India must reach out to Pakistan before the latter, through its follies and foibles, consumes itself and brings devastation and misery to this ancient land. The people of undivided India—now two sovereign nations—deserve better.

Appendix 1

Resolution adopted by the United Nations Commission for India and Pakistan on 13 August 1948

(Document No.1100, Para. 75, dated the 9th November, 1948)

THE UNITED NATIONS COMMISSION FOR INDIA AND PAKISTAN

Having given careful consideration to the points of view expressed by the Representatives, of India and Pakistan regarding the situation in the State of Jammu and Kashmir, and Being of the opinion that the prompt cessation of hostilities and the correction of conditions the continuance of which is likely to endanger international peace and security are essential to implementation of its endeavours to assist the Governments of India and Pakistan in effecting a final settlement of the situation, Resolves to submit simultaneously to the Governments of India and Pakistan the following proposal:

PART I
CEASE-FIRE ORDER

[A] The Governments of India and Pakistan agree that their respective High Commands will issue separately and simultaneously a cease-fire order to apply to all forces under their control in the State of

Jammu and Kashmir as of the earliest practicable date or dates to be mutually agreed upon within four days after these proposals have been accepted by both Governments.

[B] The High Commands of Indian and Pakistan forces agree to refrain from taking any measures that might augment the military potential of the forces under their control in the State of Jammu and Kashmir. (For the purpose of these proposals '-forces under their control" shall be considered to include all forces, organised and unorganised, fighting or participating in hostilities on their respective sides).

[C] The Commanders-in-Chief of the Forces of India and Pakistan shall promptly confer regarding any necessary local changes in present dispositions which may facilitate the cease-fire.

[D] In its discretion, and as the Commission may find practicable, the Commission will appoint military observers who under the authority of the Commission and with the co-operation of both Commands will supervise the observance of the cease-fire order.

[E] The Government of India and the Government of Pakistan agree to appeal to their respective peoples to assist in creating and maintaining an atmosphere favourable to the promotion of further negotiations.

PART II
TRUCE AGREEMENT

Simultaneously with the acceptance of the proposal for the immediate cessation of hostilities as outlined in Part I, both Governments accept the following principles as a basis for the formulation of a truce agreement, the details of which shall be worked out in discussion between their Representatives and the Commission.

A.
(1) As the presence of troops of Pakistan in the territory of the State of Jammu and Kashmir constitutes a material change in the

situation since it was represented by the Government of Pakistan before the Security Council, the Government of Pakistan agrees to withdraw its troops from that State.

(2) The Government of Pakistan will use its best endeavour to secure the withdrawal from the State of Jammu and Kashmir of tribesmen and Pakistan nationals not normally resident therein who have entered the State for the purpose of fighting.

(3) Pending a final solution the territory evacuated by the Pakistan troops will be administered by the local authorities under the surveillance of the Commission.

B.

(1) When the Commission shall have notified the Government of India that the tribesmen and Pakistan nationals referred to in Part II A2 hereof have withdrawn, thereby terminating the situation which was represented by the Government of India to the Security Council as having occasioned the presence of Indian forces in the State of Jammu and Kashmir, and further, that the Pakistan forces are being withdrawn from the State of Jammu and Kashmir, the Government of India agrees to begin to withdraw the bulk of their forces from the State in stages to be agreed upon with the Commission.

(2) Pending the acceptance of the conditions for a final settlement of the situation in the State of Jammu and Kashmir, the Indian Government will maintain within the lines existing at the moment of cease-fire the minimum strength of its forces which in agreement with the Commission are considered necessary to assist local authorities in the observance of law and order. The Commission will have observers stationed where it deems necessary.

(3) The Government of India will undertake to ensure that the Government of the State of Jammu and Kashmir will take all measures within their power to make it publicly known that peace, law and order will be safeguarded and that all human and political rights will be guaranteed.

C.

(1) Upon signature, the full text of the Truce Agreement or communique containing the principles thereof as agreed upon between the two Governments and the Commission, will be made public.

PART III

The Government of India and the Government of Pakistan reaffirm their wish that the future status of the State of Jammu and Kashmir shall be determined in accordance with the will of the people and to that end, upon acceptance of the Truce Agreement both Governments agree to enter into consultations with the Commission to determine fair and equitable conditions whereby such free expression will be assured.

The UNCIP unanimously adopted this Resolution on 13-8-1948. Members of the Commission: Argentina, Belgium, Colombia, Czechoslovakia and U.S.A.

Appendix 2

Simla Agreement, 2 July 1972

July 02, 1972

The Simla Agreement signed by Prime Minister Indira Gandhi and President Zulfikar Ali Bhutto of Pakistan on 2nd July 1972 was much more than a peace treaty seeking to reverse the consequences of the 1971 war (i.e. to bring about withdrawals of troops and an exchange of PoWs). It was a comprehensive blue print for good neighbourly relations between India and Pakistan. Under the Simla Agreement both countries undertook to abjure conflict and confrontation which had marred relations in the past, and to work towards the establishment of durable peace, friendship and cooperation.

The Simla Agreement contains a set of guiding principles, mutually agreed to by India and Pakistan, which both sides would adhere to while managing relations with each other. These emphasize: respect for each other's territorial integrity and sovereignty; non-interference in each other's internal affairs; respect for each others unity, political independence; sovereign equality; and abjuring hostile propaganda. The following principles of the Agreement are, however, particularly noteworthy:

- A mutual commitment to the peaceful resolution of all issues through direct bilateral approaches.
- To build the foundations of a cooperative relationship with special focus on people to people contacts.
- To uphold the inviolability of the Line of Control in Jammu

and Kashmir, which is a most important CBM between India and Pakistan, and a key to durable peace.

India has faithfully observed the Simla Agreement in the conduct of its relations with Pakistan.

SIMLA AGREEMENT

Agreement on Bilateral Relations Between The Government of India and The Government of Pakistan

1. The Government of India and the Government of Pakistan are resolved that the two countries put an end to the conflict and confrontation that have hitherto marred their relations and work for the promotion of a friendly and harmonious relationship and the establishment of durable peace in the sub-continent, so that both countries may henceforth devote their resources and energies to the pressing talk of advancing the welfare of their peoples.
2. In order to achieve this objective, the Government of India and the Government of Pakistan have agreed as follows:-

   - That the principles and purposes of the Charter of the United Nations shall govern the relations between the two countries;
   - That the two countries are resolved to settle their differences by peaceful means through bilateral negotiations or by any other peaceful means mutually agreed upon between them. Pending the final settlement of any of the problems between the two countries, neither side shall unilaterally alter the situation and both shall prevent the organization, assistance or encouragement of any acts detrimental to the maintenance of peaceful and harmonious relations;
   - That the pre-requisite for reconciliation, good neighbourliness and durable peace between them is a commitment by both the countries to peaceful co-existence, respect for each other's territorial integrity and sovereignty and non-interference in each other's internal affairs, on the basis of equality and mutual benefit;

- That the basic issues and causes of conflict which have bedevilled the relations between the two countries for the last 25 years shall be resolved by peaceful means;
- That they shall always respect each other's national unity, territorial integrity, political independence and sovereign equality;
- That in accordance with the Charter of the United Nations they will refrain from the threat or use of force against the territorial integrity or political independence of each other.

3. Both Governments will take all steps within their power to prevent hostile propaganda directed against each other. Both countries will encourage the dissemination of such information as would promote the development of friendly relations between them.

4. In order progressively to restore and normalize relations between the two countries step by step, it was agreed that;

- Steps shall be taken to resume communications, postal, telegraphic, sea, land including border posts, and air links including overflights.
- Appropriate steps shall be taken to promote travel facilities for the nationals of the other country.
- Trade and co-operation in economic and other agreed fields will be resumed as far as possible.
- Exchange in the fields of science and culture will be promoted.

In this connection delegations from the two countires will meet from time to time to work out the necessary details.

5. In order to initiate the process of the establishment of durable peace, both the Governments agree that:

- Indian and Pakistani forces shall be withdrawn to their side of the international border.
- In Jammu and Kashmir, the line of control resulting from the cease-fire of December 17, 1971 shall be respected by

both sides without prejudice to the recognized position of either side. Neither side shall seek to alter it unilaterally, irrespective of mutual differences and legal interpretations. Both sides further undertake to refrain from the threat or the use of force in violation of this Line.
- The withdrawals shall commence upon entry into force of this Agreement and shall be completed within a period of 30 days thereof.
6. This Agreement will be subject to ratification by both countries in accordance with their respective constitutional procedures, and will come into force with effect from the date on which the Instruments of Ratification are exchanged.
7. Both Governments agree that their respective Heads will meet again at a mutually convenient time in the future and that, in the meanwhile, the representatives of the two sides will meet to discuss further the modalities and arrangements for the establishment of durable peace and normalization of relations, including the questions of repatriation of prisoners of war and civilian internees, a final settlement of Jammu and Kashmir and the resumption of diplomatic relations.

Sd/-
(Indira Gandhi)
Prime Minister

Republic of India
Sd/- (Zulfikar Ali Bhutto)
PresidentIslamic Republic of Pakistan

Simla, the 2nd July, 1972

Appendix 3

The Lahore Declaration

The following is the text of the Lahore Declaration signed by the Prime Minister, Mr. A. B. Vajpayee, and the Pakistan Prime Minister, Mr. Nawaz Sharif, in Lahore on Sunday:

The Prime Ministers of the Republic of India and the Islamic Republic of Pakistan:

Sharing a vision of peace and stability between their countries, and of progress and prosperity for their peoples;

Convinced that durable peace and development of harmonious relations and friendly cooperation will serve the vital interests of the peoples of the two countries, enabling them to devote their energies for a better future;

Recognising that the nuclear dimension of the security environment of the two countries adds to their responsibility for avoidance of conflict between the two countries;

Committed to the principles and purposes of the Charter of the United Nations, and the universally accepted principles of peaceful coexistence;

Reiterating the determination of both countries to implementing the Simla Agreement in letter and spirit;

Committed to the objective of universal nuclear disarmament and nonproliferartion;

Convinced of the importance of mutually agreed confidence building measures for improving the security environment;

Recalling their agreement of 23rd September, 1998, that an environment of peace and security is in the supreme national interest of both sides and that the resolution of all outstanding issues, including Jammu and Kashmir, is essential for this purpose;

Have agreed that their respective Governments:

- shall intensify their efforts to resolve all issues, including the issue of Jammu and Kashmir.
- shall refrain from intervention and interference in each other's internal affairs.
- shall intensify their composite and integrated dialogue process for an early and positive outcome of the agreed bilateral agenda.
- shall take immediate steps for reducing the risk of accidental or unauthorised use of nuclear weapons and discuss concepts and doctrines with a view to elaborating measures for confidence building in the nuclear and conventional fields, aimed at prevention of conflict.
- reaffirm their commitment to the goals and objectives of SAARC and to concert their efforts towards the realisation of the SAARC vision for the year 2000 and beyond with a view to promoting the welfare of the peoples of South Asia and to improve their quality of life through accelerated economic growth, social progress and cultural development.
- reaffirm their condemnation of terrorism in all its forms and manifestations and their determination to combat this menace.
- shall promote and protect all human rights and fundamental freedoms.

Signed at Lahore on the 21st day of February 1999.

Atal Behari Vajpayee—Prime Minister of the Republic of India

Muhammad Nawaz Sharif—Prime Minister of the Islamic Republic of Pakistan

Appendix 4

Major Terrorist Organizations Based in and Operating from Pakistan

LASHKAR-E-TAIBA (ARMY OF THE PURE)

- Formed in 1990 in the Kunar province of Afghanistan, the Lashkar-e-Taiba (LeT), also known as Jama'at-ul-Dawa, is based at Muridke near Lahore. It is headed by Hafiz Muhammad Saeed and its other important leaders are Yahya Mujahid (spokesman of the outfit), Maulana Abdul Wahid and Abdullah Muntazir. Saeed's son, Talha, looks after the LeT activities at its base camp in Muzaffarabad, POK, while his son-in-law, Khalid Wajeed, is reportedly part of the outfit's office in Lahore. Saeed's brother-in-law, Abdul Rehman Makki, is the second-in-command of the LeT. Zaki-ur-Rehman Lakhvi, one of the masterminds of the 26/11 Mumbai terror attack, is another high-profile LeT leader.
- LeT's ideology is drawn from the radical Wahabi school of thought and subscribes to violence and jihad to achieve its goal of restoration of Islamic rule in India and the surrounding nations. It considers India, the USA and Israel as its prime enemies. The terror outfit comprises cadres from Pakistan, Afghanistan and has some representation from Sudan, Central Asian Republics, Turkey, Libya, Bahrain, etc.
- Apart from being linked with the Taliban and al-Qaeda,

it is closely mentored by Pakistan's ISI which generously funds and equips it besides training its cadres. LeT's network extends to Germany, Saudi Arabia, the UK, the US, Bangladesh, Southeast Asia besides having modules inside India. It also supports Islamist groups fighting the US in Iraq.
- The LeT is legally outlawed in India and the US has designated the LeT as a Foreign Terrorist Organization (FTO) since December 2001. It is also banned in UK and many other Western nations. The UN too proscribed it in May 2005 while the military regime of General Pervez Musharraf also banned it in Pakistan on 12 January 2002. To circumvent the ban, it however, re-emerged as the Jamaa't-ul-Dawa. Currently, Hafiz Muhammad Saeed is under arrest in Pakistan for his involvement in the Mumbai terror attack, yet the LeT continues with its anti-India tirades openly and frequently in Pakistan.

JAISH-E-MOHAMMAD (ARMY OF THE PROPHET)

- Jaish-e-Mohammad (JeM) was launched in January 2000 in Karachi by Maulana Masood Azhar after he was released from an Indian jail consequent to the hijacking of Indian Airlines Flight IC 814 in 1999. Azhar continues as its leader. For its formation, the terror outfit reportedly received assistance from the ISI, Afghan Taliban, Sunni outfits operating in Pakistan and even from Osama bin Laden. The ISI has been the prime force in its creation with it deriving its cadres from terrorists associated with Harkat-ul-Mujahideen.
- Headquartered in Bahawalpur in Pakistan's Punjab, JeM derives its inspiration from the Deobandi ideology.
- JeM seeks the withdrawal of Indian security forces from J&K. It was instrumental in the attack on the Indian Parliament on 13 December 2001 and the attack on the Pathankot airbase in January 2016. It has carried out several attacks on the Indian security forces inside J&K including the Uri attack

on the infantry brigade headquarter in September 2016.
- The JeM has been designated as a terrorist organization by the UN, India, the US, Pakistan, Australia, UK, UAE and Canada. It is also responsible for several attacks inside Pakistan against foreigners, Christians and minorities. It was also involved in the murder of American journalist Daniel Pearl.
- JeM maintains close links with the Afghan Taliban, al-Qaeda elements and is a prominent member of the ISI-sponsored United Jihad Council, an umbrella organization of thirteen to sixteen militant organizations masterminding terrorist activities in J&K.

LASHKAR-E-JHANGVI (LEJ)

- Formed in 1996, the LeJ is a Sunni–Deobandi terrorist group comprising radical sectarian terrorists of a breakaway group of the Sipah-e-Sahaba Pakistan (SSP). It derives its name from Maulana Jhangvi, the co-founder of SSP. Prominent leaders include Akram Lahori and Riaz Basra. Its leadership mostly comprises veterans of the war against Soviet occupation in Afghanistan.
- A majority of its cadres are drawn from the Sunni madrasas (seminaries) in Pakistan. It consists of many loosely coordinated groups in various parts of Pakistan while its training centres are located at Muridke and Kabirwala in Khanewal district. It has around 300 active cadres.
- The LeJ aims to transform Pakistan into a Sunni state. It maintains close links with the Afghan Taliban and, along with the Taliban militia, has fought the Northern Alliance. Also, both these outfits have frequently taken part in the massacres and terrorist acts against Shias in Afghanistan. Being a part of the overall Deobandi movement, the LeJ derives operational support from other Sunni terrorist outfits. Its cadres have trained at Harakat ul-Mujahideen's Khalid bin Waleed training camp in Afghanistan besides

- having its own training camp near the Sarobi Dam in Kabul.
- For years, LeJ has been receiving funds from Saudi Arabia. In addition, it is funded by several wealthy businessmen/smuggler syndicates in Karachi.
- The LeJ was proscribed by President Pervez Musharraf in August 2001. The Nawaz Sharif administration has also taken strict action against the LeJ resulting in casualties to many of its cadres and leadership.

SIPAH-E-SAHABA PAKISTAN (SSP)

- The SSP is a Sunni sectarian outfit founded in 1985. It has frequently targeted the Shia community in Pakistan. It also operated as a political party and contested elections. It is alleged to have been set up at the behest of General Zia-ul-Haq as an Islamic counter to pro-democracy forces, as also, as a reaction to the Iranian Revolution which indirectly fanned Shia militancy in Pakistan.
- Allama Ali Sher Ghazni is the patron-in-chief of SSP while Maulana Zia-ul-Qasmi serves as the chairman of its Supreme Council. The SSP also aims to make Pakistan a Sunni state and restore the Khilafat system. It is staunchly anti-US.
- Most of the SSP cadres come from the Punjab province, and Sargodha, Jhang, Multan, Bahawalpur and Muzaffargarh towns are considered as SSP strongholds. Many of its senior leaders have been killed in various intra-terror acts. The SSP has been at the forefront targeting all non-Sunni Muslims and minorities in Pakistan.
- The SSP has forged close links with various Central Asian terrorist groups, like the Islamic Movement of Uzbekistan (IMU). It is also linked to Ramzi Ahmed Yousef, the mastermind of the 1993 bombing of the World Trade Centre in New York.
- The SSP has received state funding to construct and operate Wahabi and Deobandi madrasas besides generous funds

from many Persian Gulf countries. Although the Pakistan government, under US pressure, banned the SSP in 2002, Pakistan military and intelligence officials continue to maintain close links with it.

HARAKAT-UL-MUJAHIDEEN (HUM)/HARAKAT UL-ANSAR

- Based in Pakistan, the HUM is a militant Islamist group that operates primarily in Kashmir. The HUM operated terrorist training camps in eastern Afghanistan till they were destroyed by Coalition air strikes. It is based in Muzaffarabad, Rawalpindi and some other towns in Pakistan while it conducts insurgent activities inside Kashmir. It lost some of its cadres in 2000, owing to defections to the JeM.
- HUM is also aligned to the radical political party Jamiat Ulema-i-Islam (Fazlur Rehman faction). Its former long-time leader, Fazlur Rehman Khalil, was also linked to Osama bin Laden. Its current leader is Farooqi Kashmiri.
- HUM is also linked to another Kashmiri militant group, Al-Faran, which had kidnapped five foreign tourists in Kashmir in 1995 and subsequently murdered them. It has carried out many terrorist acts within Kashmir till date. Reportedly, it has armed supporters both in J&K and in the POK region.
- It solicits donations for its activities from Saudi Arabia other Gulf countries, Pakistan and Kashmir.
- HUM was primarily responsible for the hijacking of the Indian Airlines Flight IC 814 in 1999 which resulted in the release of terrorists Masood Azhar and Ahmed Omar Sheikh (convicted later for the murder of journalist Daniel Pearl).

AL-BADR (THE FULL MOON)

- Tracing its origins to a radical outfit of the same name in erstwhile East Pakistan which was rabidly anti-Bengali, Al-Badr came into existence in Pakistan in 1998. Its cadres earlier operated under the umbrella of Hizbul Mujahideen. The group has also operated under Afghan warlord Gulbuddin Hekmatyar in the 1980s. Its current chief is a Punjab resident, Bakht Zameen. It has, reportedly, a cadre strength of 200 including 120 foreign terrorists. The headquarters of Al-Badr is in Mansehra in Pakistan while it has a field set-up in Muzaffarabad, POK. Training camps have set up at these places and also one at Kotli, POK.

- Al-Badr maintains close links with the ISI and JeI in Pakistan and with the al-Qaeda, the Taliban and Hekmatyar's Hizb-e-Islami in Afghanistan.
- Its funding can be traced to sources in Saudi Arabia; it also receives financial assistance from the Pakistani government.
- Al-Badr and LeT are the two Kashmiri terrorist groups who employ suicide squads as a tactic. Al-Badr has endeavoured to spread its tentacles in the Indian hinterland, though without any success so far.
- Al-Badr has been banned by India since 2004 while the US has included Al-Badr in its list of FTOs.

HARKAT-UL-JIHAD-AL-ISLAMI (HUJI)

- A Pakistan-based terrorist outfit, the formation of HuJI has its origins in the Soviet–Afghan war. After the end of the Afghan War, it reoriented its mission to fight for fellow Muslims in J&K and supports the secession of J&K from India and merging it into Pakistan. It also has an affiliate in Bangladesh.
- Belonging to the radical Deobandi school, it is working for increased Islamization in Pakistan and Islamic rule in India. It also derives inspiration from Osama bin Laden and the Afghan Taliban.
- With a cadre strength of 600-750, HuJI has a presence in some countries other than India and Pakistan. It has set up several sleeper cells in UP, Andhra Pradesh, Maharashtra and Rajasthan while, reportedly, a number of SIMI (Students

Islamic Movement of India) cadres have also joined the HuJI.
- The HuJI has fought alongside Taliban leader Mullah Omar against the Northern Alliance in Afghanistan. From its strongholds in Afghanistan in Kandhar and Khost, it has launched operations inside Uzbekistan, Chechnya and Tajikistan.
- The HuJI maintains close links with the ISI, Taliban, al-Qaeda, LeT and JeM. Meanwhile, coordinated by the ISI, this outfit's Bangladesh affiliate maintains links with various anti-India militant groups, like the ULFA and Manipur-based People's United Liberation Front (PULF) in India's Northeast. Its Bangla affiliate has carried out numerous terror attacks in Bangladesh.
- The HuJI is a banned terrorist organization in India under The Unlawful Activities (Prevention) Act, 2004, while the US designated HuJI as an FTO in March 2008.

AL-QAEDA AND AL-QAEDA IN INDIAN SUBCONTINENT (AQIS)

- The al-Qaeda, since decades, has symbolized the rise of radicalism in Islam and managed a global footprint while spreading its violent ideology. It aims to establish an Islamic caliphate and rejects the idea of nation-states even if they are governed by Muslim rulers. It is intensely anti-US, anti-Shias, and an inspiration for most Islamist terror groups. Formed by the notorious terrorist kingpin Osama bin Laden, al-Qaeda has a sizeable presence in many countries. It deliberately maintains a low profile in Pakistan but coordinates the functioning of many terror tanzeems in Pakistan for their terror operations in Afghanistan and India. Its members in Pakistan hail from well-to-do families and many are university graduates.
- The AQIS came into existence in September 2014, and according to the al-Qaeda chief (after bin Laden's death)

Ayman-al-Zawahiri, the AQIS owes total allegiance to the al-Qaeda. The AQIS has pledged its loyalty many times to Zawahiri and Taliban leader Mullah Omar. The current leader of the AQIS is Asim Umar whose origins and parentage are shrouded in mystery. Asim Umar is a skilled orator and a well-known 'Internet propagandist'.
- The AQIS also follows the Salafist ideology of al-Qaeda and is working to establish an Islamic Emirate in Afghanistan and the rule of the Sharia in the Muslim world.
- The AQIS is active in Afghanistan, supporting the Taliban and has many of its cadres located in the FATA region and along the terrorist havens near Durand Line.
- Ansar al-Islam, the Bangladeshi branch of the AQIS, is heavily involved in terrorist activities in Bangladesh, targeting minorities and moderate Bangladeshi Muslims including secular-minded university professors, bloggers and writers.
- Many counter-terrorist experts opine that one of the reasons for the creation of AQIS was a reaction to the rise of ISIS in Syria and Iraq and the rivalry between these two factions in South Asia will be one to be analysed to comprehend the dynamics of terrorism in the region.

TEHRIK-I-TALIBAN PAKISTAN (TTP)

- One of the most violent and ruthless terrorist organizations, TTP was formally established in December 2007 by militant kingpin Baitullah Mehsud. Based primarily in FATA and the areas bordering the Pak-Afghan border, apart from Pashtuns, it has a strong presence of Uzbeks, Arabs, Chechens and even some Punjabis in its ranks. Mehsud, suspected to be killed by a US drone attack in August 2009, was succeeded by Hakimullah Mehsud and on his death by Maulana Fazlullah.
- The TTP's objectives are to combat foreign troops in Afghanistan, enforce the Sharia and carry out 'defensive jihad' against the Pakistan Army. It has carried out several

terror attacks against Pakistan Army assets as targeted government offices, universities, police stations, markets, airports, foreign missions and organizations. Its most devastating terror act, condemned the world over, was its attack on the Army Public School in Peshawar in December 2014, killing over 140 innocent school children and staff. It claimed that the attack was in retaliation to Pakistan Army's counter-terror operation Zarb-e-Azb. A month earlier, Jamaat-ul-Ahrar, one of the TTP's breakaway groups had carried out a dramatic bombing at the Pakistani side of the Wagah border, killing over sixty people. In June 2014, along with the Islamic Movement of Uzbekistan (IMU), the TTP had attacked the Karachi airport causing many casualties.
- The TTP had reportedly set up a base in Syria to fight alongside rebels opposed to Syrian President Bashar al-Assad.
- Without any tangible proof, Pakistan claims that the TTP is supported by the Afghan intelligence and even India's R&AW.
- The Pakistan government has tried a few times, though unsuccessfully, to initiate talks with the TTP, which remains the strongest anti-state jihadi group in Pakistan.

SUMMATION

There are countless terrorist groups in Pakistan including some splinter groups that have broken away from their parent organizations over leadership differences or the extent of radicalization issues. Though some terrorist outfits have been proscribed, time and again, by the Pakistani government, they continue to exist under newer nomenclature while continuing with their nefarious agendas. The Pakistani Deep State continues to maintain close links with Afghanistan-based tanzeems like the formidable and large Afghan Taliban and the intensely anti-US Haqqani network. Many US lawmakers have complained about ISI diverting funds allotted by the US to Pakistan to combat terror in the region finding its way to the Haqqani network, Afghan Taliban, LeT and JeM.

Bibliography

Ahmed Rashid. 2012. *Pakistan on the Brink: The Future of America, Pakistan, and Afghanistan*. New Delhi: Penguin.

Ahmed Rashid. 2008. *Descent into Chaos: The World's Most Unstable Region and the Threat to Global Security*. London: Penguin.

Amarinder Singh. 1999. *Lest We Forget*. New Delhi: Paula Press.

Ayesha Siddiqua. 2007. *Military Inc.: Inside Pakistan's Military Economy*. London: Pluto Press.

B. Raman. 2002. *Intelligence: Past, Present and Future*. New Delhi: Lancer Publishers.

Carey Schofield. 2011. *Inside The Pakistan Army: A Woman's Experience on the Frontline of the War on Terror*. London, New Delhi: Biteback Publishing, Pentagon Press.

C. Christine Fair. 2014. *Fighting to the End: The Pakistan Army's Way of War*. New Delhi: Oxford University Press.

Christophe Jaffrelot. 2016. *The Pakistan Paradox: Instability and Resilience*. New Delhi: Penguin.

Daniel S. Markey. 2013. *No Exit from Pakistan: America's Tortured Relationship with Islamabad*. New Delhi: Cambridge University Press.

Darshan Khullar. 2009. *Pakistan: Our Difficult Neighbour and Allied Issues*. Ambala Cantt: Pushpa Books.

Hein G. Kiessling. 2016. *Faith, Unity, Discipline: The ISI of Pakistan*. New Delhi: HarperCollins Publishers.

Husain Haqqani. 2016. *Pakistan: Between Mosque and Military*, revised ed. New Delhi: Penguin.

Husain Haqqani. 2016. *India vs Pakistan, Why Can't We Just Be Friends?* New Delhi: Juggernaut Books.

Indrajeet Singh. 2015. *Pakistan, ISI and Hunt for Terror*. New Delhi: Gaurav Book Centre.

Ira Pande. 2009. *The Great Divide: India and Pakistan*. New Delhi: HarperCollins Publishers.

James Ridgeway. 2005. *The 5 Unanswered Questions About 9/11: What the 9/11 Commission Report Failed to Tell Us*. New Delhi: Penguin.

Jaswant Singh. 2009. *Jinnah: India-Partition-Independence*. New Delhi: Rupa Publications India.

J.N. Dixit. 2002. *India-Pakistan in War and Peace*. New Delhi: Books Today, The India Today Group.

Khaled Ahmed. 2016. *Sleepwalking to Surrender: Dealing with Terrorism in Pakistan*. New Delhi: Penguin.

Kuldip Singh Bajwa. 2008. *India's National Security: Military Challenges and Responses*. New Delhi: Har Anand Publications.

Maroof Raza (ed.). 2009. *Confronting Terrorism*. New Delhi: Penguin.

Maleeha Lodhi (ed.). 2014. *Pakistan: Beyond the 'Crisis State'*. New Delhi: Rupa Publications India.

Pakistan, Hamoodur Rehman Commission of Inquiry into the 1971 War. 2007. *The report of the Hamoodur Rehman Commission of inquiry into the 1971 war, as declassified by the Government of Pakistan*. Lahore: Vanguard Publishers.

Pervez Musharraf. 2006. *In the Line of Fire: A Memoir*. New York: Free Press.

Rajesh Kadian. 1992. *The Kashmir Tangle: Issues and Options*. Kent, UK: Asia Publishing House.

Rana Banerji. 2014. *The Pakistan Army: Composition, Character and Compulsions*. New Delhi: KW Publishers.

Shekhar Dutt. 2014. *India's Defence and National Security*. New Delhi: Har Anand Publications.

Shuja Nawaz. 2014. *Crossed Swords: Pakistan, Its Army, and the Wars Within*. Karachi: Oxford University Press.

S.K. Datta. 2015. *Inside ISI: The Story and Involvement of the ISI, Afghan Jihad, Taliban, Al-Qaeda, 9/11, Osama bin Laden, 26/11 and The Future of Al-Qaeda*. New Delhi: Vij Books India Pvt Ltd.

Stephen P. Cohen. 1984. *The Pakistan Army*. Berkeley, California: University of California Press.

Stephen P. Cohen. 2016. *The South Asia Papers: A Critical Anthology of Writings by Stephen Philip Cohen*. New Delhi: HarperCollins Publishers.

V.P. Malik. 2013. *India's Military Conflicts and Diplomacy: An Inside View of Decision Making*. New Delhi: HarperCollins Publishers.

Vazira Fazila-Yacoobali Zamindar. 2008. *The Long Partition and the Making of Modern South Asia: Refugees, Boundaries, Histories*. New Delhi: Columbia University Press.

Wajahat Habibullah. 2014. *My Kashmir: The Dying of the Light*. New Delhi: Penguin.

Index

Abbasi (Brigadier), 38
Abbasi, Zaheer-ul-Islam (Major General), 38
Abdullah, Sheikh Mohammad, 8, 14, 16-17, 19
Actual Ground Position Line (AGPL), 41, 177, 186-87
Afghan guerrillas, 163
Afghan National Army (ANA), 138-39
Afghan National Security Forces (ANSF), 141
Afghanistan
  American newly calibrated policy, 143
  attitude towards Pakistan, 128
  Benazir Bhutto's support to extremist elements, 132
  as a buffer state, 127
  civil war in, 132
  defeat of the Soviet Army, 131
  Durand Line, 127-129
  foreign policy, 140
  Iran's interests, 140
  neutrality during 1971 war, 129
  opposed Pakistan's entry into the UN, 128
  Pakistan's duplicitous policies, 151-152
  Pakistan's misgivings, 128-129
  Pakistan's unflinching strategic objectives, 134
  radical Islamism in, 129
  strategic significance, 126
  Sunni-Islamist Pashtun elements, 133
  Zia's Afghan policy, 130
Ahmad, Tajuddin, 75
Ahmadiyya sect, 36, 107
Ahmed, Khalid, 168
Ahmed, Mahmood (General), 64, 135
Ahsan, Syed Muhammad, 73
Akhundzada, Mawlawi Haibatullah, 138
Aksai Chin, 186
Alam, Masarat, 107
Al-Badr, 107, 208-09
Ali, Mubarak, 3
Ali, Rao Farman, 75
Aligarh Movement Aligarh Movement, 4, *See also* Khan, Ahmed
All Parties Hurriyat Conference (APHC), 105
Al-Qaeda, 37, 46, 65, 67, 84, 106, 135, 137-138, 142, 145, 150, 154, 156, 191, 210-211

Amu Darya, 153
Anglo-Mohammedan Oriental
    College, 4
Arakanese Muslims (Rohingiyas), 62
Armoured Personnel Carriers
    (APC), 44
Army Strategic Forces Command
    (ASFC), 31–32
Army Welfare Trust, 100
Article 370, 109, See also J&K
Aslam, Mohammad, Lieutenant
    General, 63
Attatürk, Mustafa Kemal, 37
Auchinleck, Sir Claude, 30
Aurora, J.S., 78
Awami League (AL), 35, 72–73
Azad Kashmir, 22, 46, 105
    provisional government of, 22
Azad, Maulana, 7
Azhar, Maulana Masood, 106, 165
Aziz, Tariq, 181

Babar, Naseerullah Khan, 54
Babbar Khalsa, 113, 117
    blowing up of Air India Flight
    182, 117
Bahria Foundation, 100
Banerji, Rana, 38, 62–63
Bangladesh, birth of, 8, 78
Barnala, Surjit Singh, 118
Basit, Abdul, 185
Beg, Aslam (General), 34, 39, 61,
    86, 92, 94
Bhindranwale, Jarnail Singh, 113
Bhutto, Benazir, 38, 55–57, 60–61,
    63, 65, 67, 86, 132, 149, 173,
    177
    exile in UAE, 65
    assassination of, 173
Bhutto, Zulfikar Ali, 36, 48, 51–56,
    61, 71–72, 78, 80, 82, 86, 101,
    113, 129–130, 187
Bogra, Mohammad Ali, 161
Boundary Commission, 16–17
Brar, K.S. (Major General), 116
Brown, William, 18
Brownmiller, Susan, 74
Brzezinski, Zbigniew, 57, 85
Bugti, Nawab Akbar, 53
Bush, George, 135, 143, 150

Cariappa, K.M., 23
Carter, Jimmy, 57, 85, 147
Cawthorne, Walter Joseph, 47
Ceasefire line (CFL), 50
CENTO, 146, 153, 161
Central Asian Republics (CARs), 13,
    57, 126, 134, 140, 165–166, 185
Central Intelligence Agency (CIA),
    48, 53–54, 57–59, 94, 115,
    146–147, 156, 180
Chaudhry, Iftikhar, 61, 65, 173
Chauhan, Jagjit Singh, 118
Chidambaram, P., 174
Chief Martial Law Administrator
    (CMLA), 49, 51, 70
China–Pakistan Economic Corridor
    (CPEC), 109, 140, 164–165,
    183, 189
Clinton, Bill, 87, 149
Clinton, Hillary, 133, 155
Cohen, Stephen, 11, 28, 33, 84, 110,
    189
Cold Start Doctrine, 42, 89
Creek, Sir, 32, 177, 184–185
Crocker, Ryan C., 144
Culture of Entitlement, 99, 101

'D' Company, 67
Damdami Taksal, 116

David, Noel (Lieutenant), 21
Davis, Raymond Allen, 156
Deobandi 'mujahideen', 36
Dixit, J.N., 181
Dogra, Rajiv, 66, –67
Drone strikes, 157
Dulles, John Foster, 146
Durrani, Asad, 61, 122
Durrani, Mahmud (General), 180

East Pakistan, 1, 8, 33–36, 42, 48,
    51–52, 69–77, 79, 120, 147
Eisenhower, Dwight D., 82
Enlai, Zhou, 161

Fair, Christine, 36, 78, 84–85, 145,
    153, 160
Fatemiyoun, Liwa, 140
Fatwas, 156
Fauji Foundation (Fauji Group),
    64, 100
Federal Investigation Agency, 184
First Kashmir War, 12–13, 15, 17,
    19, 21, 23, 25–27, 35, 47
Frontier Corps (FMF campaign), 31
Frontier Gandhi, *See* Khan, Abdul
    Ghaffar Khan
Frontier Works Organisation
    (FWO), 100

Gambhir, Eenam, 191
Gandhi, Indira, 70, 76, 78, 83, 86,
    114–115, 147, 187
Gandhi, Mahatma, 6, 16, 18
Gandhi, Rajiv, 60–61, 118, 177
Geelani, Syed Ali Shah, 107
Geneva Accord, 86
Genocide in 1971, 74–75
Ghani, Abdul Lone, 107
Ghani, Ashraf, 137

Gilani, Mubarak Shah, 62
Gill, K.P.S., 111–112, 117–118
Global War on Terror (GWOT),
    135, 142, 144–145, 150,
    157–158
Gracey, Douglas David (General),
    23
Grare, Frederic, 134
Gul, Hamid, 58–60

Habib, Yubus, 61
Haqqani, 3, 17, 29, 37, 132, 137,
    145, 149, 156, 170, 178–191
Harakat-ul-Jihad-al-Islami (HuJI),
    107, 122, 209–210
Harakat-ul-Mujahideen (HuM), 106,
    208
Hari Singh, Maharaja, 14, 16–17,
    19, 21, 103
Hasina, Sheikh, 125
Hayden, Michael, 180
Headley, David Coleman, 66, 174,
    See also Mumbai 26/11 terror
    strike
Hekmatyar, 37, 54, 58–59, 129,
    131–132, 137, 149
Hindu–Muslim riots, 17
Hizbul Mujahideen (HM), 106
Holbrooke, Richard, 155
Husain, Syed, 171
Hussain, Syed Rifaat, 180

Ibrahim, Dawood, 66–68
Indian Independence Act, 16
Indian Muslim Separatism, 3–6
Indian National Congress (INC),
    14–16
India–Pakistan divide
    amelioration in, 182
    attack on India's Parliament, 92,

88, 106, 171
bilateral trade through Wagah, 173
bus services, 172
ceasefire along the LoC (2003), 172
Composite Dialogue Process (CDP), 177
confidence building measures (CBMs), 172
Hindu–Muslim rivalry, 170
IC 814 plane hijacking, 64
J&K is the core issue, 188
Kargil conflict, 171
MFN status to Pakistan, 185
Modi's Leadership, 175–76
Mumbai attack (2008), 173
Non-Discriminatory Market Access (NDMA) to India, 185
normalization of trade ties, 185
opposing ideologies, 178
Pak opposition for UNSC membership, 190
Pakistan's Kashmir obsession, 169
Pakistan's Kashmir policy, 172
rail and road links, 172–73
reducing the risks of nuclear accidents, 172
smuggler syndicate, 115
truck service on the Srinagar-Muzaffarbad, 172
US role, 171
Vajpayee's Lahore bus yatra, 171
Indo–Pak war (1965), 82
Indo–Pak war (1971), 53, 77–78, 122, 129
aftermath of, 78
prisoners of war, 78
surrendering of Pakistan Army, 78

Indo–US strategic partnership, 158
Indus Waters Treaty, 13, 177, 183, 187
Insurgency, 108–110
International Atomic Energy Agency (IAEA), 83, 88, 163
International Security Assistance Force (ISAF), 151
Inter-Services Intelligence (ISI), 8, 8, 37, 39, 43–44, 46–68, 95, 104–125, 130, 132, 135–138, 151, 156, 163, 173–176, 180, 182–183, 186
Mumbai train blasts (2006), 66
Diabolical Mission, 104–106
insurgency in J&K, 108
Mumbai 26/11 terror strike, 66
nefarious activities, 120
Northeast, 121–24
Operation TOPAC strategy, 66
role, 68
secessionism in Punjab, 111
support to Bangladeshi anti-India forces, 122
terrorist actions, 66
training camps for young militants from the Valley, 105
unconstitutional powers, 68
Inter-Services Public Relations (ISPR), 158
Iqbal, Allama, 5
Iranian Revolution, 57
Islami Jamhoori Ittehad (IJI), 60–61
Islamic bomb, 42
Islamic Crutch, 34–38
US support, 39–40
Islamic State (IS), 108, 138, 142, 191
Islamist radicalism, 136

J&K
  accedes to the Union of India, 21–22
  anti-India endeavours in J&K, 12
  Article 370, 109
  Benazir Bhutto's support to extremist elements, 132
  ceasefire, 24–25
  core issue for Pakistan, 188
  Hindu–Muslim riots, 17
  insurgency, 108–110
  internationalization of the Kashmir problem, 26
  paid agents in the Valley, 105
  Pakistan's involvement in militancy, 171
  separatist leaders, 107–108
  stone-pelters, 109
  UN resolution of ceasefire, 24
  UN Resolutions for a plebiscite, 188
Jadhav, Kulbhushan, 183, 186
Jaish-e-Mohammad (JeM), 106, 165, 171, 175–76, 191, 205–06
Jamaat-e-Islami (JeI), 36–37, 52, 122
Jamaat-ud-Dawa (JuD), 107
Jamaat-ul-Faqra, 62
Jamiat-ul-Ansar (JuA), 106
Jammu Kashmir Liberation Front (JKLF), 105–106
Jinnah, Mohammad Ali, 2–3, 5–8, 10–11, 14–16, 18, 23, 36, 145, 169–170, 193
Junejo, Muhammad Khan, 58

Kahuta Research Laboratories (KRL), 94–95
Kak, Ram Chandra, 16
Kakar, Abdul Waheed, 63
Kallue, Shamsur Rahman, 61

Karachi Nuclear Power Plant (KANUPP), 83
Karakoram Highway (KKH), 109, 162, 186
Kargil conflict (1999), 10, 44, 87, 92, 104, 150, 152, 171
Karzai, Hamid, 136–137, 142
Kasab, Ajmal, 66, 174, 186
Kayani, Ashfaq Parvez (General), 34, 40, 64–65, 131
Kerry, John, 155
Kerry-Lugar-Berman) Bill, 155
KGB, 54, 59–60, 115
Khadamat-e Aetla'at-e Dawlati (KHAD), 54, 59–60
Khalistan Commando Force, 113
Khalistan Liberation Force, 113
Khalistan, 66, 112–114, 117–118
Khalistani terrorists, 111–113, 116–119
Khan, A.Q., 83, 93–94, 163
Khan, Abdul Ghaffar Khan, 9
Khan, Ahmed, 4
Khan, Akbar (Major General), 18, 24
Khan, Ayub (General), 9, 11, 33, 35, 47–51, 70, 81, 128, 146, 153, 162, 179
Khan, Feroz Hassan, 81, 87, 94–95
Khan, Ghulam Ishaq, 60, 63
Khan, Jilani, 55–56
Khan, Liaquat Ali, 18, 23, 145
Khan, Mohammad Daoud, 129
Khan, Munir Ahmad, 83
Khan, Sahibzada Yaqub, 73
Khan, Tikka, 55, 73, 75
Khan, Yahya (General), 36, 51–52, 70, 72–75, 77–78, 82, 147
Khan, Zulfiqar Ali, 61
Khosa, Tariq, 184

Khyber Pakhtunkhwa (KPK), 31–32, 54, 96, 101, 127
Kidwai, Khalid, 91
Kiessling, Hein G., 105, 114–115, 117, 122
Kissinger, Henry, 76–77, 147, 163

Laden, Osama bin, 65, 67, 84, 150, 156
Lahore Declaration (1999), 43, 177, 202
Lambah, Satinder, 181
Lashkar-e-Jhangvi (LeJ), 206–207
Lashkar-e-Taiba (LeT), 66, 106–107, 154, 171, 173–174, 176, 191, 204–205
Lawyers Movement (2007–2008), 65
Leghari, Farooq, 63
Longowal, Sant Harchand Singh, 117
LTTE, 62
Lugar, Richard, 155

Mahanta, P.K., 124
Mahmood, Bashiruddin, 84
Malacca Dilemma, 164
Maley, William, 132
Malik, Akhtar, 50
Malik, GM, (Lt. General), 38
Malik, Yasin, 106–107
Mansour, Mullah, 138
Maritime, Chinese assistance, 41–42
Markey, Daniel S., 155
Massoud, Ahmad Shah, 54, 131
Maududi, Maulana Abul A'la, 37
Menon, V.P., 15, 21
Milbus, 97–98, 101–102
Military dictator in Pakistan, 11
Military Doctrines, 40–43
Military equipment of Pakistan, 31–32

Mirza, Iskander, 35, 47, 49
Missile Technology Control Regime (MTCR), 95, 164
Mountbatten, Lord, 16–17, 21, 25, 30
Movement for the Restoration of Democracy (MRD), 56
Mujahideen, 36, 51, 58, 85, 105, 130–131, 153
Mukti Bahini, 70, *See also* East Pakistan
Mullen, Admiral Mike, 156
Mumbai 26/11 terror strike, 37, 66, 154–55
Musallah-e-Afwaj-e-Pakistan, 28
Musharraf, Pervez (General), 34, 37, 39, 53, 61, 63–65, 94, 106, 135–137, 144–145, 150, 154–155, 171–174, 177, 181, 188–189
Muslim League, 3–6, 9, 14–16, 56, 71
  ascendancy of, 5
  birth of, 4
  homeland proposal, 5

Nasir, Javed, 62–63
National Command Authority (NCA), 31
National Conference (NC), 14
National Investigation Agency, 108
National Liberation Front of Tripura (NLFT), 122
National Logistics Cell (NLC), 100
National Security Advisers (NSA), 183
National Security Council (NSC), 63
National Socialist Council of Nagaland (NSCN), 122–124

National Unity Government (NUG), 137–138, 141
Nawaz, Shuja, 26, 29, 35, 71, 99
Nehru, Jawaharlal, 2–3, 6, 8, 14–17, 19, 25, 112, 146, 170, 177
Nehru-Liaquat Agreement, 177
New Capability of War Fighting (NCWF), 42
Niazi, Amir Abdullah Khan, 74
Nixon, Richard, 76–77, 147, 163
No First Use (NFU) doctrine, 43
Noon, Feroze Khan, 48
Northeast, 66, 120–121, 123–125
　ISI involvement, 121–124
　Nefarious Stratagems, 124–125
Northern Distribution Network (NDN), 151
Nuclear capability, 42, 88–89
　civilian programme, 82
　evolution and expansion, 81–87
　initial years of nuclear build-up, 84
Nuclear Doctrine, 89–93
　China's assistance to Pakistan, 90, 93
　first use of nuclear weapons doctrine, 92
　flexible response strategy, 92
　Nuclear Command Authority, 91
　Strategic Plans Division, 90
Nuclear explosions, 80–81
Nuclear Proliferation, 93–96
Nuclear Security Summit (NSS), 95
Nuclear Suppliers Group (NSG), 95, 165, 190

Obama, Barack, 143, 154–155
Omar, Mullah, 64, 84, 138
Operation Black Thunder, 118–119
Operation Blue Star, 114–118
Operation Enduring Freedom, 135–136, 150–152
Operation Eraze, 23
Operation Gibraltar, 115, 50, 82, 147
Operation Grand Slam, 50
Operation Gulmarg, 18
Operation Neptune Spear, 156
Operation Parakram, 88
Operation Searchlight, 74
Operation TOPAC, 104
Operation Vijay in February 1948, 22
Operation Woodrose, 117
Operation Zarbe-Azb, 157
ORBAT, 31
Organisation of Islamic States (OIC), 148

Pakistan Army, 8, 11, 18, 22–23, 26–39, 42–43, 47, 51, 62, 64–65, 68, 71, 74–75, 77–78, 81, 89, 92, 113, 131, 133, 137, 147–148, 157–158, 182, 192
　Islamization of the armed forces, 39
　Kashmiris from Pakistan Occupied Kashmir (POK), 33
　Punjabi-dominated, 32
　radicalization among junior ranks, 44
Pakistan Atomic Energy Commission (PAEC), 82–83
Pakistan Muslim League (PML), 56, 71, 145
Pakistan Nuclear Regulatory Authority (PNRA), 95
Pakistan People Party (PPP), 35, 48, 56, 60, 71–72, 82
Pakistan Rangers (PR), 31

Panthic Committee, 114
Partition, 1–10, 12–14, 16–17, 29–30, 35, 43, 47, 104, 112, 168, 170, 179
  communal genocide, 2
  distribution of revenue and population, 29–30
  division of military assets, 30
  historical Perspective, 2–3
  Indian Muslim Separatism, 3–6
  Mohajirs, 9, 34
  objective, 2
  Post-Partition violence, 7
Pasha, Ahmad Shuja (Lieutenant General), 65, 180
Patel, Vallabhbhai Patel, 3, 6, 15, 19, 26, 170
Pearl, Daniel, 62, 64
People Liberation Army (PLA), 45, 101, 122
Personnel Reliability Programme (PRP), 95
Pressler Amendment, 85
Psychological warfare, 44, 114

Qazi, Ashraf, 63, 190

Rabbani, Burhanuddin, 54, 129, 136
Radical Islamist separatists, 104
Rahman, Mujibur, 8, 71–72, 78, 125
Rangers (paramilitary force), 100
Ranjit Rai, Dewan, 21
Ranjit Singh, Maharaja, 13
Rashid, Ahmed, 126, 131
Reagan, Ronald, 57, 85, 149
Rehman, Akhtar Abdul, 58
Religious extremists, 104
Reprocessing Plant Agreement, 148

Research and Analysis Wing (R&AW), 38, 56, 59–60, 115, 186, 191
Rice, Condoleezza, 180
Russian expansionism, 121

Saeed, Hafiz, 154, 174, 184, *See also* Mumbai 26/11 terror strike
Salem, Abu, 66
Sandhu, Balbir Singh, 114
Saran, Shyam, 167
Sazeman-e Ettela'at va Amniyat-e Keshvar (SAVAK), 54
SEATO, 146, 153, 161
Sen, L.P. (Brigadier), 22
Sepoy Mutiny (1857), 4, 32
Shah, Shabir, 107
Shah, Zahir, 58, 129
Shaheen Foundation, 100
Shanghai Cooperation Organisation (SCO), 183
Sharif, Nawaz, 37–38, 56, 62–64, 67, 81, 86–87, 94, 149–150, 175, 182–183, 191
Shiromani Gurdwara Parbandhak Committee (SGPC), 114
Siachen Glacier, 186–187
  demilitarization of, 186
Siddiqa, Ayesha, 97–98
Siliguri Corridor, 121
Simla Accord, 86
Simla agreement, 43, 78, 104, 177, 187, 198–201 #see page 201 for correction, 198, *See also* Lahore agreement
Singh, Amarinder, 25
Singh, Amrik, 114
Singh, Gulab, 13–14
Singh, Hari, 14, 16–19, 21, 103
Singh, Jaswant, 6

Singh, Manmohan, 174, 177, 181, 188–189
Singh, Mehar (Captain), 21
Singh, Narain (Colonel), 19
Singh, Rajendra (Brigadier), 19–20
Singh, Ranjit, 13
Singh, Subheg, 114
Sinha, S.K. (Lieutenant General), 120
Sino–Indian tensions, 162
Sino–Pak cooperation, 163
Sipah-e-Sahaba Pakistan (SSP), 207–208
Sood, Vikram, 191
Sovereign Nation, Birth of, 77–79
Soviet Occupation Forces, 58
Special Communications Organisation (SCO), 100
Special Services Group (SSG), 53, 115
Standstill Agreement, 18
Subsidiary Intelligence Bureau (SIB), 48
Sundarji, K. (Lieutenant General), 116
Syed, Ghulam Murtaza, 9

Tablighi Jamaat, 37, 62
Tactical nuclear weapons (TNWs), 32, 42–43, 80, 89, 93
Taliban, 37, 46, 65, 84, 130–133, 135–143, 149–150, 153–154, 186, 191
  Bad Taliban, 133, 136
  good Taliban, 133, 136
Tamil extremists (LTTE), 62
Tashkent agreement (1966), 51, 177
Tehrik-i-Taliban Pakistan (TTP), 65, 133, 154, 157, 186, 191, 211–212

terror attack at the Army School, 133
Tellis, Ashley, 189
Terror tanzeems, 59, 65–96, 107, 180, 191–192
Terrorist Organizations
  Al-Badr, 107
  Harkat-ul-Jihad-al-Islami (HuJI), 107, 122, 209–210
  Harakat-ul-Mujahideen (HuM), 106, 208
  Hizbul Mujahideen (HM), 106
  Islami Jamhoori Ittehad (IJI), 60–61
  Jaish-e-Mohammad (JeM), 106, 165, 171, 175–176, 191, 205–206
  Jamaat-e-Islami (JeI), 36–37, 52, 122
  Jamaat-ud-Dawa (JuD), 107
  Jamaat-ul-Faqra, 62
  Jamiat-ul-Ansar (JuA), 106
  Lashkar-e-Jhangvi (LeJ), 206–207
  Lashkar-e-Taiba (LeT), 66, 106–107, 154, 171, 173–174, 176, 191, 204–205
  Tehrik-i-Taliban Pakistan (TTP), 65, 133, 154, 157, 186, 191, 211–212
Thapa, Sher Jung (Colonel), 24
Thimayya, K.S. (General), 23, 25
Tiger Memon, 66–67
Treaty of Amritsar, 13
Treaty of Peace, Friendship and Cooperation, 76
Truman, Harry, 146
Trump, Donald, 138, 140, 142–143, 165–166
Two-nation theory, 2, 6–10, 78, 103, 113, 169

United Liberation Front of Assam
  (ULFA), 122–123
United Nations Commission for
  India and Pakistan (UNCIP),
  23
United Nations Commission,
  194–197
United Nations General Assembly
  (UNGA), 161
United Nations High Commissioner
  for Refugees (UNHCR), 1
United States Naval Forces Central
  Command (NAVCENT), 163
US–Pak relation
  Anti-US narratives, 152–159
  economic and military sanctions,
    149
  effects of Kargil War, 150
  F-16 fighters supply, 149
  honeymoon period, 148–149
  military and economic assistance,
    149
  mistrust, 149–150
  Operation Enduring Freedom,
    150–152
  trajectory of, 157

Vaidya, A.K. (General), 116
Vajpayee, Atal Bihari, 81, 86, 168,
  203
  bus yatra from Amritsar to
    Lahore, 86
Varshney, Ashutosh, 7

Wassom, Herbert M., 59
Water and Power Development
  Authority (WAPDA), 100
Weinbaum, Marvin, 126
World Trade Centre (WTC), 135

Yamin, Brigadier Tughral, 152

Zakiur-Rehman Lakhvi, 174, 176,
  184
Zardari, Asif Ali, 37, 63, 154, 174
Zia, Khaleda, 122
Ziauddin, Khawaja (General), 63–64
Zia-ul-Haq, General, 33, 36, 40, 48,
  55–58, 66, 105
  Afghan policy, 130
  anti-Soviet jihad, 130
  Islamization of the Pakistan
    Army, 37